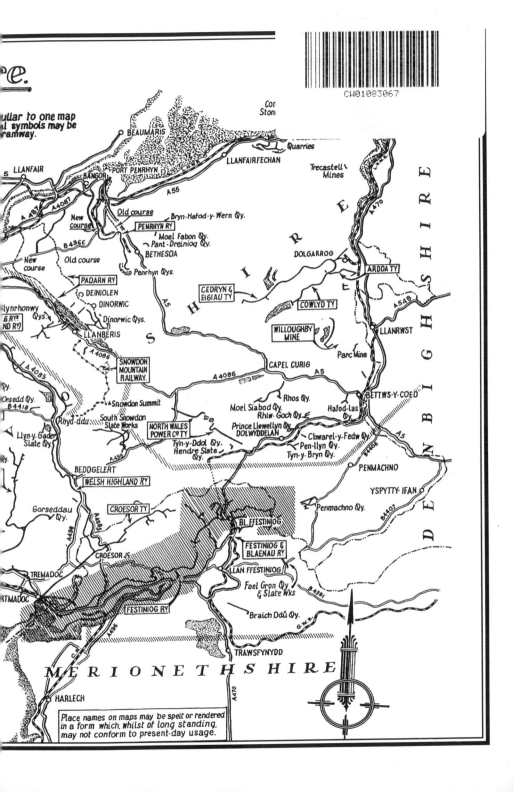

e.

...ular to one map
...l symbols may be
...ramway.

Cor...
Ston...

BEAUMARIS

Quarries

LLANFAIR
LLANFAIRFECHAN
Trecastell
Mines
BANGOR
PORT PENRHYN
A55
Old course
New
course
Bryn-Hafod-y-Wern Qy.
PENRHYN RY
Moel Fabon Qy.
Pant-Dreiniog Qy.
B4366
DOLGARROG
New
course
Old course
BETHESDA
ARDDA TY
PADARN RY
Penrhyn Qys.
CEDRYN &
EIGIAU TY
DEINIOLEN
...lynrhonwy
.G.RY·
.ND RY·
DINORWIC
Dinorwic Qys.
A5
COWLYD TY
A548
LLANBERIS
WILLOUGHBY
MINE
LLANRWST
A4086
Parc Mine
SNOWDON
MOUNTAIN
RAILWAY.
CAPEL CURIG
A4086
A5
...y.
Orsedd Qy.
B4418
Snowdon Summit
BETTWS-Y-COED
Rhos Qy.
Moel Siabod Qy.
Hafod-las
Qy.
Rhyd-ddu
South Snowdon
Slate Works
Rhiw-Goch Qy.
A5
Llyn-y-Gader
Slate Qy.
NORTH WALES
POWER Cº TY
Prince Llewellyn Qy
DOLWYDDELAN
Chwarel-y-Fedw Qy.
Pen-llyn Qy.
B406
...y.
Tyn-y-Ddol Qy.
Hendre Slate
Qy.
Tyn-y-Bryn Qy.
A498
BEDDGELERT
WELSH HIGHLAND RY
PENMACHNO
Gorseddau
Qy.
CROESOR TY
YSPYTTY-IFAN
Penmachno Qy.
B4407
BL.FFESTINIOG
CROESOR Jc
FESTINIOG &
BLAENAU RY
...RTMADOC
TREMADOC
LLAN FFESTINIOG
Foel Gron Qy
& Slate Wks
B4391
FESTINIOG RY
Braich Ddû Qy.
G.W.R.
TRAWSFYNYDD

M E R I O N E T H S H I R E

HARLECH

A470

Place names on maps may be spelt or rendered
in a form which, whilst of long standing,
may not conform to present-day usage.

D E N B I G H S H I R E

NARROW GAUGE RAILWAYS IN NORTH CAERNARVONSHIRE

Volume 3
THE DINORWIC QUARRY & RAILWAYS, GREAT ORME TRAMWAY
and other
RAIL SYSTEMS

Hunslet Engine Works,
Leeds. Dec 1st 1905

Specification.
OF A
TANK LOCOMOTIVE.

Gauge of Railway **2** feet **10½** inches.

GENERAL ARRANGEMENT

The Engine to be generally as shown by ~~————~~ *Loco Dg Plate* No. **829** having **Outside** cylinders **7"** diameter and **10** stroke **Four** coupled wheels placed ~~inside~~ the frames, **axles** with ~~outside~~ bearings, the **feed-water** to be carried in **a "Saddle"** tank , and the fuel in bunker at the **Left side**

BOILER

The Boiler and Outer Fire-box to be made of the best Siemens-Martin mild steel plates, having a tensile strength of not less than **26** tons per square inch, and an elongation of **20** per cent in **10** inches. The **barrel** to be **6** ft. **8** ins. long, and **3** ft. **2** ins. ~~————~~ diameter, plates **½** thick ; ~~————~~ to be made of one plate, longitudinal seam to be **butt** joints and double rivetted. The **fire-box** shell to be **3** ft. **7½** ins. long, and **2** ft. **8** ins. wide between the frames, and at the bottom **3** ft. **0½** ins. below the boiler barrel, plates **½** thick, **smoke-box** tube plate to be **½** thick and rivetted to barrel by strong angle ring. The boiler to be efficiently stayed throughout for a **working pressure** of **140** lbs. per square inch. A **manhole** to be rivetted on top of shell over the fire-box, fitted with a cover, carrying the safety valve and steam cocks. The fire-box shell to be raised above the boiler barrel so as to form a steam chamber and contain the regulator valve. **All rivet holes to be drilled,** all plate edges to be machined and all rivetting as far as possible done by machine.

FIRE-BOX

The Inner Fire-box to be made of **best selected copper plates, 3** ft. **1½** ins. long, by **2** ft. **2½** ins. wide at the bottom, and, **3** ft. **2** ins. deep inside ; the sides and crown made in one plate **½** thick, tube plate **¾** thick where tubes pass through, and **½** thick below tubes ; back plate **½** thick except round fire-hole **¾** thick, rivetted together with copper rivets. The **sides of fire box** to be stayed to the shell with **copper stays** ⅞ in. diameter, placed as near 4 inches centres as they will pitch equally, screwed into both plates, and rivetted over at each end ; the **crown of fire-box** to be stayed by **strong wrought iron girder stays,** and protected by two fusible **safety plugs.** The fire-hole ring to be fitted with a renewable steel protection plate.

I. A.

Note that this Specification for a locomotive (possibly DONALD ?) for Darbishires Ltd., Penmaenmawr quotes a gauge of 2 ft 10½ ins., rather than the working gauge of 3 ft.

NARROW GAUGE RAILWAYS IN NORTH CAERNARVONSHIRE

Volume Three
THE DINORWIC QUARRY and RAILWAYS, THE GREAT ORME TRAMWAY and OTHER RAIL SYSTEMS

by
James I.C. Boyd

THE OAKWOOD PRESS

© Oakwood Press & J. I. C. Boyd 1986

British Library Cataloguing in Publication Data
A Record for this book is available from the British Library
ISBN 0 85361 328 1

First Edition 1986
Reprinted 2001

Printed by Cambrian Printers Ltd., Aberystwyth, Ceredigion.

Published by The Oakwood Press, P.O. Box 13, Usk, Mon., NP15 1YS.
E-mail: oakwood-press@dial.pipex.com
Website: http://ds.dial.pipex.com/oakwood-press

CONTENTS

Foreword vi

Author's Note vii

Preface viii

Acknowledgement ix

Sources x

Part 6   THE DINORWIC QUARRIES AND RAILWAYS   1770 TO 1969   1

Part 7   THE GREAT ORME TRAMWAY & TRAMROAD 133

Part 8   OTHER RAIL SYSTEMS 162

Part 9   THE ALUMINIUM CORPORATION LTD. 211

Part 10   CONWAY VALLEY – RAILWAY PROPOSALS 214

Part 11   LLANBERIS LAKE RAILWAY (RHEILFFORDD LLYN
            PADARN) 219

Index to Text 223

Index to Drawings and Maps 226

[References will be found as appropriate at the end of each Part.]

v

FOREWORD

By E. H. Douglas Pennant

The last time that a member of the Penrhyn family wrote a foreword, at the author's invitation, for a book about local railways was when the Rt. Hon. Hugh Napier, 4th Baron Penrhyn of Llandegai, my great-uncle, wrote the foreword to Charles E. Lee's book, which also included a section on the Penrhyn Railway. It is therefore an honour, for me, to be invited to write the foreword to this book.

It is a fact that Caernarvonshire had large mineral deposits, including slate, which attracted speculators and landowners to tap the source. Some were successful and as a result of their success, railways such as the Penrhyn were built to transport the product to the coast, from where it would be exported.

From the year 1768, in the days of Hugh Warburton and John Pennant, when they leased to tenants the right to quarry slate from what became Penrhyn Quarry, Bethesda, until 1973 when Lady Janet Douglas Pennant sold the remaining 51% of shares she held in the quarry to Marchwiel Holdings Ltd., my family has been involved in the slate industry for just over two hundred years.

The section on Penrhyn not only deals with the railway and the locomotives that worked on it and in the port and quarry, but also with the ships associated with it, which carried the slate to other parts of the country and Europe. Other sections of the book deal with the Dinorwic Quarry Railway, the tramroads in the mines of the Trefriw and Llanrwst areas, the reservoir construction lines west of Dolgarrog and also the Great Orme Tram.

At home, I have the other books in the series of which this book is the latest, so the author is not unknown to me. When I first met him in early 1984 at the archives at the University College of North Wales, it was a pleasure and an honour to be invited to write this foreword.

I have enjoyed the other books he has written and I hope that all who read this book will enjoy doing so. I wish Mr. Boyd every success with his latest volume.

Penrhyn, 1985   E. H. Douglas Pennant

AUTHOR'S NOTE

An Author's Note having already appeared in Volume 2, it is unnecessary to repeat its content as it adequately covers the substance of that volume and this; it was intended initially to publish in one large treatise, hence a certain amount of repetition will be found in the introductory material to Volumes 2 and 3.

Colwall, Herefordshire.   James I.C. Boyd.
April, 1986.

PREFACE

This is the third and last volume in a series to cover a part of North Wales where lay some of the earliest railways in the Principality, if not in the world. They were certainly the first built to carry slate, that intractable roofing material which is most economically carried by water. Herein lies the competition between the great 19th century quarry/landowners who used the railways to achieve the most efficient transport between quarry and sea, a critical factor in not only their own survival but for whole communities both on land and water. The most efficient railway system could ensure domination of a market and as that market grew less, so more effective did the railway system have to become.

Over the period of almost forty years since the last in this series was published, an explosion of Further Education, and the spread of radical beliefs has given enormous emphasis to the social impact of commerce and industry, with the result in the subject under consideration here that publications on the slate industry (for instance) have completely lost sight of the technology of the industry itself, in exchange for social impact. One cannot overlook the change from agricultural to industrial communities which took place in certain parts of North Wales, but the manner and means of this revolution, the detail of the pockets of industrial expertise almost always in isolation from the remainder of the country, the initiative and individuality of the end-products . . . these have become the neglected basic issues and in this final publication an effort has been made to correct this ill-balance.

The railways herein were of infinite individuality, reflecting the character of the owner. Unlike railways in other parts of the Kingdom, they were not territorially ambitious, governed by remote Boards of Directors in far-away London or subject to scrutiny by Board of Trade inspection. They operated under an umbrella of semi-feudal relationship between landlord and employee (sometimes landlord/tenant and employee/tenant – a far more demanding situation) in a pattern of employment which few other railwaymen would have accepted and yet clearly was largely accepted and appreciated by those involved! Changes were slow until the business was threatened; when changes came they did so with consuming rapidity. From horse-power to steam-power within a matter of months, or from ancient tramway to modern railway in as short a time; no Directors of a share-holding company could develop at such pace, let alone the ponderous undertakings in public ownership!

In short, we may look back on an age where imagination, ambition, drive, confidence and success in a few men could ensure the employment of hundreds. And the lynch-pin of that complex was none other than the railway!

ACKNOWLEDGEMENTS

This work has involved over one hundred persons in the three decades of preparation, and besides the fact that many are no longer living, it would be impossible to mention each by name; among those deceased are the Engineers of the Penrhyn and Dinorwic undertakings, and many of their colleagues also. Survivors amongst the employees may still be found in The Welsh Slate Museum and at the National Trust's Museum in Penrhyn Castle; their reminiscences together with those who have come forward from retirement to help, have given life to the script. Sources less closely-connected include Eric Foulkes who made his extensive researches into Penrhyn archives available to me, loaned his unpublished notes and checked my first rough draft. Next, Douglas Carrington, who has been especially interested in Dinorwic and published a small book on the subject, has shared his knowledge with me and supervised my rough draft. The unselfish collaboration of these two good friends has saved me hours of tedious research and added beyond measure to my personal experiences of these two sites.

Visits to archival depositories in Wales have become opportunities of real pleasure, no less because of the helpful and friendly welcome which always awaits! These include Gwynedd Archives at Caernarfon, The Library Archives at University College of North Wales, Bangor, The Welsh Industrial & Maritime Museum at Cardiff with its branch, The Welsh Slate Museum, Llanberis; here Gareth Williams, Tomos Roberts, Stuart Owen-Jones, Dafydd Roberts and their supporting staff have tended to make me linger in their company for longer than was really necessary for my objectives!

Roy Fenton has ensured that with his close knowledge of coastal shipping, I was fully informed on the maritime links of these Welsh quarries; Dr. C. V. Waine gave me details of individual ships. Bernard Roberts, Philip Hindley and Victor Bradley with their keen curiosity in railways on industrial sites, have helped me over many points of locomotive and rolling stock details; Ivor E. Davies, full of years and experience, assisted with many aspects concerning local history and the granite industry, as did Eric Jones with Dolgarrog notes. W. H. Roberts (Port Dinorwic) recalled his life as a guard on the Padarn Railway, Iowerth Jones and J. K. Jones of Bangor their personal reminiscences of Penrhyn.

Edmond Douglas Pennant has spent much time retrieving archive material from his ancestors' collections, and has contributed a Foreword. Much of the material from his patient work has been used herein.

No writer can afford to be without the fullest collection of photographic material; C. C. Green, Ifor Higgon, Eric Hannon, Hunslet Holdings PLC, E. D. Chambers and David Chatfield have been especially generous in this regard.

As to drawings, several capable persons have contributed either from their own collections or made a special assignment to my requirements. In this respect Chris. G. Down, Philip Hindley, Alan Holmes, Alan Kidner, G. R. Page, W. A. D. Strickland and Don Townsley should be mentioned, not omitting Tony F. Rushworth who made available the work he did for Mr. Carrington's book.

Finally, to the small team whose contribution is without measure: John M. Lloyd who is responsible for the greater part of the drawings, maps and diagrams – to meet his exacting standards some have been re-draughted up to half a dozen times. Jeremy Wilkinson has supplied a stream of supporting information ranging from statutory statistics, through commercial information to the valuable availability of technical services at manuscript stage . . . and that is not all! Then in the ultimate my wife must address herself to the assemblage I have made from so many sources and proceed to construct an acceptable typescript: on the way I expect her to know every subject as well as I do, to be on personal terms with my associates, assist me with research, entertain my collaborators, insert missing facts from the formidable array of material in this study and keep callers at bay. The finished work must be well typed, grammatically correct, and impeccably spelled. The story must be crystal clear – these are her standards! She more than anyone else involved will dispel an enquirer's illusion that writing railway history is a casual, speedy, free-time relaxation . . . and equally that it is either financially rewarding or undemanding.

A simple list of appreciation must follow:

J. L. H. Bate and D. E. Bick	Mining information
Rev. E. A. Boston	Access to preserved rolling stock
M. Cowley	Use of drawings
Emlyn Evans (Gee & Sons, Denbigh)	Background publications
Mrs. Catherine Hughes	Translations
Peter Hughes	Quarry information
L. Humphries	Quarry information
Dr. K. A. Jaggers	History
Gwynfor P. Jones	Quarry histories
Hugh R. Jones	Engineer, Dinorwic
H. A. Lewis	Translations
Dr. Jean Lindsay	Quarry histories
W. John Milner	Dinorwic Quarry material
A. S. R. Parsons	Loan of unpublished essay
Douglas Rendell	Photographic work
Ernie Roberts	Quarry information
Dr. E. A. Shearing	Genealogical and architectural notes
Einion Thomas	Penrhyn Estate information
Rev. H. Thomas	Reminiscences
P. Vaughan-Davies	Penmaenmawr & Welsh Granite Quarry material

SOURCES

A NOTE ON SOURCES TO VOLUMES 2 AND 3

Two main sources of information have been used herein; firstly, the close personal familiarity of the author with all systems which survived to 1940 and, secondly, such records of these systems which have come available during and since their demise.

Private railways which formed the greatest mileage herein are especially difficult to research as owners naturally treat their records as not for public scrutiny. In the case of the Padarn Railway instructions went out to burn all paper-work when the railway closed and little recent paper-work has survived . . . if indeed there ever was the close written account such as fortunately has been made available concerning the Penrhyn Railway – and which is still coming to light. So it is these two historic lines, whose ancestry goes back to the earliest days of rail transport, cannot enjoy equal status.

The Dam Disaster at Dolgarrog in 1925 carried away many of the records of the North Wales Power & Traction Co. Ltd and its associated interests. Ironically, the circumstances surrounding the many small tramways can often be pieced together from company records whilst the unique Great Orme Tramway – so relatively modern – is embarrasingly rich in material!

Some variation in the presentation of place names will be noted; for examples there is documentary evidence for the vernacular at Penrhyn of Felin-Fawr Slab Mill (not Felin-Fawr slab mill) or Spoon Points (not spoon points) and this characteristic has been followed. Elsewhere documentation is scarce and does not support this presentation e.g. galleries with the same name at Penrhyn and Dinorwic would be Twlldyndwr Level and Twlldyndwr level respectively.

General National Library of Wales: Manchester Central Reference Library: The Science Museum: The Bodleian Library: The J. S. Wilkinson Collection: Clwyd Record Office: The National Museum of Wales: The House of Lords Record Office: The Public Record Office: Festiniog Railway Archives: Institution of Civil Engineers: Gwent Record Office.

Periodicals and Annuals The Quarry Manager's Journal: The London Gazette: The Stock Exchange Official Intelligence: Bradshaw's Railway Manual: The Engineer: Engineering: The Railway Magazine: The Railway Times: The Railway News: Stone Trades Journal: The Quarry: Industrial Railway Record: The Stock Exchange Year Book: The Mining Yearbook: Skinner's Mining Manual: Skinner's Register of Defunct Companies.

Other sources are listed under ACKNOWLEDGEMENTS, and to avoid a long list of book titles and newspapers, appropriate footnotes have been given to specific sources in the text. A detailed list of directories, registers and maps is given on p.274 of Volume I, and is applicable also herein.

With special reference to the content of Volumes 2 and 3, Accident Reports published by H.M.S.O. are relevant to the Great Orme Tramway, The Museum of English Rural Life to the use of oxen, and the extensive records held at the City of Birmingham Reference Library have wide-ranging application.

Note on Maps and Diagrams

Those drawn herein may not always be to scale and care must be exercised where, in order to show detail, some exaggeration has been necessary.

Care must also be taken with Ordnance Survey maps; those of similar date but differing scales do not always agree, especially in the detail of such places as quarries. The plans of quarries and port arrangements have been prepared in the knowledge that in these areas railways were being subject to continuous alteration. Where documentary evidence has been available, this has been used in preference to Ordnance Survey maps.

Note on Place Names

No attempt has been made to bring Welsh place names into the modern form, but the spelling of the period has been retained. Many records were kept for years without the correction of place name mis-spelling and something of a compromise has been attempted throughout.

Note on abbreviations of Titles

B.R.	British Railways
C.C.R.O.	Caernarvonshire County Record Office (more recently – Gwynedd Archives)
C.E.G.B.	Central Electricity Generating Board
C.&H.R.	Chester & Holyhead Railway (Company)
F.R.	Festiniog Railway (Company)
G.W.R.	Great Western Railway (Company)
L.N.W.R.	London & North Western Railway (Company)
N.W.P.&T.C.L.	North Wales Power & Traction Co. Ltd (ex North Wales Power Co.)
P.&W.G.C.L.	Penmaenmawr & Welsh Granite Co. Ltd
P.B.S.S.R.	Portmadoc Beddgelert & South Snowdon Railway (Company)
P.R.O.	Public Record Office, Kew
U.C.N.W.	University College of North Wales, Bangor
W.H.R.	Welsh Highland Railway (Company) – a Light Railway

Note on motive power in certain more obscure locations

The Birmingham Locomotive Club Pocket book 'F' of 1968 INDUSTRIAL & INDEPENDENT LOCOMOTIVES & RAILWAYS OF NORTH WALES – almost the only publication available – is used wherever necessary. In 1982 the compilers stated that certain lists 'dogmatically published in the past . . . may contain errors of fact'. Wherever possible the authors of the Pocket Book have collaborated to bring information herein up to date.

Note on changes effected by statute since 1962

The content of this volume largely ceased to exist during the 1960s. It ignores therefore:

Changes of place names etc. brought about by Local Government re-organisation in April 1974. In consequence the titles of the period are retained (e.g. Carnarvon or Caernarvon and not Caernarfon) and present-day titles do not appear e.g. Gwynedd.

The change to decimal money – almost all transactions herein were made before this was introduced.

The change to metric measurement, which was seldom used in the period concerned, save for an occasional exception.

PART 6
THE DINORWIC QUARRIES AND RAILWAYS

(Quarries open by 1770: closed 1969)

THE DINORWIC SLATE QUARRIES CO. LTD.
Registered November 1951

OWNERS: *Acquired*

(1)	Thomas Assheton-Smith (senr.)	see text
	(1752–1828)	
(2)	Thomas Assheton-Smith (jnr.)	1828
	(1776–1858)	
(3)	George William Duff-Assheton-Smith[1]	1859
	(1848–1904)	
(4)	(Sir) Charles Garden Assheton-Smith[2]	1904
	(1851–1914)	
(5)	(Sir) Robert (Robin) George Vivian Duff[3]	1914
	(1876–1914)	
(6)	(Sir) Charles Michael Robert Vivian Duff[4]	1914
	(1907–1980)	

NOTES

1. Assumed additional names Assheton-Smith 1859.
2. Assumed Assheton-Smith in lieu of Duff 1905. Created baronet 1911.
3. Did not assume Assheton-Smith: killed in World War I shortly after succession to title.
4. Assumed additional names Assheton-Smith 1928: relinquished names 1945.

DINORWIC RAILWAY

24½ in. gauge	Open	by 1824
(over rail centres)	Closed	May 1843

PADARN RAILWAY

4 ft gauge (inside rails)	Open	3rd March, 1843
		(Horse worked)
	Open	23rd November, 1848
		(Steam worked)
Workmen's Train	Started	August 1895
	Ceased	8th November, 1947
Last train		27th October, 1961
Officially closed		3rd November, 1961

1

QUARRY TRAMWAYS

First noticed	1813
Last steam working	November 1967

Port Dinorwic Siding
Open 10th March, 1852   Closed 30th October, 1961
Llanberis branch
Open 1st July, 1869   Closed 7th September, 1962

THE ASSHETON-SMITH INHERITANCE to the former Crown Manors of Vaynol and Dinorwic, Caernarvonshire.

The Asshetons are reputed to be descended from the feudal lords of 'Assheton-under-Lyne' and later to have been of Kirkby, near Leeds. Thomas Assheton acquired Ashley Hall, Bowdon, Cheshire, and on the death of his uncle, Captain William Smith of Tedworth, Hampshire – who died without issue – Vaynol, (or Vaenol, a property lying between Caernarvon and Bangor) and other properties passed to him. Captain Smith was a son of a former Chancellor of the Exchequer who was later Speaker of the House of Commons, the Right Hon. John Smith, and his acquisition of Vaynol is recalled by the curious tale of one Sir William Williams who left this 3,000 acre Estate to King William III. When the King learned of the gift he asked what sort of a fool was this man who had no relatives or friends to whom he could leave it? Tradition has it that Smith, then the Speaker and a party to the conversation, said 'It matters not who has it, for it is nothing but barren rocks'. To this the King replied, 'Then I give it thee, Smith'.

When Thomas Assheton inherited, he added the name and arms of Smith to his own and in due course the property passed to his second son, the elder having died young. He became Thomas Assheton-Smith (1752–1828); the property then passed to his son Thomas (1776–1858) and then George William Duff (1848–1904) a nephew who acquired it in the will of his great uncle's widow in 1859; thereafter the Estate remained in the Duff family during the period covered by this account. Ashley Hall was sold to Lord Egerton of Tatton, Knutsford in 1846. The two Thomas heirs, spanning the period before the property passed to the Duffs, developed the slate quarries and created the railway system to serve them. The second Thomas would spend summers at Vaynol and his winters elsewhere. He was well known for his other interests, which included swimming, cricket, rowing, and being keenly interested in maritime matters, his inventiveness in design of sailing and later, steam yachts, brought him into contact with the leading ship builders and designers of the times. His passion for horses and hunting was a by-word; both at his London home and Vaynol he built indoor railway systems. That at Vaynol led from the kitchen to the dining room, the trains of hot food entering through a trap door in the wall and leaving, empty, by another. These railways were based on the quarry incline system and at Vaynol the weight of sufficient empty dishes etc. going downwards raised the full ones on the inclined track. This crockery was carried on a wheeled platform 'brought . . . within the dining room by means of connecting ropes, the hot and smoking trucks coming up . . . a similar device took him upstairs to bed when old and asthmatic in his London home . . .'[1] Another aspect of his character was that 'He taught himself arithmetic after leaving Eton and on autumn visits to Vaynol would check the books and accounts by visiting the quarry offices at the Port'.

HISTORICAL SUMMARY OF RAIL TRANSPORT inside and outside the Quarry (1770–1970)

The Dinorwic Quarry railway system was once, like that at Penrhyn Quarry, one of the largest private railway undertakings with significance both in longevity and mechanical innovation. Some extensive records survive concerning the building of the railways connecting Quarry and seaboard, but many records were destroyed in recent years, or not kept or never made . . . it could be that once the cost of construction had been met, subsequent fiscal accounts were of little lasting value. Fortunately the valuable accounts of the building have been saved. Certain remaining physical features remain unexplained, and the legend of an early railway lacks confirmation. The main system outside the internal quarry network may be shown:

1) A legendary tramway c.1800 along the shore of Llyn Padarn: extent unknown.
2) The Dinorwic Railway 1824–43: superceded by The Padarn Railway.
3) Schemes to replace The Dinorwic Railway, probably in the late 1830s and especially at the 600–700 ft contour: none completed.
4) The Village Branch, linking the original Dinorwic area quarries with the Mill at the Big Quarry: possibly built by c.1843.
5) The Padarn Railway, completed December 1842 to replace The Dinorwic Railway.
6) The Padarn-Peris Tram Line replacing part of 5) at its eastern end.

The circumstances leading to the building of these railways were almost identical with those at Penrhyn. These two slate quarries were always to the fore in output and dominated the North Wales industry perpetually, and they enjoyed many years of owner-working, an advantage which a quarry lessee could never equal on commercial terms.

Their transport was in advance of their competitors, being owners of the land over which their routes lay; and their scale of business was such that they could pioneer transport fashions with the backing of workshop facilities, even though they were geographically beyond the influence of, and regular familiarity with, the general development of railways in the country as a whole. As at Penrhyn, the derivative at Dinorwic was inventive, idiosyncratic and exclusive, and was in both places linked to the trade situation.

The expansionist period in the trade was of about 85 years duration (1793–1877) in which total trade output rose from 45,000 to 504,000 tons, with many ups and downs between. In North Wales business had weakened in 1794 due to a Slate and Stone Tax (the effects of Horse Tax have already been suggested; Vol. 2 pp. 7–8) designed to placate the tile and brick manufacturers who had borne a tax for the previous ten years, which effectively added 20% duty to all slate shipped coast-wise, except to Ireland. In practice, due to war, Welsh ships working to the English Channel refused to sail beyond Milford Haven except when protected in convoy, and this paralysed much of the available business; worse, when the rate of Slate Tax was increased it decreased the Irish trade too, but fortunately at that time both Penrhyn and Dinorwic were more closely linked with a growing demand from the Industrial Revolution in England, than by having much Irish custom. This was a new market, though even they were hit by the Tax and in 1802 when only half their output was sufficient to meet orders, riots due to unemployment broke out. It has been seen previously that at Penrhyn this position was put to constructive use in the building of a railway, but Assheton-Smith, being at that time not personally involved in the Quarry, limited himself to road improvements.

After better times, 1803–12, trade worsened again and there was a small loss on working in 1817 when the two quarries realistically came together to agree on slate prices and uphold profit margins – with considerable effect on railway development at a later stage – their consequent domination of the Welsh market was to influence every Welsh slate railway proposal for the next sixty years. Business collapsed again by the mid-1820s by which time Dinorwic had built its first railway (. . . which may not, if tradition is to be believed, have been its pioneer rail undertaking). There was up to then 'a period of extravagant speculation in slate quarries . . . and widespread unrest among quarry-men'. Assheton-Smith was anxious to mitigate circumstances which would create more unrest among his workforce, which was already angered by his claim to the Estate and the enclosures which ensued; he followed the Penrhyn example in 1823–4 and using unemployed labour, built a railway, a much-needed outlet. A period then followed when trade held up and underlined the fruits of co-operation; in 1831 Slate Tax was abolished and next year profits rose to £12,000. More expansion followed, and in 1840 output was twice that of 1830, and

Thomas Assheton-Smith Jnr. (who succeeded his father in 1828) found his Quarry again under pressure for improved rail links; by the 1830s he was seeking ways to implement or replace the 1824 railway. By chance or design the resultant Padarn Railway, for which materials had been ordered as early as 1841, was also begun in a time of depression and later, steam locomotives were on trial when business once again was languid. Such bold steps may have been far-sighted moves to efficiency, or to uphold employment and certainly to maintain profits on a reduced turnover. Foresight was well rewarded, for by 1850 Dinorwic possessed the most modern railway system in the slate trade, steam-worked and on a rail gauge and structure free of physical limitations, and having 'pick-a-back' trains which anticipated the modern container system by a century and more . . . albeit such methods were already in use on the Liverpool & Manchester Railway by 1830!

Having related the main development of railways hereabouts, it is not necessary to follow the vagaries of the slate trade any further except to note that Lord Penrhyn too, was obliged to build a steam-worked railway at a later date and it is arguable which Quarry showed more initiative in railway development. Dinorwic enjoyed superior transport for several decades, but the need to trans-ship quarry wagons both onto and off the Padarn Railway (especially for the short journey down the Port Incline) increased labour costs as the workforce established its existence and right to better wages and employment conditions. The Penrhyn system allowed quarry wagons to work from Mill to ship's side without such labour costs, but unlike it the Padarn line was almost level throughout.

Turning now to the Quarry. The mountain of Elidir contains a vast bed of slate rock; at the time it was quarried on the north side by the Pennants and on the south by Assheton-Smith – Sir John E. Eardley-Wilmot described the mountain as a 'colossal plum cake out of which two boys are each trying to take the largest slice he can'. Assheton-Smith, restricted by the two lakes on his southern flank, would soon be extracting rock even from below lake level and by 1858 his workings were 1800 feet between top and bottom, 1420 ft above Llyn Peris; they formed an excavation over 700 acres in extent and collectively this was dubbed The Big Quarry although it did not embrace all the then-workings – these never formed one convenient site. Even in the immediate Assheton-Smith era, Fenton was able to write 'there are two or three works going on at the same time, at no great distance from each other, being separated by a stratum of hard stone which runs parallel to the slate . . .'. This enormous hole has engulfed many smaller satellite pits on its periphery and with the need to dump rock rubbish (esti-mated at 20 tons for every ton of slate) always at crisis-point, many of these pits were filled with rubbish later. The final commercial title of 'The Dinorwic Slate Quarries Co. Ltd.' was truly apt.

S. Lewis in his 'TOPOGRAPHICAL DICTIONARY OF WALES' (4th Edit. 1850) is hardly complimentary about the district '. . . the scenery is uninteresting and unpleasing – there are no trees. The soil is cold and unproductive'. The first quarries hereabouts were smallish pits to the south east of Dinorwic village; among them was Allt-Ddu (at first known as Chwarel Griffith Ellis after the lessee) and Bryn-Glas, both grown large enough to be mapped in 1771; some of them coalesced into bigger pits and their original location is only known by hearsay – Bryn-Glas was obliterated by tipping (also the original quarry hospital). There were other small workings on the shore of the lakes and some of these excavations survive due to having tipped their rubbish into the lake and not into each other; this tipping into the water at various points created several delta.

Groups of men (neither quarrymen nor farmers but an amalgam of both) divided their time between these occupations as season demanded; some increased their quarry time as the call for slate increased, for many had worked slate on the manor long before Assheton-Smith inherited, and at first he enabled them to continue this practice by charging a rent, but when he moved into quarrying personally it unsettled these operators and there was some civil unrest. The first manor lease (for 21 years) was made in 1787 to The Dinorwic Slate Co. formed by Assheton-Smith's agent Thomas Wright, Hugh Ellis and William Bridge (as Manager) who at first concentrated on working the quarries (or pits) near the village of Dinorwic. Far-reachingly, they began 'The Great New Quarry' (possibly on a site near Garret) in 1788, the genesis of the ultimate site, but transport was to prove the restrictive bottleneck to expansion. The immediate method was to take slates 'in hampers on horseback' up over the Bwlch-y-Fachen ridge and down through the hamlet of Fach-Wen to Pen-Isa'r-Waen where the slates were transferred to two-wheel carts: however, it was often found more convenient as time went by to lower slate by sledge down a road to Cei-Newydd on Llyn Padarn, and boat it along Padarn Lake to meet the carts – more will be said of this system, later.[2] The carts threaded unsuitable roads to reach, originally, Caernarvon, but later the north side of a small creek on the Menai Straits (the embarkation point for the Moel-y-Don Ferry) known as Aber-Pwll.

In 1802 Caernarvon was being abandoned in favour of improvements at Aber-Pwll (made in 1793 and again in 1809) to make it a much more convenient shipping point. Shipping became even more brisk after the building of Assheton-Smith's road (or 'The Slate Road' as contemporary maps showed it), built in 1812 to link Allt-Ddu and Felin-Heli (Salt Water Mill), the alternative name for Aber-Pwll. This road came down the escarpment behind the creek via Nant-y-Garth, and most of it is still a highway; when the first railway was built it followed the course of this road in some measure. Strangely, Assheton-Smith did not secure his first lease of the quays and buildings on the south side of the creek here until February 1845 (being then given a 31 year lease, 5th July, 1844, from the Crown at £25 per annum) and the entry then made was that the area was 'never before in lease'; this land was titled Llanfair-ys-Caer.

Moel-y-Don took its name from the Anglesey point of destination and its mediocre facilities may be judged by it being served by a small rowing boat on windless days and a tiny gaff-rigged vessel otherwise. In 1788 it had been arranged with Lord Boston (landowner in the Parish of Llanfair-ys-Caer) to begin construction of a better road between Llanddeiniolen and Moel-y-Don, Assheton-Smith and his quarry lessees agreeing to share the cost; to encourage the carters (mainly small farmers) to use broader wheels, reduced tolls were offered to those who responded. The evidence of precise dates for early road and railroad building at this period is scarce, but within a generation of these times John Hughes of Fron-Heulog, Dinorwic, entered a local history in a Caernarvon eisteddfod in 1867 with the information: "Next came the iron road from Velinheli to Dinorwig Quarries, which was built in 1822–23" and he adds that the cart road had been built in 1807–8; on Saturday afternoons the local people turned out to keep it in repair. This would be Assheton-Smith's 'Slate Road' which was heavily used by 1812, displaying notices alongside proclaiming it was private and had been 'built by Assheton-Smith, William Turner, Thomas Wright & Hugh Jones' (i.e. those operating the Dinorwic Slate Co. since 1809).

The initial Quarry company foundered in 1807 when Ellis died and when two years later the lease expired, Assheton-Smith worked the Quarry himself with three partners, and feeling their livelihood to be under threat, some tenants rioted at Llanddeiniolen. To the west Glynn Griffith of Bod-y-Groes ultimately took over the working of Bryn-Glas, Allt-Ddu and Chwarel-Fawr[3]; he challenged Assheton-Smith's take-over in the Courts, but the case was settled outside (it would have been an invidious situation for those concerned for the decision to have gone against Assheton-Smith who had become High Sheriff of Caernarvonshire in 1783). Assheton-Smith now experienced a difficult period, for after establishing his right by the Enclosure Acts of 1806 and 1808 to legal ownership of the commons, he began a series of enclosures of them which further embittered the squatters who had heretofore considered it their right to live and quarry where they wished.

With reference to these lessee's early transport difficulties, Bridge wrote to Ellis as early as September 1788 re 'Dragging Slate down a steep Hill and carrying the Drag up again . . . few will undertake at any price'. Ellis was recommended, whilst on a visit to Liverpool, to order timber baulks 40–50 ft long and 13 in square 'for the Making of a Rail Road to convey slates down from Bryn-glas, to where the carts can take them up . . .'. So the first quarry incline was built and operative by 1789. It fell from near the east side of Bryn-Glas Quarry to near Y Cei on the most northerly point on the shore of Llyn Peris, a historic quay on that lake which owed its origins to the long-established boat transport system between the two lakes before the building of the first valley road in 1802.[4] In practice the incline was somewhat less in length than when first considered and in later years is believed to have formed the basis of the lower portion of the former 'A' incline – now tipped over. Hemingway, writing before 1835, says the 'mode of conveying the slates down the almost precipitous descent to the margin of the lake was formerly singularly awkward . . . and dangerous. The carts, each conveying about 1 ton slates in winter and two in summer, were drawn down a serpentine path by one horse in front and one hooked on behind . . .' but by 1836 another writer could proclaim '. . . on subsequently witnessing the improvements and corresponding advantages of the inclined plane . . .'. Although Bridge clearly intended it should carry rails all the way, this would have been far too lengthy for the equipment (ropes etc.) of those times and probably the lower and less steep portion was used by carts and sledges. Fenton recommends readers to 'cross Pont-y-Bala over the River issuing out of the upper lake, look at a handsome cottage of Mr. Ashton Smith's called Glan Bala . . . on a pretty knoll . . . ascend to the Slate Quarries by a sloping acclivity of about a Mile, running on the side of an immensely high hill forming the boundary of the lake . . .'. At no stage does Fenton mention a 'rail road' which may indicate there was none at the time, for elsewhere he carefully records their existence and about here he laments their absence.

Earlier inclines on which horses pulled carts (later sledges) with a horse following to provide brake power had been recorded by Rev. W. Bingley[5] before 1804, but this correspondence proposes that a railway be carried on the timbers. At this period slates were loaded into boats not only at Y Cei but also at the newer Cei-Newydd (New Quay) on the Padarn shore whence they worked their way at least as far as the west end of Padarn at Cwm-y-Glo or Pen-y-Llyn for slate transfer for stockpiling; these open boats were much at the mercy of inland water and frequently foundered with all hands. This water-borne transport kept Dinorwic free from impositions of the Horse Tax!

From 1789 The Dinorwic Slate Co. had a fleet of 26 boats with crews[6] available but how the passage between the two lakes was achieved through the shallow waterneck is still unclear – it may have been by tram road – in the 1970s an 80 year old quarryman admitted 'that it was even a mystery in his own childhood' but suggested that shallow-draught sledge-shaped boats especially designed for this Pont-y-Bala link may have been dragged through the shallows by horses; copper ore boats had used this route before the quarries opened, and the channel was probably deeper.

Early transport costs for the alternative road routes were then 9d. per ton but such was the inefficiency of the method that during the winter huge stocks of slate built up at the Quarry and quayside. In 1812 Assheton-Smith had built the aforementioned 'Slate Road' on his own account, to link Dinorwic Village through Deiniolen with Aber-Pwll, and for the first time carts could take goods direct between the two. In the poor season of 1822 he reduced his tenant farmers' rents by 20%, but to those carting his slates the reduction was only 10%! Fenton has more to say, for he deplored Assheton-Smith's procedures: 'From these Quarries a road for Seven Miles to a shipping place on the Menai . . . has been lately made, where his slates are perpetually carrying, carts and men being employed in the business; so that it is to be lamented (and perhaps Mr. Smith himself will lament) that there was not at first a rail road made, which would not have required so many horses to tend it, an advantage that the neighbourhood of the Penrhyn Quarries feel, in consequence of such improvement'. (It could be that Fenton was somewhat biased – he had been royally entertained at Penrhyn Castle but not at all at Vaynol!)

The reformed Dinorwic Slate Co. of 1809 embraced William Turner (a Lancastrian well experienced in mining and quarrying in The Lake District and Wicklow), Hugh Jones of Hengwrt (the banker) together with the aforementioned Thomas Wright. Development soon took on a more earnest appearance and the building of a series of inclines from Peris shore to 'The Great New Quarry' was begun. In 1821 Assheton-Smith took over the entire Quarry on his own – an arrangement to last for 15 years – by then one of the two largest in Wales. By 1816 Dinorwic's inclines were multiplying and tramways were being built to link them; on the inclines hemp ropes gave way to chains, and chains to wire ropes[7] so by 1831 all principal movements were being made by railed vehicles, relegating wheelbarrows (of which there were prodigious numbers), packhorses, and carts to minor duties.

This late and full entry of Assheton-Smith into the affray may account for his late entry into the railway era in the mid-1820s. So long as it mainly affected his tenants, there was little encouragement for him to do more than keep the roads in reasonable state; moreover, Lord Penrhyn's railroad was having troubles of its own and two decades after building evidenced uncertainty about the most suitable form of track. While Assheton-Smith's quarries spread their workings over a vertical distance of 2000 feet and though Penrhyn also faced this problem, his railroad did not enter the quarry premises at the highest level; why Assheton-Smith chose to build his first railway along roughly the same course as his 1812 road rather than at the lowest point (to which all output might be lowered) is curious, but it could be that at the time it was judged that a line at this level would suffice for the existing workings; after all, no one would have dared to believe that output would be more than doubled in the next 15 years. Assheton-Smith was not without advice – a newspaper correspondent writing in 1810 was recommending him to follow one Penrhyn example; it 'would be an inclined plane, with proper apparatus attached', a method which was in fact soon adopted on a growing scale. An overwhelming case for a railway was made where demand for road haulage grew to such intensity, whilst the cost of operating horses had grown on account of war, that hauliers were now playing off one organisation against another for their services and in consequence it was costing more to transport to Felin-Heli than ship from thence to Liverpool.[8] Herein lay the stumbling block of all quarry operators; whilst the cost of slate at the quarry was much the same in every place, its cost at the port of shipment might cripple the business.

Within the Quarry, rock extraction along shelves, developed horizontally along a contour and named 'galleries', was evolved before 1799; by 1830 there were five principal galleries; these were not as sophisticated as the organised system of working galleries at Penrhyn Quarry which was exploited in 1812 by James Greenfield its manager. By 1816 Dinorwic Quarry's internal transport system showed some evidence of an integrated pattern of gallery tramways to connect, by means of incline(s), other gallery levels and these inclines lowered materials to mill premises where the rock could be processed. By the 1840s Assheton-Smith's income from the quarries – it was frequently said – was upwards of £100,000 a year.

Legend of an Early Tramway

In a recent biography of the Quarry, Emyr Jones records a legend of earlier times, one of many passed from generation to generation;[9] this tale is based on the childhood stories heard by Isaac Lloyd, a quarryman who died in the 1960s at a great age. A tramway of 2 ft gauge was said to exist along the north shore of Llyn Padarn – perhaps coinciding with the course of the later Padarn Railway. It would be helpful if some later evidence was available perhaps to indicate (for instance) that such a line linked the north shore quarries on Padarn-side with Cei-Newydd. Or, that it was forged between Y Cei and Cei-Newydd to run on a narrow apron of rubbish at the foot of the heights above Glan-y-Bala and perhaps link up with the first-suggested; the usefulness of the latter to avoid the 'narrows' between the lakes would be undeniable. This would in part supercede the need for slate boats, which of course were in use until the opening of The Dinorwic Railway in 1824. Of the existence of Cei-Newydd by 1793 there is no doubt, and there must have been a road down Allt-Wen side to reach it; up to six carts might be found there unloading at any one time, with the necessary boats to take away the slate.

The Dinorwic Railway (1824–1843)

There is nothing legendary about the next venture designed to replace the 1812 "Slate Road" cartage method but it suffered the same drawbacks in that the slate had to be hauled uphill to surmount the Fach-Wen ridge, en route for Aber-Pwll. The new line was 7 miles long

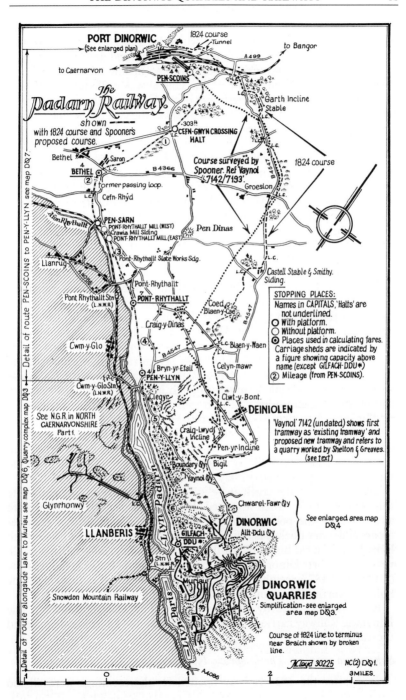

PORT DINORWIC
(See enlarged plan)
1824 course
Tunnel
to Bangor

to Caernarvon
A 499
PEN-SCOINS

The
Padarn Railway.
shown
with 1824 course and Spooners
proposed course.

Garth Incline
Stable

303ft
CEFN-GWYN CROSSING
HALT
①

Bethel
4
Saron
BETHEL
②
former passing loop.
Cefn-Rhŷd

B 4366

Course surveyed by
Spooner. Ref Vaynol
7142/7193.

1824 course

Groeslon

Afon Rhythallt
PEN-SARN
PONT-RHYTHALLT MILL (WEST)
Crawia Mill Siding
PONT-RHYTHALLT MILL (EAST)
③
Pont-Rhythallt Slate Works Sdg.

Pen Dinas

Castell Stable & Smithy.
Siding.

Llanrug
Pont-Rhythallt
Pont Rhythallt Stn.
(L.N.W.R.)
PONT-RHYTHALLT
Craig-y-Dinas
④

Coed
Blaen-y-Cae
Blaen-y-Waen
Celyn-mawr

STOPPING PLACES:
Names in CAPITALS,'Halts' are
not underlined.
○ With platform.
○ Without platform.
⊙ Places used in calculating fares.
Carriage sheds are indicated by
a figure showing capacity above
name (except GILFACH-DDU*).
② Mileage (from PEN-SCOINS).

Cwm-y-Glo
Bryn-yr-Efail
PEN-Y-LLYN
Cwm-y-Glo Stn.
(L.N.W.R.)
Clegyr
④

Clwt-y-Bont.
DEINIOLEN

See N.G.R. in NORTH
CAERNARVONSHIRE
Part 1.

Craig-Lwydi
Incline
Pen-yr Incline
⑤

'Vaynol' 7142 (undated) shows first
tramway as 'existing tramway' and
proposed new tramway and refers to
a quarry worked by Shelton & Greaves.
(see text)

Boundary Qy.
Bigil
Vaynol Qy.

Glynrhonwy

LLANBERIS

Chwarel-Fawr Qy.
DINORWIC
Allt-Ddu Qy.

See enlarged area map
DQ4

GILFACH-
DDU*
⑥
Stn.
(L.N.W.R.)

Snowdon Mountain Railway

Muriau

DINORWIC
QUARRIES
Simplification-see enlarged
area map DQ3.

Braich

Course of 1824 line to terminus
near Braich shown by broken
line.

JCLloyd 30225   NC(2) DQ1.
3 MILES.

A4086   1   0   1   2

Detail of route PEN-SCOINS to PEN-Y-LLYN see map DQ7.

See map DQ 6, Quarry complex map DQ3

Detail of route alongside Lake to Muriau see

and was the next natural answer to the problem of carrying away the output of the then major workings which lay along its contour; in the west it approached Felin-Heli from the northeast and descended steeply to the creek, a part requiring a rope-worked incline; along the course there were two adjacent inclines; the course was well-engineered and extended into the Braich department of the Quarry in the east, where it terminated. Lewis (in 1850) gives £25,000 as the cost of the line. It was given the title The Dinorwic Railway and proved inadequate almost from the start; the need to haul slate uphill was unacceptable; the enormous growth in demand meant that workings at some distance from it had to take their slate uphill to the line to load it and finally some of the most productive parts of the Quarry were well below it and nearer the lakes' shore. Assheton-Smith wrote in March 1826 complaining of the problems of lifting the loads over the ridge on the existing line. The increase in productivity is well indicated by the number of employees; 1828 – 300 men and boys; 1832 – 800; 1843 – 1,900; (and in 1858 – 2,400; and by 1873 – 2,800). The initial capacity of the line was 150 tons daily.

The gauge of the new railway was a nominal one of 24½ in. measured over the centres of rails, the wheels having a double flange which embraced the rail. In the House of Commons Enquiry into the Festiniog Railway (1836) George Homfray in evidence on contemporary trackwork stated that Dinorwic's was a 'cast-iron road – Pennant's' (i.e. The Penrhyn Railway) 'is of round Bolt'. Homfray said he preferred the wrought iron rails of the Festiniog Railway, maintaining the track was stiffer and did not sink so much, though he added that Lord Penrhyn had by then taken up his cast-iron rails and substituted wrought-iron. At the same Enquiry Assheton-Smith, speaking of his new line, said that slate was being 'let up three inclines, about 100 tons per day', which could hardly have been an economical method of transport to reach The Dinorwic Railway level. He also agreed that 'much of the slate' (he wished to quarry) 'lay under the line of the railroad'!

The wharves in the creek at Felin-Heli had to grow in line with slate shipments, and by 1828 accepted 200 ton vessels: 60–70 ships were already using the port and in due course there were further enlargements and a dry dock was built; yet further impetus came in 1849 when Rees Jones moved his shipyard from a declining Barmouth (he built 28 vessels at Port Dinorwic including 21 schooners and the barque ORDOVIC of 1877, weighing 825 tons; it was the largest sailing ship to be built in North Wales) and from 1853 an Outer Dock was begun.

Rendered obsolete by the building of The Padarn Railway, The Dinorwic Railway carried its last train in May 1843 and was dismantled thereafter.

Schemes to supplant The Dinorwic Railway

Soon after the 1824 railway opened its shortcomings were all too obvious and, like the contemporary Nantlle Railway to the south, in busy trading there was a perpetual temptation to quarry away the good slate beneath its tracks and thrust the railway to one side. It happened on both systems. Assheton-Smith wrote to his agent J. Millington:

London. 8th March, 1826

I have been glad to hear from you and Turner that the quarries are going well but I hear further expences [sic] for additional rail Road will be required. I wrote to Turner to say what was absolutely necessary must be done and to get an agreement drawn up by Mr. R. Williams [his local solicitor] with Mr. B. Jones for the addition wanted which I conclude you have heard of. This will be a considerable drawback on the profits which have not as yet much exceeded what they were before the rail Road was made . . .

Thos. A-Smith (signed)

Thoughts and indeed actual surveys turned towards something bigger and better; they tended to concern themselves with serving the Victoria department of The Big Quarry which The Dinorwic Railway did not reach. Plans and similar spade-work occupied the early and mid 1830s – one undated proposal (which survives) came from Spooner & Sons, Portmadoc, and coincides with the period when James Spooner's survey for a Festiniog Railway was taking actual form. At the Quarry end, Spooner's line would have left Victoria and crossed the foot of the old 'A' inclines to the east of the latterday A4 incline. (There still exists an earthwork stretching westwards from the head of the later A2 incline, and though it would be convenient to associate this with a possible start on the Spooner idea, this work is not on the same contour: furthermore, the diagram shows that hereabouts Spooner intended his line to run through one of three tunnels.) The surviving Plan, hand-tinted but lacking many features to locate it exactly, would have worked westwards about the 600 ft contour, passed south of the Fach-Wen Quarry after curving sharply above Bedw-Argoed, and then swung north-west through two tunnels and cross-country to Ynys-Llech-Arian ('Ynys Llecheyryn' on the Plan). Thereafter it would follow the 1824 railway ('Present Railway') through Groeslon to Garth-Fach where it left it, and diverging westward, fell down a small valley past Cefn ('Tan-yr-Wlfa') and so to the head of the later-day Padarn Railway Port Incline at Pen-Scoins. There is no Section to the Plan and no inclines are marked, so perhaps a Festiniog Railway-like fall (bearing in mind that that line at the time was to have inclines in lieu of a tunnel) for gravity working was intended in a distance of 7 miles 30 chains over a fall of c.370 ft? Referring to the incomplete earthwork just mentioned, this may still be followed across the Vivian Quarry excavation (not then worked at this height). Above the Quarry Hospital it ceases abruptly, perhaps due to a change of policy.[10] Meanwhile the route could have been used in truncated form and products lowered by the Vivian Incline to Cei-Newydd, on Padarn side.

Traditionally this unfinished scheme has always been linked with another based on a proposed focal point on Padarn shore at Bedw-Argoed to which boats might bring Peris-side products. A railway would have run from here (at least) to Pen-y-Llyn . . . and may indeed have already existed thus far in the shape of the legendary system of c.1800. Be that as it may, it is certain that by closing The Dinorwic Railway – or at least diverting some of its traffic – by means of a scheme to extend the Allt-Ddu Quarry rubbish-tipping tramway which skirted the north edge of the Big Tip (Domen-Fawr) (and which is still a clear footpath) the quarries east of Dinorwic village, denied their Dinorwic Railway, could have moved their output along such an extension which at its western tip would have formed an incline down to Bedw-Argoed.[11] The truncated gallery ending on the hill above the hospital together with the 'Domen-Fawr' scheme, have always been a legend as forming one great scheme; if the scheme was arrested on the realisation that a superior plan would be to continue a Padarn-side railway eastward past Bedw-Argoed, under Glan-y-Bala by a tunnel and thus into Muriau and Hafod-Owen below the Victoria Level on Peris-side, the conception of the Padarn Railway as built is clear. Some have thought the change of plan was also due to land-ownership problems: Gruffydd Ellis's diary of c.1850 ('Cof Lyfr') recalls that the Allt-Ddu to Padarn-side link was long contemplated, and that in 1845 Assheton-Smith gave £13,500 for Fach-Wen Quarry 'consisting of 300 acres mainly of rock for which Lord Newborough's grandfather had paid £800. There were three reasons which [sic] Mr. Smith bought it, first so that he could build a railway through it, second he could dump rubbish from Allt-Ddu there and thirdly to get farms for his quarrymen; and a good plan it was . . .'. (Lord Newborough's royalty for slate carried over his land was ½d. per ton, amounting to £70–80 per annum, i.e. c.38,000 tons carried over the Padarn Railway).

How remarkably close to the truth this diary proves to be is confirmed in correspondence between Lord Newborough (owner of Fach-Wen) and Edwin Shelton (its lessee) in 1839–40.[12] It appears that by 1840 'Smith's agents . . .' had ascertained some background to Fach-Wen 'even to the sum it was bought for a century ago'. They knew 'Shelton had tried and failed . . . proof that the whole thing was good for nothing'. Smith had agreed to re-purchase the land for £13,500 giving as his reason that the land was the only site in the district where he could obtain slate 'It being the only one on that side of the Lake which does not belong to me . . .'. Locally it was then well-known that Smith was employing James Spooner to survey for a new railway which would have to pass through Fach-Wen 'I understand Mr. Spooner is engaged early and late in completing for Mr. Assheton-Smith the Plans and Sections for a Railway through Fach-Wen' (20th April, 1840) – (Shelton to Lord Newborough). His Lordship had two problems; firstly to obtain the best price, and secondly that his tenant would need to sell his lease; Shelton had to pay royalty to Newborough on any slate won, but long ago had proved Fach-Wen unworthy of further exploitation, so he hoped Newborough would help him to dispose of the lease and find a buyer for 'machinery and rails at the Quarry'. Ellis' diary is confirmed throughout this exchange of letters, namely that Smith needed Fach-Wen through which to build his Spooner-surveyed new railway, and that until it was his, there would be no railway! Further, that Shelton had no legal means of preventing Smith from building a line over his leased land, whoever was the land-owner, and that a 'party from Manchester' was interested in Glynrhonwy and Fach-Wen, but not intending to buy both. Shelton writes finally (24th August, 1840) 'Fach-Wen, I am convinced will never pay to be worked without a Railroad Communication and therefore can only be of value to Mr. Smith . . .' revealing that Shelton intended to hold on in the hope of a good price for his lease. The incomplete earthworks before-mentioned along the Spooner survey, abandoned in favour of a lake-shore site for the new railway, could be evidence of Smith's problems in having an 'island' owned by Newborough in the way of his plans!

The foregoing correspondence includes reference to the existing line when Smith complains to his Agent, Owen Roberts (19th February, 1840):

> I would recommend altering your old road by degrees making it upon your new property with better levels and substituting malleable for cast iron. The first part to be altered should be that from the Bwlch Inclines to Castell – we can have inclinations of Road by making an Inclined Balance about Midway betwixt. The Cost of forming an inclined road would be but smaller and an Extra Incline would be so far from delaying, expedite the working, because the Horses would be able to tread with so much greater ease, and the Inclines to draw up the Slates from Victoria and under Braich may be very easily effected as was proposed to you two years since at an easy Cost.

The next sentence is very significant, emphasising that though Smith considered the existing Railroad unworthy of further improvement, he was at the same time full of doubts as to the outcome of the Spooner survey and prepared to urge Roberts to improve the eastern end of the Railroad (as above) albeit this length would have survived as a feeder – so it was proposed – to any new mainline.

> But nevertheless, if I did anything at all about a new or improved line of Railway I should much prefer going to the expense of £10,000 (Tomos Estimate) at once and get rid of these sets of Inclines.

Sometimes writing twice in one day, Shelton goes to great lengths to convince Newborough that Smith only wants the land for a railway and that he (Shelton) had already spent £5000 (this included costs pre-viously incurred by Thomas Jones of Glynrhonwy prospecting on behalf of Owen Roberts), by Thomas Pritchard for Shelton and 'by Hugh Jones and others whom I repaid for making the new road' . . . 'the results were uniformly unsatisfactory'.

Ellis' diary emphasises that even after The Padarn Railway along the lakeshore had opened, Assheton-Smith – for reasons which are no longer apparent – was trying to link Fach-Wen with Allt-Ddu by rail . . . perhaps demand was so pressing that even the small Fach-Wen Quarry, now in his own hands, was capable of development? Ellis adds a few useful dates of some of the smaller quarries' opening dates, all being swallowed up in The Big Quarry later: Wellington (or Diphwys) 1810; Clogwen-y-Gigfrau 1811; Braich c.1822; Matilda 1826 (named after lessees wife); Victoria 1827 ('an old quarry worked by the old people for hundreds of years'). Ellis emphasises the growth in population; in the Fach-Wen district there were 13 houses in 1785 and 140 by 1850.

The Village Branch

After closure of the 1824 rail outlet some means had to be found to give the older Allt-Ddu district workings a link with the sea. As the Domen-Fawr – Bedw-Argoed scheme was not prosecuted, a railway running in the opposite direction and linking the periphery of Allt-Ddu pit near the course of the 1824 line with the main Mills of The Big Quarry at the top of the later A4 incline was built at uncertain date, but clearly not long after The Dinorwic Railway carried its last load. Names have varied for this line, sometimes known as The Doctor's Road, The Village Tramway or simply, The Mills Branch. It had operating problems as the line ran uphill to the Mills; both it and the feeder branches were horse-worked until the 1890s, when improvements in grade and curvature made it suitable for steam locomotives, but some horse-haulage survived hereabouts until the beginning of the First War.

The Padarn Railway (1843–1961)

The decision to build a 4 ft gauge,[13] pick-a-back method, railway on the chosen site must have been largely determined by what to avoid in the methods tried and found wanting at that time, and the choice of route at the lowest altitude would, on the completion of an incline system, be a natural outcome. Construction was carried out most speedily and as had been said, coincided with a time when quarry labour was available. Though their plans were not used, the Spooners were called in as consultants and may have actually been responsible for the ultimate course. From its western end at the head of a 2 ft gauge (nom.) incline dropping down to the Port, it left Pen-Scoins and climbed gradually as a single line, reached and passed along the north shore of Padarn and then by means of a tunnel, terminated at the north shore of Llyn Peris at Muriau. The length was 7m. 5ch. To facilitate the building, a temporary railway was laid the full length of the route; construction began in May 1841 and was complete by March 1843.

James Spooner's fee was £58 16s. 0d., and the railway cost almost £35,000. Nearly everything was built by local labour, from civil engineering and track assembly to rolling stock, though non-local materials were obtained from South Wales or England, for instance. Between 3rd March, 1843 and 10th February, 1848 trains were drawn by horses in each direction – there was no gravity working – for the conception was basically a more sophisticated and larger version of the 1824 line, using similar operating methods but adopting the pick-a-back procedure of carrying the loaded quarry wagons on rail-transporters or Host Wagons. The initial arrangements at Port Dinorwic between 1843–1845 remain in doubt; the new railway's Port Incline-foot abutted land which was not leased from the Crown until 1845 and a temporary scheme must have obtained. Considerable alterations to track, curvature, clearances and the opening out of tunnels then ensued [a mid-route 46 yd. tunnel (probably at Llech-y-Fulfran, where there is now a rock cutting) was opened into a cutting and the 460 yd Glan-y-Bala tunnel was given an enlarged bore to suit], to enable steam locomotives to take over the working from horses. At first the line was named The Padarn Rail Road, later The Padarn Railway, but from about 1880 the name The Dinorwic Quarry Railway became official. It was to survive as the ultimate quarry–port link and served its original purpose until 1961. More recently the Llanberis Lake Railway, a tourist system, has been built on part of the site running along the shore of Llyn Padarn.

Equally anxious to tap this lucrative source of traffic were the standard gauge railways; a Caernarvon extension (nominally independent but part of the Chester & Holyhead Railway) reached Port Dinorwic on 10th March, 1852 and a branch was built down to the quays using in part some of the formation of the 1812 Slate Road. Some business in carrying slate from the quayside in standard gauge wagons then robbed the previous sea-borne tonnages of a part of their total, and this traffic tended to grow in more recent times.

The Padarn-Peris Tram Line: 'The Tram Line'

The most easterly portion of The Padarn Railway led through a tunnel at Glan-y-Bala, forced upon the builders of the line by the proximity of rock face to the waters between the lakes (but tunnelling would be easy to those rockmen whose work in the Quarry involved tunnels on its tramways). This bore had one horizontal ventilating adit opposite Pont-y-Bala; at some time castellated walling and an ornamental stone entrance at the west mouth were added, these matching nearby features. From 1848 rubbish from Vivian Quarry and elsewhere began to be tipped hereabouts, and soon formed a great apron pushing out into the lake; Cei-Newydd was buried, but it had already been replaced by the Railway. By 1870, the site known as

Gilfach-Ddu (Black Nook) had been used for the erection of work-shops,[14] stores, and railway sheds alongside an existing store yard; and the old 'A' inclines were abandoned in favour of a more westerly group which came down beside the Padarn Railway terminus here. Thus, the area close to the west mouth of the tunnel became the focal point of the Quarry tramways which were also led into the works. A development of this was to convert the Padarn Railway track through the tunnel into Quarry-Gauge, and truncate it in a new terminus just west of Gilfach-Ddu complex where Quarry wagons might be run on and off 4 ft gauge trains. This new Quarry-Gauge line was worked by horses, but in 1870 a steam locomotive was placed on it and the converted section was named 'The Tram Line'. By the early 20th century further tipping round the Glan-y-Bala bluff enabled the Tram Line to be brought out of the tunnel and re-laid (together with a road along the same route), so a new road-rail link by-passing the tunnel was created: the tunnel was still in use in April 1899 for it was then lit by '30 lamps' whilst a Royal Train passed through it.

Larger engines were constructed for the new route to enable long trains of slate wagons to be brought from the most easterly part of The Big Quarry to the loading station. The tunnel had employed 8–12 horses which were replaced by one locomotive; this was in time sent to work in the Quarry and ultimately engines of a larger type were specifically ordered for The Tram Line. From about 1899 the tunnel lay disused, only to come into life again during World War II as a factory; after the Quarry closed it was a workshop for a period and more recently the Central Electricity Generating Board has used it as a route for cables on its pumped storage reservoir project inside Elidir mountain. The west mouth now measures 12 ft × 12 ft. Like the Village Branch, The Tram Line was regarded as a separate entity in the whole railway organisation! An inventory in 1877 valued its 1,310 yards of 56 lb. chaired rail at £363 – the Tramway was therefore rather less than half a mile long.

Such was the improved potential for traffic at the new Gilfach-Ddu terminal that in 1873 the L.N.W.R. proposed to extend its Llanberis branch round the head of Padarn to a new terminus between the lakeshore and Padarn Railway at a short distance from that system's engine shed and coaling platform. This plan was never carried into effect.

Early Quarries and their Rail Links

A Plan of the Quarry and Dinorwic Railway prepared by R. Lloyd Ellis in 1836, together with references in Ellis' diary, emphasises the difficulties in choosing an altitude suitable to terminate that Railway. Listing the workings roughly from west to east which lay along The Dinorwic Railway course there were: Chwarel-Fawr, Allt-Ddu, Adelaide (and buried here, Bryn-Glas), Vaynol, Raven Rock and Garret ('The Old Quarry'), Harriet, Matilda, Morgan's, Sophia and Braich. The Railway's route was a compromise to serve each as nearly as possible. The distance from first to last quarry thus served was approximately 1,400 yards.

In a separate group of workings, and at the time of the Plan without confirmed rail communication, was a cluster below the above-listed and nearer the Peris-shore: Ellis, Turner, Bryn-Llys, Hafod Owen (or Wellington), Millington, Victoria (or Diphwys), which later found themselves better placed for the terminus of The Padarn Railway. Lastly the group of smaller quarries along and above the Padarn shore and from the west included Boundary, with above it Fach-Wen (leased to Shelton & Greaves in 1834, losing Shelton in the early 1840s and becoming Greaves' Quarry by 1864 . . . only producing 550 tons yearly at that time . . . perhaps emphasising land boundary doubts hereabouts), Vaynol, Ladas and Vivian. Additionally there were quite a dozen smaller quarries in this area both above and at the water's edge, all in easy reach of The Padarn Railway but leaving no surviving traces of any intrinsic connection.

By 1843 all working faces were served by tramways laid in 'iron rails'; there were portions of The Big Quarry where a layer of whinstone dividing its upper and lower parts was left standing as a pillar, 'Big Dyke', an eye-catching feature. Though an over-simplification, it may be said that the rail system ultimately became linked to the two main incline systems, the westerly at Garret and the easterly at Braich. Today the original and amended routes of both these incline systems are still clearly visible; from these two trunk routes the galleries branched west and east, whilst some gallery lines passed over or below them. Galleries were at intervals of 75 vertical feet. There were also independent inclines of considerable length in various other parts of the Quarry; to reach deeper pits and galleries within the mountain itself certain galleries tunnelled into the hillface and entered craters which, surrounded by their own satellite gallery systems, were only accessible through such tunnels. An alternative to tunnelling was to make deep cuttings; a number of these were a feature of The Big Quarry. By 1858 there were about 23 miles of tramways and wire-roped inclines, the 18 inclines averaging 600 ft long . . . by 1960 this tramway mileage had grown to almost sixty, and there were also 15 miles of compressed air piping.

The accounts give little insight, but confusingly refer to each fresh working as 'new quarry' without identification; one such opened in 1832 had new inclines from the start and these were on a scale as never before. Thomas Jones (millwright) built the components which were shipped into Port Dinorwic and carried by the railway; winding drums sent in parts were assembled on the site; Baldwin & Co. of Bilston, Staffs. supplied iron tanks which were taken to Liverpool and shipped to Port Dinorwic. Thomas Gladstone made the ropes and Bayley Bros.

cast the iron bars for the inclines' tracks . . . all these were brought together over the winter of 1831–2 and made some interesting east-ward-bound loads for the railway. In 1848 a further quarry was opened at the top of Raven Rock (for once, the site is named) but now the incline materials, brought by sea, were taken to The Big Quarry foot by The Padarn Railway . . . in trains hauled by steam. To judge from the materials supplied where water was available some of these inclines must have worked on the water balance system – the later wire ropes had a breaking strain of 30 tons.

By the late 1850s Port Dinorwic could hold 120 vessels in its two docks.

Dates are infrequent for this period, but Morris' diary notes the opening of Terfyn Incline (the penultimate on Garret) on 13th August, 1868, 230 yards long (No. A8). The same source records that a steam locomotive first worked on the summit at Braich (1,480 ft) on 7th March, 1878, which suggests a de Winton product in Pen-Garret Department.

These remarkable achievements were essential, for all was formerly not well; in May 1873 the 'CARNARVON & DENBIGH HERALD' referred to the unplanned development which had occurred during the years up to the 1870s, so that 'within the memory of those now living the whole concern was one of chaos. At that time it was probably worked profitably for the time being, but certainly not with an eye to the future. The present ambition is to get all the galleries level, apply a tramway to each of them and dispose of all the rubbish in the lake'.[15] Boundaries between quarries were scarcely marked out and the land division between Wellington and Victoria, for instance, was simply a wooden post driven into the bed of the lake. Land boundaries between Wellington, Sophia and Harriet had become unknown. A period of tremendous planning ensued; evidence is found among the new 'A' inclines and the Gilfach-Ddu complex formed around a rectangular yard 80 × 60 yards in that fortress-like citadel.

The same newspaper describes it all; wagons (all of which were stated to have been built on the premises – which was not true), the 48 ft diameter waterwheel to drive the Works (supplied by de Winton and having its water brought from the other side of the valley), and the new village built for the quarrymen. One street therein, Pant Eden, had the latest device . . . a tramway down its centre to bring coal to the door.

Latterday Railway Networks in the Quarry and the End of an Era

It was the construction of the Padarn Railway which had the greatest effect on the internal railways in the Quarry, as was the subsequent removal of its terminus from Muriau to Gilfach-Ddu; the latter alter-ation was preceded by the resiting of the existing 'A' inclines to a situation further west, to bring their foot into the Gilfach-Ddu area

Plate I "Llanberis Slate Quarries The Property of T. Assheton Smith Esq."   *per J.S. Wilkinson*

Plate II The Allt-Ddu area seen from above Allt-Ddu Quarry. Loco Shed *(centre left);* Village Branch *(extreme left)*; Domen-Fawr *(centre to right)*: 1968.   *J.I.C. Boyd*

Plate III The Village Branch looking west from The Mills towards the Allt-Ddu complex - at this time the line had been abandoned: January 1968. *J.I.C. Boyd*

Plate IV The Lower portion of Graig-Lwyd Incline at Cribau on the 1824 Dinorwic Railway is still very evident: November 1966. *J.I.C. Boyd*

Plate V 'Port Siding' signal box looking south on the now-lifted Bangor-Caernarvon line. The Port Branch fell down to the Dock in the right distance. The 1824 Dinorwic Railway made its way from right to left across the middle of this scene, en route from the Port to the foot of Garth Incline. This line was abandoned in 1843; the standard gauge did not arrive until 1852: 1952.

J.I.C. Boyd

Plate VI A surviving feature of the Dinorwic Railway is the western mouth of the tunnel just outside Port Dinorwic: 1982.

J.I.C. Boyd

Plate VII A probable form of Dinorwic Railway track before abandonment, showing T-bulb rail and two forms of chair (one making the rail joint). The wooden sleeper is not of that period. (Garrett Incline. A8). *J.I.C. Boyd*

Plate VIII Slab sleeper with later form of chair; Dinorwic Railway period.
J.I.C. Boyd

Plate IX Chairs of the Dinorwic Railway era style, to hold T-bulb rail.
J.I.C. Boyd

Plate X Port Dinorwic before the alterations of 1896 showing former bridge; the former Dinorwic Railway terminated on the right hand wharf.   *Gwynedd Archives*

Plate XI Port Dinorwic looking up the berths towards the Dry Dock; the VELINHELI moored on right, and loading slates: c 1912.   *Gwynedd Archives*

Plate XII The full extent of four-tracked Incline C1: c 1895.   *Gwynedd Archives*

Plate XIII Vivian Quarry Inclines with bridge over Padarn Railway (*right*) to bring out rubbish. Note the Travelling Platforms on this form of incline, and slate wagons on 4 ft. gauge transporters below the bridge: c 1895.   *Gwynedd Archives*

Plate XIV The full extent of The Big Quarry, with Llyn Peris below, before the turn of the century. There are

amways thereon which disappeared long before present-day memory. *J.I.C. Boyd*

Plate XV WILD ASTER on typical Quarry duty. The loco is too heavy for the adjoining track, so the rubbish wagons behind have a hawser on the rear wagon which is attached to the 'Car Cyrn' slab wagons (*far right*): this will pull the latter along the parallel line where WILD ASTER cannot go!

per T.H. Morris

Plate XVI A Ruston & Hornsby rail tractor leaves a typical rock tunnel, propelling modern 'Car Cyrn' wagons of slabs en route for the Mill. *Gwynedd Archives*

Plate XVII ALICE peeps from her enforced hibernation in the engine shed on Australia level, the top of the Quarry. Work had then ceased there: 1960. *D.L. Chatfield*

Plate XVIII Seven years after the previous scene, ALICE still moulders and the level has the abandoned atmosphere of permanency about it. *J.I.C. Boyd*

Plate XIX In such shelters as these, locomotives might lurk during blasting operations.   *J.I.C. Boyd*

Plate XX An untypical 'Tank Incline' type Travelling Platform; whilst elsewhere this type was operated by filling and emptying a water tank on the Traveller it was not so latterly at Dinorwic where control was solely by the brake on the winding drum!   *J.I.C. Boyd*

Plate XXI The Mills, looking up inclines A5, A6 and A7 towards Garrett. *D.L. Chatfield*

Plate XXII The tricky practice of bringing out a run of slabs from a spur on the C inclines; note the wagons of rubbish (*left*) and the tactically-placed beam of timber some way below them; the beam was lifted out when the rubbish wagons took up the weight of the slab wagons. *Gwynedd Archives*

Plate XXIII Civil engineering features were on a huge scale, but were everyday construction to men whose task was working with rock. *J.I.C. Boyd*

Plate XXIV A typical level showing stub points in chaired track to carry steam locomotives, the track passing under a slab-supported incline embankment.   *J.I.C. Boyd*

Plate XXV The Mills. Wagons of slab await processing. The dinner-hour is in progress, the men have gone to the Cabanau and the only sound is of wind moaning in the roof: 1965.   *J.I.C. Boyd*

Plate XXVI Slate wagons are loaded at Hafod Owen before being taken over The Tram Line to Gilfach-Ddu: 1931.   *S. Bale Ltd.*

Plate XXVII Following on from above, loaded slate wagons leave Hafod Owen behind a Tram Line engine. 'The Big Dyke' is a distinctive pillar of rock: c 1905.   *from an official brochure*

itself, and this allowed excavation and tipping to obliterate some of their site. There was of course a continuous pattern of change within the Quarry, and as fresh working faces were opened, the portable temporary tracks were lifted and moved forward as required; fresh sites (known as Departments) were begun and some of the older filled up with rubbish. Inclines, mills, workshops, smithies and locomotive facilities might disappear completely in the interest of a source of new materials or the replanning of the railway system; the face of the mountain became one of slow but inexorable change and at an unrecorded date the 'C' inclines were considerably altered. Of these obsolete sites little remained as rubbish spewed down from above and engulfed all surfaces of little future portent.

By the mid 1930s the Quarry employed 3,000 men and boys; its output was c.350 tons a day or c.100,000 tons per year (of which that amount shipped had declined to 37,200 tons). The pick-a-back wagons of the Padarn Railway carried four 2 ton slate wagons each (each slate wagon carrying about 1¾ ton of slates) and a typical train formation of 16 wagons might carry c.110 tons per trip; thus the 350-ton daily output required 200 slate or 50 transporter wagons each way daily over the railway, requiring three train rakes to be loaded, transported and returned to the quarry on average Monday–Saturday; in practice additional runs might be made Monday–Friday so that work would cease at noon on Saturday. At this date there were 22 galleries in the main quarry (the highest at 1,500 ft), each running across the face of the mountain over an elevation of about 2,000 ft and with its own individual railway system of which an average length was 1 mile. Each gallery had its own railway motive power with attendant facilities of shed, repair work, coal, water etc. and was connected to the remainder of the Quarry system by incline(s), some as steep as 1 in 2. Each gallery had a main line (usually steam worked, and some had blast shelters to protect the loco during blasting) and branches in lighter track materials were worked by hand or in certain cases, rail tractors. Track materials varied according to the status of the line. The total gallery mileage of that time was said to exceed 60 miles, all of 1 ft 10¾ in. gauge, and by the mid 1950s there were over 2,000 quarry wagons of all kinds.

For economic reasons the details of which are outside the scope of this account, the Quarry was closed down during July 1969 and was auctioned in December 1969 and June 1970.

Among the reasons for decline was an ever-lessening demand for slate which followed the short-lived World War II boom (it has continued into the 1980s); such quarries as now survive are few in number and having limited output, enjoy a reasonable trade. But Dinorwic is not among them. The slate rock which had provided that natural source of wealth remains, but access to it after over 150 years of quarrying – not all done with the next generation in mind – made the removal of overburden become less economic with rising wages. In due course 75%

of costs was attributable to wages, which themselves were low compared with those obtainable elsewhere; also young men were no longer
attracted to conditions inseparable from quarry work. In 1959–60 the
Company re-opened a basic quarry on adjacent Marchlyn, following a
spectacular collapse of part of the working face in The Big Quarry in
the late 1950s and early 1960s which demonstrated time was running
out for some of the Departments.[16] Initially Marchlyn had a primitive
railway system, but here and elsewhere transport turned to heavy earthmoving equipment and construction of rough roads; the writing was on
the wall for all tram lines. Marchlyn proved to be a failure.

On the Padarn Railway slates continued to be taken to the Port for a
further fourteen years after the Workmen's Train had ended, and
where steamships were involved in coastal deliveries until 1957. On
27th October, 1961 the last train went to Pen-Scoins; by then rail
transport was reduced to a run of under ten wagons, once daily. Pittrail
Ltd. obtained the contract for demolition of the Padarn Railway, and
for a time road lorries took deliveries away from Gilfach-Ddu and
occasionally delivered to the Port for shipment. At the Quarry the
Padarn Railway materials were cut up for scrap and the workmen's
coaches, brought from their sheds, were made into what became a
familiar Dinorwic funeral pyre – set alight after being drenched with
petrol. Some parts, including doors, were removed and found other
strange uses; of the passenger stock, the Saloon has survived.

Within the Quarry the gallery system was being run down; by 1964
only three steam engines were in service, NO. 1, DOLBADARN and HOLY
WAR; the last-named survived the others and worked until November
1967. The Company had installed new plant at Muriau for making
roofing materials from waste and this produced some export business; a
tithe of railway working survived along the old Tram Line until suddenly, on 10th July, 1969, closure of the undertaking ended employment for the 350 men who were the last of hundreds to spend their
working lives on Elidir. The cost of borrowing money for new projects
which showed insufficient return for Debenture interest put the
Company into liquidation.

Following auctions on 12th and 13th December, 1969, equipment
from Quarry and Port was sold – a host wagon, complete with brake
van and three slate wagons, was already at the Narrow Gauge Railway
Museum at Tywyn. FIRE QUEEN, the Saloon and a velocipede duly
found a home at Penrhyn Castle, certain Quarry engines were purchased for further use on what was to be a new railway laid on Padarn
shore (see p.219); all the Hunslet and other engines found buyers at
this or on previous occasions. More recently Gilfach-Ddu Works with
its great water wheel, together with surrounding parts of the Quarry,
have become an Industrial Museum of Slate Quarrying, though not
confined to Dinorwic itself in its ambitions.

Portions of former locations of railways and tramways (the Port has become a yacht-basin and Marina) the Works (now a Museum) together with part of the Padarn course now forming the Llanberis Lake Railway, are still being developed, entirely due to imaginative public bodies or private citizens. At the Gilfach-Ddu Museum the personality of the quarryman and the ethos of the slate quarry can be recalled by all, but for the few who lived and worked among such an unique railway system – which appeared to enjoy such everlasting properties – the sound of a quarry engine working the new lakeshore railway and carried by the breeze which moans round the rubbish tips, is to fan the embers of a memory which no Museum can re-create.

(Of the later disposal of parts of the Quarry, the building of a Pump Storage Scheme by the Central Electricity Generating Board and the later history of the Dinorwic site, this account pays no regard.)

THE DINORWIC RAILWAY

(opened by 1824; closed May 1843)

Following the acquisition of the Dinorwic Slate Co. by Assheton-Smith, William Turner, Hugh Jones (the Dolgellau Banker) and Thomas Wright in 1809, great impetus was put into improving the transport system. First came (as already noted) The Slate Road opened by 1812, along which tenants could cart slate if broad-wheeled carts were employed. The Company had by now switched from water to land transport and out-goings for 30th June–30th September, 1812 show:[17]

Paid for quarrying slates, clearing, tradesmens' bills, erecting buildings etc.	£1133. 14. 5½d.
Paid for carriage of slates down from the quarries, loading, and repairing new road, straw and storage etc.	£828. 1. 3¼d.

and perhaps due to the greater efficiency of the new road the Quarry was obliged to improve its methods and rail transport appears for the first time: (1st Jan–1st April, 1813)

Paid Quarrying etc and for making Rail Road	£1360. 11. 2d.
Loading, and repairing new road (as above)	£780. 3. 0½d.

After July, repairs to Rail Road feature again, but thereafter only the new road and the erection of cottages in the Quarry. When early in 1823 a new road was driven to the top of Raven Rock in the Quarry, knowledge of a Quarry–Port rail link proposal is in the air – and John Hughes' recollections suggest work had begun before Newborough's George Bettiss received a letter from Griffiths of Pwllheli (Newborough's solicitor) recommending that railway construction should soon begin, especially that of 'The Llanberis Quarry Railway'.[18]

'Mr. Jones of Plasgrove' was given the work of building the line, and received his first payment in the year ending 30th June, 1824 (£900); he finished the job and had had his final payment on 10th March, 1825, his total being £9000. Within the same Contract he was to supply 200 wagons at £7 each – by March 1825 a further 60 had been added to his order. In May that year the line had been extended 'at the Quarries and at the Inclines £231. 0. 0d.' and with exchange of land between Smith and Rice-Thomas along Nant-y-Garth, walling was begun. Some was by Robert Lloyd but farmers whose land was taken for the line were paid to do their own walling. H. Robert Williams had been appointed surveyor and was still measuring land taken from farms in summer 1825; his total fee was a little over £100. In June 1825 Evan Evans (mason) had £60 for erecting 'Stable at the Quarry for the Waggon Horses and other buildings'.

Jones the contractor was back again in autumn 1825 'laying additional length of Rail Road at Brynllys Qy. & turnouts at the foot of Raven Rock & other places', further employment for him in 1826 concerned 'Iron for the New Road . . . bottom of Raven Rock to the new Quarry & other places' (£540. 18. 0d.) and at that time Mr. Roberts made '3 large Waggons for the purpose of carrying large slate slabs £21. 15. 0d.' so perhaps until then the line only carried slates? At Brynllys they then erected a water-wheel, and the parts were brought up by train. Contemporary opinion held that the railway was nevertheless inadequate, and this may be confirmed by the continuing extensions then being made to it!

In September 1826 Captain Williams (ship's master) had brought 'Iron from Liverpool to make a Railway on the Upper Incline in the Raven Rock Quarry' and boundary walling on the main line continued. Not until the quarter ending December 1825 is there reference to traffic, when £586. 13. 0d. is paid 'for carriage of Slates' but no names are given; however, from October 1826 Daniel Roberts is the named contractor for carriage; no tonnages or rates are given but he received £663. 16. 9d. and £651. 6. 10d. on 2nd October and 30th December respectively. He was allowed to charge for 'ale consumed by the Carriers'. Clearly he was retained for over a·decade and his Payment's Books for 1838–40 reflect growing traffic in the Railway's closing years; horses were bought in Anglesey for an average of £14. 18. 0d. each and Horse Tax cost four guineas for the six-month period. On average a new horse was bought every month, and their costs included 'Salts, spices and ale for Horse 2. 6d.' and 'Caskia Powder at Stabal 2. 6d.'. In the period of these books, four purchases of 'Inclain Rope' were made, and 2000 Boat Nails, 2000 Shoeing Nails and 4 lb. chain were bought.

Passing largely over Assheton-Smith's own land the Railway required no statutory authority, though clearly some territorial liberties were intended, as when Lord Newborough's attention was drawn to the proposed route, it was quickly amended. The earliest accounts survive from May 1829 when Thomas Roberts was in full charge of the undertaking (he would be either Manager or Superintendent) and all bills were passed through him for payment. Physically the Railway was divided into three levels because of the incline near the Port at Garth, and the mid-route pair of inclines at Graig-Lwyd; though not worked as a balanced incline (as were the foregoing) there was a steepish fall into the Port in favour of the load. Operation was by horses (but not gravity) and the three levels from Quarry to Port were (a) Braich Quarry to head of Upper Graig-Lwyd incline, (b) foot of Lower Graig-Lwyd incline to head of Garth incline, (c) foot of Garth incline to the boundary of the Port area: the tracks at the Port were separately documented and recorded. Unlike operation on neighbouring slate railways, the men in charge of trains detached the horses at inclines, walked them and picked up fresh rakes of wagons at the other end. The positions of stabling points were: Allt-Ddu; foot of Lower Craig-Lwyd; 'Stablau Newydd' (where the railway came alongside the 1812 road); head of Garth incline. Port horses or manpower were used on the lowest level. The Quarry authorities provided the horses, and not the men who contracted for the work; the positions of the stables appear regularly in the accounts for deliveries of straw, bran, oats and in summer, vetch, for horse feed.[19]

The Quarry and Railway accounts are generally not separated and this makes identification difficult; for instance, in winter 1829 Towers of Bangor Foundry supplied sleepers, likely to be iron ones for the Quarry because Dinorwic Railway sleepers were of stone or slab. Thomas Gladstone & Co. of Liverpool supplied 'ropes for inclines', and Wood Bros. '3 chains had for the inclines on the Railroad £74 6s. 4d.', and in spring 1830 Towers sent 'rowlers' and iron rails for £19 15s. 7d. – these would be chain rollers and rails for inclines – spelling errors are frequent; in May 1832 Thomas Jones was paid £1 7s. 0d. for 'making slippers for the railway' (previously the term 'Railroad' was mostly used) – these would be stone or slab. A note in January 1833 states the Quarry profit had exceeded £12,000. As to the demise of the first railway, Lewis' (4th Edit. 1850) says '. . . the old tramway has been wholly removed'. On 30th August, 1831, the 'NORTH WALES CHRONICLE' said briefly: 'Last Tuesday a boy fell on Mr. Smith's quarry railway from Llanberis to Moelydon, and was run over.'

The Route (incorporating field notes first made in 1945)

The Railway began at a height of about 970 ft and 8¼ m. from Port at an unnamed quarry (according to the Estate Survey of 1832) immediately above 'Braich & Hafod Owen Quarry' which lay above Llyn Peris shore: it ran west and north passing several small workings to its north side (unnamed) into the parish of Llanberis above Pant-y-

Ceubren – a farm now engulfed by rubbish. Just within the parish it passed the south end of Raven Rock Quarry with its northern extension, Garret Quarry; there was a branch into the former, and a small lake opposite the junction. Beyond came a cottage and weighing machine, another lake on the north side and, to avoid these sheets of water, the line meandered for some distance. All the foregoing length has long been buried by tipping.

The course can be identified today by a very short length of embankment east of the Allt-Ddu group of pits; a tramway course of later construction round the south edge of these pits was not the Dinorwic Railway proper, but a deviation to avoid additional quarry work – this later earthwork with some slab sleepers is very clear – it is crudely constructed. At its western end it joins the 1824 course, here to be found beyond and above the roadway (where it has again disappeared) on the west lip of Allt-Ddu; all trace has been lost due to the southward extension of Allt-Ddu Quarry. From here onwards the course rises, running on the north side of the 1812 Slate Road (the tramroad traces on the other side are later systems), curves round and above Chwarel-Fawr pit (erroneously named 'Allt-Ddu' on the Estate Plans 1832!) and so past Tan-y-Fawnog and the site of Dinorwic House – which gave its name to the district. At Bron-y-Foel the line crossed to the south edge of the Slate Road and at Bigil traversed an embankment to reach the head of the Upper Graig-Lwyd Incline.

On a clear day this makes a superb viewpoint; to the southwest the cliffs of Lleyn, the Irish Sea ahead, the coast of Anglesey and nearer, the Menai Straits. A nearby house carries the name 'Pen-yr-Incline'. The Upper incline is the longer; at its foot there is Caer-Main and a sharp short left-hand curve: the Lower incline begins, at its top the walls of a drumhouse survive, and there are traces of a shelter for its brakesman (5¾ m. from Port). At the foot is Cribau, a cluster of ruins relating to the railway doing duty as stables, weigh-house and warehouse; there are traces of a horse-trough. The track then passed through the hamlet of Clwt-y-Bont, threading the narrow street by what today has become a pathway beside a high wall. At about 5 m. from Port a length contains both slab and stone sleepers, each of them to carry a single chair; this section is now a bridleway. Near Groeslon are two level crossing sites at Blaen-y-Waen and, with steeper hills now falling behind there comes a rough, morose and sedgy countryside. For some distance the course has sunk into a marshy tract and all trace is lost; this boggy section shows evidence of a low embankment before entering Coed Blaen-y-Cae (planted after the line closed), and its trees have not taken kindly to rooting in the broken slate which had been tipped there to make a firmer foundation for the track. Now taking a more northerly tack the line curves to follow the contour and at Efail-Castell comes up alongside the Slate Road once again, this time on a sharp curve where there remains a little evidence of the site of the former stables and siding. The Spooner Survey shows there to have been 'New Stables' further down the road at a point opposite Ynys-Llech-Arian, suggesting Efail-Castell had been superceded by the time of his Plan. Following the road first on the left and then on the right hand the railway reaches Groeslon crossroads at which point some old maps show the route incorrectly on the west side of the cross. The track, once over the Pentir – Caernarvon road, remains on the right of it to near Cae-Gwydryn where, owing to a land dispute, it crossed and recrossed the road in a matter of a few yards . . . all on the level as elsewhere with road crossings. The Slate Road now falls steeply at the head of Nant-y-Garth whilst the Railway held up into a small woodland at Garth-Fechan where there survives a section of stone-block sleepers. Passing through a reverse curve to maintain a steady fall, 'a cottage and croft' were passed, and near Garth Farm the head of Garth Incline (330 ft above sea level) is reached with its stable.

The line thence drops into the cwm below, now a wooded valley and from the incline foot there averaged a fall of 1 in 90 for the last mile to the Port, first following the valley bottom and crossing the Quarry Road to run for a short distance along its southern edge. It recrosses the road in a matter of yards and curved round the northern flank of a piece of high ground (much of it obliterated later in the making of the standard gauge Port Siding). The course today may be followed as a narrow lane leading to the east edge of the Caernarvon – Bangor road opposite a gateway in the wall of Vaynol Demesne; here the line ran below and alongside the road (which has been widened and partly effaces the railway course) and then turns sharply west under the road by a stone-built tunnel, 30 yards long, 6 ft high and 8 ft wide; its east mouth is sealed but the western end survives. The First Edition O.S. map confirms the course then led between the road and the Nant-y-Garth stream, falling now at 1 in 47 in the narrow wooded ravine; it crossed the stream – now a channelled course – above a muddy creek at the head of Aber-Pwll inlet and reached the quays along the north side of the creek. At no time in the life of the Dinorwic Railway did it terminate on the south side, for the lease of Crown land there was not obtained until 5th July, 1844.

It must be added that due to the extension of the Port in later times, the alteration of Assheton-Smith's 1812 Quarry Road (which originally occupied a route from the Port which was utilised by the Port Siding) and the moving of complete roads between Garth and Port Dinorwic, much of this portion of the railway has disappeared. The Vaynol Estate Plans survive to show the whole railway, but curiously the route has only been indicated by a dotted line at this most western extremity.

The Dinorwic Railway was single line but tradition has it that between the Port and Garth Incline foot, it was doubled. If this was so, it would only have applied to the section above the road tunnel.

So much for the main line. Returning to Allt-Ddu, Ellis' map of 1836 shows a branch falling southwest from the line just above Allt-Ddu access tunnel, to serve the mill at the Quarry; this earthwork may just be discerned today.[20] There is also evidence of an incline to serve Chwarel-Goch Quarry but there is no mapped evidence by Ellis.

The Port

At the period in question this was a very rudimentary point of shipment and the slate was loaded into lighters and then handled again into ships lying in the Straits. Contemporary accounts recall 8–10 ships being loaded at any one time and there was an annual tonnage of approximately 2,500 tons, so that when a Railway was created, small craft only were using the upper reaches of the creek. As the quays were extended westwards, the Railway followed; they were at first little more than an extension of the former landing place slipway, being a jetty built onto the Moel-y-Don ferry berth. At the time of Capt. William Griffith's Port Superintendency it took on a two-piece appearance with the old inland creek separated from the newer south side portions by a swing bridge carrying the 1824 line across the creek. This arrangement survived the period of the 1824 Railway, but over the years the Port premises grew beyond recognition by stages which are described later.

In the late 1820s the Railway possibly developed wholly along the north side of the creek; there is evidence of extensions in July 1830 when there is an entry in the accounts 'Jno. Bathgate for Iron Rails for Rail Road on the Quay, Velin Heli £55 0s. 9d.' and afterwards work on a 'New Dock' was to cover mid 1830 to April 1834. A weighing machine appeared in 1835 and throughout the 1824 line's life man-power was sufficient for wagon movement; in June 1843 a horse with boy attendant took over (they cost 5/- a day). Efficiency was fairly low: incoming ships in ballast had to offload it on the beach before they could take on slate, and for many years this had to be wheelbarrowed away at 4d. per ton. Only the smallest ships could come alongside – for example, AMNITY OF STROMNESS lay offshore in April 1845 and lighterage costs to load her were 15/6d. Loaders and others employed hereabouts were in time given premises for mealtimes; these originated in a purchase from Bangor station (opened May 1848) of a 'Wooden Cottage for the end of the new quay at Port for janitor' from the Chester & Holyhead Railway for £3 16s. 0d. and served for many years.

In order to give continuity, the story of the Port has thus been taken into the first years of the 1824 line's successor.

From records of slate shipments (1845–95) from the Port a rough calculation of tonnages required along the supply railway can be made, but as tonnages taken away by rail from the Port after 1852 are not known, some allowance for greater Padarn Railway tonnages – and in slowly-increasing quantities – must be made. After 1895 there was an annual decline in shipments even though from that period the Company used its own steamers.

Year	Tons Shipped	Daily tonnage along Padarn Rly.[a] (for shipment only)	No. of P.R. transporters required up/down daily[b] (for shipment only)
1845	65,700	212	30[c]
1850	75,900	245	35
1855	64,500	208	30
1860	73,400	237	34
1865	80,000	258	37
1870	76,800	248	35
1875	69,200	223	32
1880	57,000	184	26
1885	45,200	146	21
1890	55,900	180	26
1895	65,000	210	30
1914	47,316	—	—
1919	11,392	—	—
1939	29,219 (9 months)	—	—
1942	580	—	—
	[No shipments given after 1942]		

(a) Based on 310 working days in a year
(b) Based on a transporter carrying approx. 7 tons slates
(c) Horse-hauled 1845 – later dates steam-hauled

Track

The Railway gauge was 24½ in. measured across the centres of the rails and as the wagon wheels were double-flanged and ran loose on their axles, precision was not essential. The earliest rails were of iron, and in the 1940s a number of 3 ft rails was found near the Foundry at Gilfach-Ddu; they were of rounded section and similar to the earliest Penrhyn track of 1801. They raise the question as to why Assheton-Smith should install materials (if in fact he did) which much earlier had shown their deficiencies on Penrhyn's line, but it must be said the rail section was an outline which the local foundries could easily produce – it was little better than a round bar having a foot cast at each end. Cast-iron tie-bars supported the feet of the rails by a flat-footed portion at each end of the tie-bar, the joints being simple butt type resting on the common tie-bar foot, which in turn rested in shallow recesses both square and rectangular cut in slab blocks of irregular outline, but having such recesses accurately cut 4 in. × 4 in. × ½ in. deep. The tie-bars were of shallow 'U' shaped section allowing them to be buried for the most part, though tradition again maintains the horse walked outside the track rather than between the rails. If the centres of slabs found in 1943 were undisturbed, then perhaps longer lengths of rail were ultimately introduced, 3 ft 6 in. or 4 ft long.

It cannot be proved that any of the 1824 construction was in this material, but if so it certainly did not survive the life of the Railway; other reasons for the existence of these rails/sleepers may have included (a) an early portable form for use at the working face; (b) materials produced by the Foundry for an outside customer. Piecemeal replacement is evident, with chaired 'T' section iron rails; the chairs had deep slots in them avoiding the need for a key (though some small iron ones have been noted).

Doubtless referring to this replacement track, Van Oeynhausen and Von Dechen write: '. . . a more important railway than this [i.e. The Penrhyn Railway; Author] 10 miles English long, leads from the slate quarry near Llanberis . . . the rails are 3 ft long and rest on iron cross-sleepers: they are 2 ins. high, 1½ ins. wide, not elliptical but flat and wide on top and pointed underneath'.[21]

Joints were made in longer chairs, and all chaired material was carried on slab sleepers roughly outlined – 'rough hewn for the purpose by quarrymen of advanced age who can prepare sleepers when they are unfit for any other work'. Some carried only a single chair, some were full length, the former usually of stone (from outside the district!) rather than the local slab; a section north of Clwt-y-Bont used both types at random. Some of this second phase material enjoyed an extended life in the quarries around Allt-Ddu where these materials may still be found. Full length slab sleepers measure up to 3 ft long; the chair recesses are 8 in. × 3½ in. (4 in. at butt joints) and the double-pin holes for each chair are 1 in. diameter at 5½ in. centres.

The single-chair sleepers may have been unsatisfactory and allowed the gauge to wander; there is evidence that simple tie-bars were bolted to some sleepers to keep them in gauge – though this was an uncommon feature.

Wagons

The precise form of slate wagon used at the beginning is not known – the frame-type slate wagon was already in use elsewhere in North Wales and Dinorwic is likely to have adopted a very similar pattern. The numbers of wagons may be deduced from the cost of buying lubricating oil from Hugh Griffiths (Druggist) which from November 1829 was to average £40 monthly. If no other proof of growing business was available, the building of 109 new slate wagons from the end of 1829 to May 1832 would be enough. Iron wheels came from Towers of Bangor – who also supplied iron rails and rollers – frame timbers from Humphrey Owen or the Vaynol or Trefathrin Estates and these were assembled at the Port by David Williams, the carpenter, who was paid £40 for making 27 vehicles in May 1830 and £19 5s. 0d. for making 11 more by the following January 'and finding timber for same'. In July 1832 'iron castings for waggon wheels' came from Thomas Jones and in

January 1833 Elias Parry provided 'iron castings for Rail Road wag-gons'.

In May 1837 six 'sledges' were built to carry 'heavy slabs' . . . the name being a natural outcome of the sledges once horse-hauled throughout the Quarry before the days of tramways. Jno. Davies (carpenter) and Ellis Thomas (smith) built them for £24 and £23 17s. 10½d. respectively.

Operation

By 1826 there was an average monthly output from the quarry of 1,650 tons at a cost of £200 per month (road costs alone had been £550) most of which would pass over the Dinorwic Railway and require 35 slate wagons daily in each direction. The capacity of the line was designed (according to the 'CARNARVON & DENBIGH HERALD') to carry 150 tons or 85 wagons a day (or 3,900 tons over the 26-day month). 'Two or three horses are attached to several wagons' and if Dinorwic efficiency was on a par with Penrhyn then initially two daily 18 wagon trains would suffice. Having in mind that the journey was broken into the 'level stages', Braich–Graig-Lwyd, Graig-Lwyd–Efail-Castell, Efail-Castell–Garth, Garth–Port (all except the last-named about 2 miles long between stabling points), and assuming that horses and men/boys were restricted to their own 'levels', (and did not have to work the inclines), each 2 m. 'level' would need a 'run' of nine loaded and nine empty wagon trains to pass each working day. If experience on the inclines was similar to that at Penrhyn, they would pass only 3 or 4 wagons at the very best per run and the conclusion is reached that the designed capacity even allowing for long working days would have strained men and equipment considerably; perhaps in this – and the uphill section for loaded trains near Allt-Ddu – were found the seeds of discontent. It is likely however, that such maximum operation was seldom needed, for Hemingway[22] said in 1835 '. . . to avoid this great labour and danger' (i.e. of carting slate to the Menai) 'about ten years ago a new rail-road was made from the Quarries down to the shipping place . . . by this rail-road the slates are conveyed down at an average, it is said, of about 100 tons daily throughout the year . . . a distance of about 9 miles'. None of the foregoing takes account of the necessity to pass about one empty to every two or three loaded wagons to the bottom of the inclines to assist the control of the down-going loaded, on customary experience that even if the drumbrake was highly efficient, one upgoing empty wagon plus brake was equivalent to balancing little more than two descending loaded wagons.

The Quarry put this work out to contract, though the horses – and of course, wagon trains – were all from one Quarry, a subtle difference in methods from those used on some neighbouring railways. Initially one pair of men contracted to work the traffic, to 'keep the Rail Road in repair' and 'make and repair waggons'. However, this did not apply to the inclines which were separately contracted and repairable; nor did the men have to load or unload wagons; at the Port there were men who unloaded the slate, packed it in straw (for which a Straw Shed was built), loaded the lighters and then finally transferred from lighter to ship – all by contract. Little wonder there was a special shelter at Port for the retrimming of slates which were broken during handling!

William Roberts and his partner Humphries held (perhaps a second?) operating contract for over eight years beginning in June 1830. Some of the cost entries of this time read 'Men employed on the Rail Road, carriage of slates, keeping Rail Road in repair . . .', '. . . supplying the horses and waggons for the contractor . . .' all of which costs amounted to £227 6s. 0d. for June 1830 and £224 15s. 8d. for the following month.

The sides of the line were laid out in Gorse Gardens [sic] to provide feed for the horses and the same year a Gorse Mill was obtained to cut up the feed; also Edward Evans supplied 'beans for horses, and a Patent Mill to crush oats for the horses . . .'. Stables were lit by candles in winter and they cost 1d. each. Griffiths, besides selling them oil for wagons, also supplied 'drugs for horses'. In summer vetches came from Vaynol Farm as horse feed, and there are small entries like 'repairs and horses geers [sic] £3 12s. 9d.' Roberts received two new horses, one in January 1830 for £19 and another in May for £18: the contractors were paid 1/1d. a ton for carriage, the July 1830 tonnage being 2,188 tons 15 cwt. and there is little variation in this weight for some time – the rate dropped to 11½d. in 1836 and rose to 1/3d. in November 1838 when Richard and David Roberts (sons of William?) took on a contract. In March 1843 when the life of the 1824 railway was almost ended, they received £145 5s. 3d. (@ 1/3d. per ton) for the tonnage of February 'carriage of slates down The Old Rail Road 2,324 tons 5 cwt.' and the April tonnage was 2,017. Thus the accounts began to show the existence of a new Railway and gradually the Roberts' transferred their attentions to the new line so there is a fascinating period in March 1843 when they are credited with an additional tonnage of 4,457 over the new Padarn Railway; of course track repairs were probably kept to a minimum by then, but these figures allow rough calculations on trains and subcontractors employed by the Roberts'. On the new Railway monthly tonnages in the region of 5,000 show the line carrying double the traffic of the old one.

The Railway did not usually make the news, but a sad entry in 'THE NORTH WALES CHRONICLE' (28th September, 1841) reads: 'On Friday last an old soldier was literally crushed to a shapeless mass by the fall of a quantity of superincumbent earth from the Railway Level at Velinheli. He was working as a labourer at the time.'

THE PADARN RAILWAY

(Begun 1841 – closed 3rd November 1961 (last slate train ran 27th October, 1961))

The circumstances leading to the replacement of the Dinorwic Railway were manifold and it has been seen that consideration of the method and route of replacement had long been in view, having in mind that any new route would involve the ascent of the escarpment at the back of Port Dinorwic and, so far as possible, a course which kept to Assheton-Smith land throughout. To all intents and purposes, the new railway was to be a larger version of the Dinorwic Railway, on a more suitable site and with the operating feature of being a 'transporter' link whereon slate wagons would ride, four at a time, on transporter wagons[23] – a term first noted in an inventory of 1877 – from Quarry to Port incline-head on horse-hauled trains. There would be no inclines and the gradients were not severe. Operation by contractors would be carefully transferred (as would the traffic), from the existing line to the new. There is nothing to anticipate that within five years the new Railway would be reconstructed as a steam locomotive-worked railway.

Construction

Before building began, the scheme was broken into two sections, '. . . Cefn Gwyn Cutting' [map ref. 535667] being the dividing point. A temporary track was laid as the earthworks went forward and considerable purchases of 'spikes', 'temporary wedges' and 'tree-nails' were made in October 1841, indicating it was chaired.

William Allcarde of Warrington, an 'engineer', was consulted at the start, being paid £39 10s. 0d. 'for advice respecting the Rail Road' in February 1842. The surveyor William Harland cost £58 16s. 0d. in August 1842 'for surveying work on the Rail Road' – an amount was paid to 'James Spooner & Son' in December 1842 and the nominated carrier for all materials, (planks, rail waggons etc.) from October 1841 was Owen Jones. Allcarde was recalled to inspect the work in early 1843 and received £36 18s. 0d. Evan Williams was given local supervisory control over the whole work.

All work was contracted and as was done in the Quarry it was first put out to bargain; at one time over 130 small contractors, some with men under them, were involved. Appropriate entries begin in May 1841 and end in September 1842, headed THE PADERN RAILWAY, a form of misspelling frequently found. Some entries are usefully detailed and include:

Cutting foundations	£5	6s. 3½d.
Mason Build two walls	7	11 4
Sawyer	10	14 0
Carts and cartage	6	15 6
Tunnel & incline	30	0 0
Forming Road	257	1 4
Filling bed of Road	199	5 3

(the above from loose leaves pre-June 1841). From the form of the entries it could be assumed work began at the Llanberis end, where there would be the most abundant supply of labour. Pre-June 1841 costs totalled £1,279 5s. 2d. and a total figure to 17th September, 1842 – again on a loose paper – aggregates £30,321 5s. 11d.

The western terminal was then 'Garreg-y-Walch', the form of spelling for the farm Careg-y-Gwalch – later it was Pen-Scoins or Pensconce. Two termini were building at the Quarry end, 'Muriau' and 'Quarry' and the former may have been the short branch at Bedw-Argoed (plurality of one name brings a problem here as there was also a Muriau at the Quarry end!)

Date	Builder	Details (as entered)	Cost		
July–Sept. 1841	Hugh Williams	levelling terminus @ 6d. per sq. yard	£40	5s.	7d.
	(Mason)	Muriau Terminus	3	5	4
July 1841	Thomas Closs	Cut through rock & remove rubbish to form railway @ 2/6 per sq. yard	16	6	3
" "	Richard Owen	To build breast wall & level railway for 15/- per Rood	14	1	3
June–Sept. 1841	Owen Jones	Forming & construct-ing line of Railway through the Water at 80/- per Rood	126	13	4
Aug.–Dec. 1841	Francis Jones	Cutting Tunnel at Port Dinorwic & removing rubbish £6 10 0 per lineal yard & £9 per lineal yard for opening an entrance 10 ft. × 7 ft.	356	1	6
Aug.–Dec. 1841	Owen Jones	Inclined Plane (from top end of Tunnel) etc. etc. Removing solid, widening Tunnel mouth etc.	591	4	2

Date	Builder	Details (as entered)	Cost		
20 Aug.–10 Dec. 1841	John Jones & Hu Roberts	Sinking a shaft[24] to level of turnpike road to Carnarvon @ 72/6 yard & cutting Tunnel at both ends to meet Francis Jones & Owen Jones for 150/- yard. For cutting a Place of Safety in the Tunnel 50/-	261	1	8
Sept. 1841	Wm. Hughes	. . . cutting out a foundation for Stables at Bryn Madog for 8d. per yard	4	6	8

At this time gravel was coming across Llyn Padarn by lighter for use at 'Craig-y-Dinas Buildings', the stable block near Pont-Rhyddallt. Being at some distance from the lake, it must have been offloaded from water to the temporary railway; though the accounts mention stone for stables at Tan-y-Dinas (October 1841) this would be the same destination, where cottages were built too (November 1841–June 1842). At the same time much work was going on at the 'Muriau Terminus' with deliveries of stone for an office, 'long shed', weigh tables and a house.

Gorse was frequently used as a feed for cattle and horses 'but not when in flower when it gave them wind' so in January 1843 there is noted 'turning land for planting gorse gardens at side of Road' demonstrating there was to be no wasted border of the railway boundary; a Gorse Mill was built at Glas-Coed and the next month a 'Gorse Engine' was installed there, a machine for cutting gorse as for chaff. By the end of 1841 walls and flagging stones were put in at 'The Quarry Terminal' and men were 'procuring blocks and laying rails at 15/- per dozen'. At the Port a smithy and saw pit were put in and at the top of the Port Incline Richard Owen was 'Cutting Rock at the Garreg-Walch Terminus' . . . houses were to follow here later, whilst John Davies was 'making treenails for fastening Chairs' and in the November a 'Passing Place' was formed at Clegyr costing 18/- per rood – it was complete in the next February.

William Foulke was a leading contractor and in February 1842 was 'unloading Iron Rails from Waggons at Glan-y-Bala, Pen-Llyn and Pont-Rhytallt for 6d. per Ton (367 Tons) . . . Blasting rock to widen curve at Clegir . . .' whether such 'waggons' were of road variety or running over the temporary or finished line cannot be confirmed. In

March 'Roof of Tunnel heightened' for £8, but which of the three is uncertain. Temporary rails had been laid at Pandy by the end of 1841 and next February Jno. Francis & Co. were given '2/- day' for 'Lighter taken from lower to upper lake' which reveals how un-navigable the passage must have been then.[25] This may be the same craft carried by road from Port to Pen-y-Llyn in June 1841 . . . for two guineas!

In the spring of 1842 it cost £1,046 12s. 3d. to 'completing Tunnel & Incline and Bottom Curve'; as the title Port Incline was previously adhered to consistently, this may reveal the completion of the Glan-y-Bala tunnel and foot of the original 'A' inclines at the Quarry. The 46 yard [sic] 'Level tunnel' was heightened and widened by 'a miner' for £61 11s. 0d. in November 1842 and as the line had been available since September, the bore may have been found restrictive in practice (the accounts suggest the lengths of the other tunnels were then: Port 92 yards and Glan-y-Bala approximately 430 yards). Drainage along the line was by means of an open culvert between the rails . . . the more easy because there were no cross-sleepers. Building of rolling stock began in December 1841.

To operate the line efficiently it was essential to install 'Passing Places' at regular intervals; surviving earthworks support the theory that loops were at approximately 1 mile intervals, a suggestion the accounts sustain though place names are not given.

The Route (Field notes were first taken in 1946, and are used here in the present tense for their retrospective value.)

In contrast to the description of route for The Dinorwic Railway, it is simpler to begin the Padarn Railway down at the Port.

From the quays a Quarry-Gauge incline, known as R'Allt Incline or The Incline (but in the Quarry records as Port Incline) raises the rolling stock to the Garreg-y-Walch terminus of the Padarn Railway proper, 260 ft above. Thence this stock was conveyed pick-a-back method to the Quarry where the Quarry-Gauge tracks recommenced; the Padarn Railway was thus an isolated 4 ft gauge link in the "Quarry-Gauge" chain between Quarry and Port.

In recent times the Port Incline was laid in steel bars 3 in. × 1 in. section set on edge in cast iron chairs, a longer chair being used to make a butt joint between bars; this is similar to other inclines in the Quarry. The quay lines converge – there is a weighing table – in front of a Check Office on the quay level to form a double track, the right hand used for empty wagons returning to the Quarry. The mouth of the Port tunnel, with 10 ft wide × 7 ft high[26] bore first cut in the rock face in 1841, is immediately beyond the Check Office (originally a stone-built cottage with wooden verandah), and the tracks curve into the opening. The incline does not have a regular slope but is parabolic; it crosses the ex-L.N.W.R. Bangor–Caernarvon line in a cutting below and the upper part passes through a cutting on a steep wooded slope above the roofs of Port Dinorwic; the winding drum is perched on a lip of the escarpment at the top. The village is hardly noticeable at lower levels as the tunnel carries the line beneath it and the main street. The incline was finished in September 1841.

At the summit the slate wagons run onto level track and pass beneath the winding drum by means of an open-ended shed to emerge at high level on a loading dock where, four per wagon, they are run onto the host wagons of the Padarn Railway to be carried bodily back to the Quarry. As each host wagon is loaded, it is allowed to run off the dock into a loop line where a train of similarly loaded wagons is raked; the arrival at the dock and discharge of wagons from it is assisted by slight falls in the 4 ft gauge tracks which are therefore on different levels at this place, the loaded host wagons being about 4 ft higher. No work is done by the steam locomotive; as Lewis explained in 1850 'a locomotive engine is used to draw the slates down to within 800 yards of the Port Incline . . . this is of about the same length and worked by an endless chain of above 1600 yards long'. This terminus was Pen-Scoins, a corruption of Pen-Ysgoi (an escape top) the name dating from the railway. The operating chain of which Lewis writes had six links cut off it each year to compensate for wear – this was done on a Sunday![27] There was electric bell communication from top to foot and in the days of the chain the wagons were hitched singly to the chain at intervals, eight at a time, up and down. In May 1924 a wire rope replaced the chain on Board of Trade instructions; they insisted that the load be reduced to one wagon, thus increasing the time factor almost eight times![28] Evan Evans was for many years responsible as lookout man, keeping the track in repair and oiling the chain/wire rollers (his sons, William and Thomas, were both drivers on the Padarn Railway).

The endless chain passed round sheaves at top and bottom but the replacement wire rope passes over the summit drum; a bandbrake on the drum controls the speed which moves considerably faster than the original chain. The drumhouse carries two notices:[29]

PORT INCLINE NOTICE   EXCEPT ON BUSINESS NO PERSON OR
PERSONS ARE ALLOWED ON ANY PART OF THIS INCLINE

and

PORT INCLINE   LENGTH OF INCLINE 1,250 ft. HEIGHT 296¼ ft.
MEAN GRADIENT 1 in 4¼   11/6/1924

The wagon loop at Pen-Scoins is 185 yards long and holds a maximum train of 21 wagons; loaded wagons arrive on the north side. By dint of fly shunting, the locomotive works only from the east end of the departing train and does not approach the drumhouse. The stone carriage shed or 'Coach House' beside the drumhouse is entered by a siding connection and a plaque over the door reads '1888'; the Saloon is

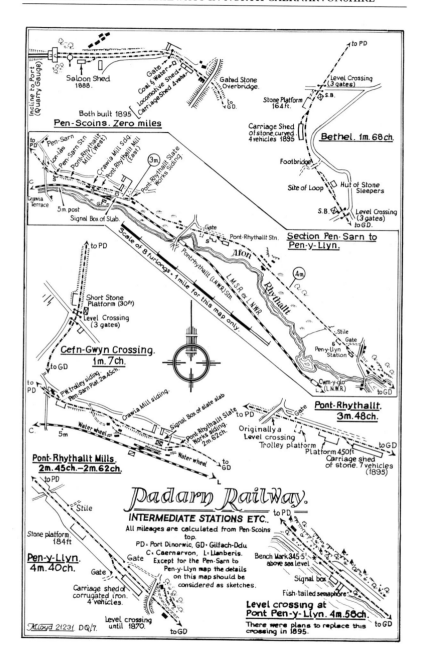

stored within. This shed replaces the original and is ornamented by a windvane showing a fox on the run – a decorative touch in keeping with the Assheton-Smith connection! Between it and the drumhouse is a short siding to hold two wagons, connected with the south loop by turntable.[30] This table is also essential to turn the first and last transporter wagons of each slate 'run': the last's load includes the guard's van and it cannot be reloaded with three loaded wagons at the Quarry unless turned onto the end of the empty return working – it is then correctly positioned to be unloaded again at the Quarry.

The simplicity of the track layouts at each end of the line, in view of the tonnages handled, stem from earliest railway practices. At Pen-Scoins the art of fly-shunting (long since illegal on main lines) overcame the primitive facilities. An approaching train would whistle twice at Cop Cefn and one of the three men on duty would man the small 'sentry-box' with its signal at the approach points. The driver would shut off steam, depress the foot treadle outside the cab sheet which uncoupled the leading wagon, and draw ahead smartly over the points to the south line (a similar treadle worked the coupling at the other end; it was on the other side of the footplate). Meanwhile the train brakes-man would be lending all his weight by standing on the brake lever on the last wagon. Once the engine was clear, the pointsman would throw the points in the track of the oncoming train – by now somewhat checked by its brakesman – and jump onto the step of the first wagon which had such a fitting for the purpose, and also carried a brake. The man would then depress the brake lever with his foot and now, with two brakesmen, the train would come to rest just short of the unloading dock, with the wagons in compression to enable them to be uncoupled in due course. Each wagon was then run forward for unloading, the men using wooden sprags between the spokes of the wheels to check unwanted movements of unbraked stock.

(Fly-shunting was unsuited to the Quarry terminus due to the adverse gradient, and wagons were drawn along a track alongside the engine by means of a chain; in this way and with the help of a 'hump' in that adjacent track, the empties were brought up to the loading dock.)

At the east end of Pen-Scoins loop the tracks converge to a single line and pass through a gate on a curve in a southerly direction – this use of field gates across the tracks was at one time commonplace on such railways in Wales. There is a semaphore signal beside the gate warning arriving trains of the state of the pointwork which is hidden by a curve in the line. There is a longish siding (by Padarn Railway standards) on the south side which contains a long stone building housing one engine (kept near the doors) with four workmen's carriages beyond it. Outside is a coaling stage and water tower; in earlier times a windmill worked the pump to fill the tank. Here onwards are some of the many bi-lingual enamel notices, mainly in white lettering with blue ground (and containing some curious lettering defaults) headed DINORWIC QUAR-

RIES RAILWAY, a title which seems to have been adopted when the Workmen's Train was introduced. There is yet another short siding to the east of this building followed by a terrace of cottages built in 1896; this place is usually named Pen-Scoins but variations in spelling are legion (the spelling used on the tokens of the Workmen's Train is peculiar to that series!).

The line traverses an occupation crossing and passes under a bridge (replacing a level crossing in November 1848) spanning the curved cutting, the bridge having a gate beneath it across the tracks. Another common product appears at the lineside here, a cast-iron WHISTLE board, with red lettering picked out on a white ground. Once out of the cutting the line begins a long straight run to the south, climbing smartly, and then falling past another cutting at Coed Pant-yr-Afallen Coppice, thence by a low embankment to the road crossing at Bryn-Pistyll (1 m. 7 ch. 302 ft a.s.l.) – known as Cefn Gwyn – which was gated and boasted a small platform 30 ft long on the west side just north of the gates. The climb from Pen-Scoins could be tricky on a greasy day but drivers eschewed using sand there as it impaired their braking on the return journey; on dry days it would blow up as the engine passed and get into the moving parts. Warning signs to show the gates were across the line take the form of red-painted rectangular target boards which lifted high above the gates when they were open to the highway. There is a crossing-keeper's hut of recent construction; these and other precautionary features at crossings resulting from the fatal accident at Bethel in 1926. Here as elsewhere, the line is solidly constructed, the low embankments being heavily supported by slab walling – easily obtainable from the Quarry – rather than earthwork. The course now turns south-west, then east over rough bogland more reminiscent of Ireland than Wales. West of the tracks the land falls, undulating in pleasant but unstriking manner to the shores of the Menai; to the east, above low foothills, the well-remembered names of many principal peaks of Caernarvonshire range upwards as backcloth – between us and them was the route of this Railway's predecessor in 1824.

At Bethel (1 m. 68 ch. 315 ft) a gated crossing protects the main road and beyond it there is a considerable platform, 164 ft long: not unique, the crossing requires three gates to span the tarmac, and there is a modernish keeper's cabin where the custodian has much time to himself! On the south side beyond is the recognisable outline of another stone carriage shed on a curved siding facing the Port and bearing the date '1895'. (The 1888 O.S.Plans show no additional railway features at this place). Just beyond again there is an unusual footbridge (2 m.) and there is clear evidence of a widening of the formation to make a passing loop. (One of the hand-operated Car Gwyllt was parked at the trackside here to the end of the line's history.) There is a lineside hut too, formed with stone sleeper blocks probably recovered when the track was relaid and the loop discontinued. The line is now running south-east and reaches Cefn-Rhyd road crossing (310 ft a.s.l.) with its three gates and hut; there is now a steeper climb.

[There are many variations in lineside notices – all Gilfach-Ddu products – which have been passed, thus:

PENSCONCE FARM & COTTAGES CROSSING,   PRIVATE RAIL-
WAY,   THE USE OF THIS CROSSING IS ON SUFFERANCE AND FROM
PENSCONCE FARM AND COTTAGES ONLY   TRESPASSERS WILL BE
PROSECUTED   W W VIVIAN;

whilst another reads:

BLAEN-Y-CAE STILE   PRIVATE RAILWAY etc. etc.

Every foot and vehicle crossing is so marked – the management intend there to be no doubt!]

With the track now on a stone embankment the Llanrug road passes beneath – this was a level crossing in former days – and hereabouts many stone sleeper blocks have been built into the earthworks. The railway now enters the shallow valley of the Rhythallt which comes in alongside as does the standard gauge Llanberis Branch from Caernarvon. The river and both railways remain adjacent until Llyn Padarn is reached when the standard gauge makes for the southern shore and the Padarn Railway skirts the northern side. On the south side of the Padarn line here is a simple 36 ft platform and opposite it a short siding to store a gangers' trolley. This is Pen-Sarn (2 m. 45 ch. 315 ft). A few yards beyond comes a short siding to the right serving Crawia (or Creuea) Mill and slightly further on were once two semaphores – one for each direction – the only ones 'en route' not connected with crossing gates. Here, as at Pen-Scoins, they were really point indicators and there was a small 'signal box'; no trace of anything remains. Almost immediately there trails in another short siding on the south side, this linking Pont-Rhythallt with the slate mills, another source of writing slate traffic for which two solid-sided wagons were available . . . they were stored at Gilfach-Ddu in 1945, derelict . . . and worked here on the rear of Port-bound trains, detached, then manhandled into the siding.

Climbing gradually, now comes Pont-Rhythallt itself, with cutting, overbridge (with ironwork by de Winton & Co), formerly a level crossing, and the river (now the Afon Rhythallt) meandering alongside (3 m. 48 ch.). A roadway appears alongside the track on the south side to serve the 450 ft platform, which has been extended at some time, and carriage shed (with siding facing the Port as usual) dated 1895. There is a wooden staging just short of the platform onto which the permanent way trolley can be run off the rails. The surroundings now take on a softer look with rocks and trees intermingling, though on the river side of the line the ground is flat, sedgy, and liable to flood. A terrace beside the line at Craig-y-Dinas is historic in that it marks the site of stables (the account book entry reads: 'Sept. 1841 Tan-y-Dinas (stables)

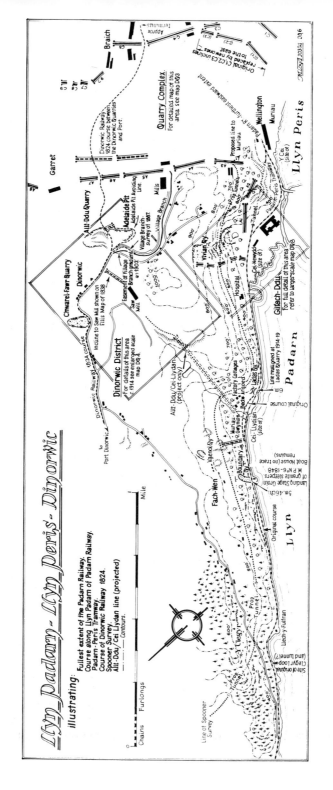

Llyn Padarn ~ Llyn Peris ~ Dinorwic

Illustrating: Fullest extent of the Padarn Railway.
Course along Llyn Padarn of Padarn Railway.
Padarn-Peris Tramway.
Course of Dinorwic Railway 1824.
Spooner Survey.
Allt-Ddu/Cei Llydan line (projected)
————— Contours.

Chains   Furlongs

Mile

Garret

Braich

Approx terminus

47
46
6¼

Quarry Complex
For detailed map of this area see map DQ3

Dinorwic Railway.
1824 Course between the Dinorwic Quarries and Port.

Original C1,C2,C3 inclines replaced by new ones to the east.

Llyn Peris

Wellington
Muriau

Cei (site of)

A7
A8
A9

Proposed line to Muriau

Padarn R. (Incline) eastway extent

Chwarel Fawr Quarry

Allt-Ddu Quarry

Dinorwic

Incline to Saw Mill shown on Ellis Map of 1838

Adelaide Pit
Adelaide Pit Avoiding Line

Village Branch survey of 1867

Mills

Saw Mill

Village Branch

Extent of Village Branch gradient c.1903

Vivian Qy.

Padarn-Peris Tramway

Hospital

Tunnel

Cei Howells (site of)

Gilfach-Ddu
For full detail of this area refer to larger-scale map DQ8

Dinorwic District
For details of this area 1914 see enlarged scale map DQ4

Dinorwic Railway 1824 course

Padarn

to Port Dinorwic

Allt-Ddu/Cei Llydan (project only)

Line realigned at Ladas Quarry 1914-19

Original course

Ladas Qy.

Factory Cottages
Factory Beds project

Muriau Gwynion (site of)

Cei Llydan (site of)

Vaenol Qy.

Boundary

Fach-Wen

Landing Stage Group of granite sleepers
5m.46ch.
W.P.No.6-1848
Boat House (no trace remains)

Llyn

Original course

Site of original Clegyr Loop (and tunnel)

Cegyr Tunnel

Llechi Fulfran

Prop Tunnel

Line of Spooner Survey

Padarn

£8 1s. 8d.') locally known as Stabla and here the 4 m. point is passed. Rising ground to the left and boggy riverside flats to the right continue to mark the route so, running south-east, the line crosses a drainage channel by a bridge incorporating a number of 4 ft gauge locomotive firebars (!) to reach Pen-y-Llyn (4 m. 40 ch.) with its 184 ft platform on the south side; the carriage shed in the siding beyond is unusually built in corrugated iron (and was moved to house a brick-making plant between 1952 to 1964 after the Workmen's Train was suspended). The road overbridge beyond, with its ironwork by de Winton & Co. and its stonework of old sleeper blocks (suggesting most had been replaced by wooden ones by that date) was built in 1870 to replace a level crossing.

Quite suddenly the lower end of Llyn Padarn comes into view from the line and there is a nasty level crossing for road users who may climb to Fach-Wen from here.[31] The gates are protected by an unusual fish-tailed semaphore with spectacles on each side of its lamp; it is connected to the crossing gates and there is a nearby signal hut (4 m. 58 ch. 354½ ft); on the south side of the line alongside the foregoing length was once a much greater area of water than now, which allowed the early slate boats to reach the stacking point at Cwm-y-Glo; drainage has altered the appearance of the land now. Back on the railway, the line has reached its summit level and now runs alongside Llyn Padarn, using a shelf of rock and slab, curbed by a stone wall abutting the lake; here and there, there are twists and turns to follow the shore, but generally the track hugs the 'promenade' built for it at the foot of the craggy rock and tree covered slopes above. Shortly, the erstwhile connections to Boundary and Vaynol (Vaenol) Quarries are passed on the left. Hereabouts, small quarries may be seen, and evidence of old quays, made from groynes of old rubbish, on the shore. In places, some straightening of the line has resulted from it being built out from the cliff above and beyond 5 m. comes Clegyr, the site of the 1841-built loop and probably also of a short tunnel of the same period.

Continuing, the view of the lake with the Snowdonia bloc ahead quite surpasses the one from the road on the other side of the water; Llanberis may be seen on the shore ahead, and in season, a smoke pall hanging over the lower terminus of the Snowdon Mountain Railway. Before 6 m. comes an interesting groyne of granite sleepers quite different from any elsewhere (size approx. 3 ft long × 1½ ft × 1½ ft) opposite the Boundary Slate Quarry (marking the edge of Assheton-Smith property); here is a small stone hut with 'W.P. No. 6 1848' cut into the lintel. In a short distance Cei-Llydan and Bedw-Argoed is reached, the little flannel factory here being converted into two cottages at the turn of the century. Little survives as evidence of the rail and quarrying activity which must once have marked this place and the line now curves round the shore and passes Ladas Quarry; it was the availability of rubbish tips from this pit which enabled the railway to be diverted lakewards in the 1914–18 period to improve alignment – at

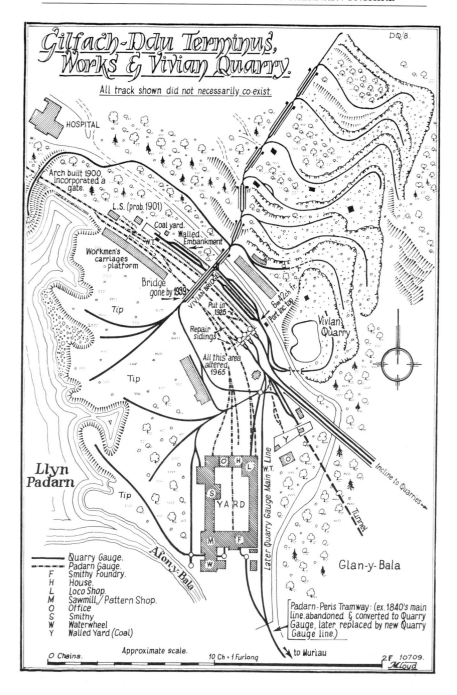

Gilfach-Ddu Terminus, Works & Vivian Quarry

DQ/8.

All track shown did not necessarily co-exist.

HOSPITAL

Arch built 1900, incorporated a gate.

L.S. (prob. 1901)

Coal yard.
W.T.
Walled Embankment

Workmen's carriages platform

Bridge gone by 1939

VIVIAN BRIDGE

Put in 1926

6m 12ch fr. Port inc. top

Repair sidings

Tip

Vivian Quarry

All this area altered 1965

Tip

Tip

Llyn Padarn

YARD

O H L
S
M F
W

W.T.

Later Quarry Gauge Main Line

Y

Incline to Quarries

Tunnel

Glan-y-Bala

Afon-y-Bala

Quarry Gauge.
Padarn Gauge.
F   Smithy Foundry.
H   House.
L   Loco Shop.
M   Sawmill,/Pattern Shop.
O   Office
S   Smithy
W   Waterwheel
Y   Walled Yard (Coal)

Padarn-Peris Tramway: (ex. 1840's main line, abandoned & converted to Quarry Gauge, later replaced by new Quarry Gauge line.)

Approximate scale.
O Chains.   10 Ch = 1 Furlong

to Muriau

2F 10709.
M.Loyd

the same time the remains of Cei-Llydan were thus obliterated. These lakeside workings were very small, but now the main Quarry is reached and, passing under a tall slender stone arch carrying a rubbish tramway from the Vivian Quarry (the arch built in 1900) there is once more a gate under the bridge; thus was the line gated at both ends. Now the elongated yard on the rubbish apron preceding Gilfach-Ddu is reached (begun 1848 and originally serving Cei-Newydd – now buried) and there are long sidings and stabling yards for stock. The main line terminates at trans-shipment platforms used by the host wagons, and in the past the wharves on the left-hand were surmounted by a handsome stone workshop building with a tower sandwiched between railway and Vivian Quarry behind; this place was the first Gilfach-Ddu headquarters.

Originally the 4 ft gauge carried on through a tunnel in Glan-y-Bala bluff, but the present terminus dates from the time when that section was converted to (nom.) 2 ft gauge (see diagram p.44). Behind the terminus (6 m. 42 ch.) the ground rises magnificently in a blanket of dwarf oaks and protruding rocks and the scale of the mountainface minimizes the Gilfach-Ddu complex below. Beyond the trans-shipment platform will be seen the narrow rock entrance to Vivian Quarry, the stone-built engine shed where FIRE QUEEN is housed [today preserved in Penrhyn Castle Railway Museum (1986)], the tunnel mouth – now disused – the "2 ft" lines in complicated trackwork serving both the Padarn–Peris Tramway beyond and the Works lines to the right. The Works themselves stand, fortress-like round a central yard, one of the most complete purpose-built buildings of their kind in the whole of Wales. Tracks of both gauges enter the Works and others sprawl over a wide area, extra mural, to spill yet even more tonnages of rubbish into the lake.

In this long railway site, the 4 ft gauge has its Workmen's Train platform on the south side, complete with stone platform and, in more recent times, given a roof to shelter the ageing carriages of the Train. Changes in layout have taken place here, and some wagon turntables – the necessity of which has been discussed – replaced by pointwork.[32] Three lines were taken up to the transfer dock, allowing three trains to be handled simultaneously – and at times even those would be insufficient: the wagon turntables lay at the dock fronts. The dock itself embodies a substantial lock to keep the host wagon closed up to it during transfer. In past years the whole yard was spanned by a wooden overbridge carried on cast iron columns; this carried a rubbish tramway from Vivian Quarry to the lakeshore tip.

The original Padarn Railway had been largely 're-modelled' by the time of closure; at the end the generous loading gauge gave a 15 ft vertical clearance and 11 ft horizontal clearance between stone walls. A gradient profile does not survive but is given as an average of 1 in 232; mileposts did not all survive either; full miles were marked with stone posts but their form is not established.

Finally, what remains of the now truncated length from here to its original Muriau terminus? There are no elderly pictures showing the Gilfach-Ddu end of Glan-y-Bala tunnel; the earliest show only the 1 ft 10¾ in. gauge system through it in the early 1870s. It was on the site of the most northerly (present-day) siding here that the 4 ft main line would have run; we cannot speculate if there was any siding hereabouts but it seems very doubtful; it is likely that the shore of the lake came close to the existing tunnel mouth. The stone engine shed (used to store FIRE QUEEN from 10th July, 1890) just outside the mouth, was built to house the Padarn–Peris Tramway engine(s) and did not exist before the tunnel was re-gauged. The tunnel mouth too, was given an ornamental stone facing with string-course and castellated effect to match the walled coal yard which was later built to the south of the mouth; it may be assumed that when first built, the bore was of similar height to that originally at the Port viz. 7 ft but containing only a single 4 ft gauge line. It would not need to be wider than 10 ft and must have been opened out at a very early date to clear the chimneys (at least!) of FIRE QUEEN and JENNY LIND which required 12 ft from the rails. The size of the present mouth is 12 ft × 12 ft. The east mouth was of smooth slabwork having three dominant keystones; it has been suggested that ornamentation was thought unncessary as there were less visitors to that area!

Traces of the former terminus at Muriau can only be conjectured; what today appears to be evidence of the old layout might be totally misleading, so much quarrying having taken place in this small area. There would have been a transfer dock and locomotive run-round, and probably housing, coaling and watering facilities for the engine. All had been swept away before a convenient edition of maps might have shown the arrangements. The distance from Pen-Scoins would have been approx. 7 m. 5 ch. with a height of 355 ft.

Track: 1843–late 1860s

Tracklaying began at the Llanberis end in June 1841 with the temporary line: this seems to have been accomplished fairly speedily – perhaps by the following September – but entries in the accounts like the one quoted regarding temporary rails at Pandy may suggest amendments or additional works.

In November 1841 iron rails were being shipped from Newport, S. Wales (ex-Ebbw Vale?) to Port Dinorwic where they were transferred to lighters; in February 1842 '20 ft bars' are quoted and from the next April several lots amounting to a cost of £1,400 were shipped in from Bayley Bros. & Co. of Liverpool. In January 1841 there is occasional reference to the Newport shipments coming into Caernarvon; perhaps Port Dinorwic could not handle it all? Shortly after this, laying began with 'Setting Rails and Blocks £143 11s. 7d.', by the same

April much of this material had been delivered to the site and was lying piled up awaiting laying. A curious result (and without explanation) is the purchase of a quantity of 'mats' to cover these stocks – perhaps it was netting to prevent pilfering? In view of their length it is assumed these rails were for the 'permanent way' and not the temporary line.

The assembly consisted of placing these rails into cast iron chairs having a base 9 in. × 5 in. and two fixing oak pins (treenails); keys secured the rails tightly in the chairs, a result which put the Padarn line right in the forefront of methods then in use. Also in trend with materials used elsewhere, the sleepers were of limestone, (and not generally the locally-available slab, or even of wood) and were shipped in from a quarry at Moelfre, Anglesey, using lighters (e.g. SLUICE) at a price of 2/6d. per ton, drilled for the treenails at Port under contract (January 1842). Apparently these cargoes were insufficient to complete the line, for in May 1842 there appears 'Blasting rock to procure blocks for laying rails for 1/3d. each 71 @ 1/3d. £4 8s. 9d.' and 'Procuring and drilling blocks for laying rails @ 15/- per dozen . . .' whilst as early as January 1842 'slate blocks and sleepers from Quarry to Bryn-y-Madog and Cae-Newydd' is entered; these blocks may have been for rail-joint support. The limestone blocks were approx. 24 in. × 12 in. × 9 in. deep into which a depression was cut to take the base of the chair, 9½ in.×5 in. with two holes 1¼ in. diam. and 4½ in. deep for the pins at 6 in. centres, and were nicely finished – unlike some of the slab used – many finding their way into lineside structures when wooden sleepers took their place in the late 1860s!

There is some evidence that to improve the support of rails at joints, the chairs adjacent to the joint were supported on a common slab; this was not a transverse sleeper. The rails were held to gauge simply by the rigidity of the blocks. Certain very large slabs have been unearthed from the lake shore section near Boundary Quarry with the imprints of chairs on them, suggesting almost whole pieces of pointwork were built on one slab.

The chair pattern was supplied by the Roodee Foundry, Chester in January 1842 and chair supplies began to reach the railway very soon; (Robert Jones, Caernarvon; Owen Thomas, Caernarvon; Roodee Foundry, Chester – all these delivered in March to July 1842). In the Caernarvon deliveries, 1,311 chairs weighed 40 cwt. and the average weight per chair over all suppliers was 20 lb. This may be compared with the same average weight of chairs used to carry the double-headed 50 lb./yard rail on the Quarry-Gauge tracks used by steam locomotives in modern times but does not confirm the rail weight. At the end of 1842 £700-worth of chairs came from Bayley Bros. Liverpool and were similar to those used on the later Chester & Holyhead Railway.

Curiously, no one made a contemporary description of the first permanent way but as late as 1905 'THE LOCOMOTIVE MAGAZINE' stated 'the railway was originally laid on stone blocks with cast-iron chairs. The rails were of wrought-iron of the "double-headed" type and had no cross ties,' by which time of course this track would be but a memory. However, a few scarce items have found their way into the North Wales Slate Quarrying Museum at Gilfach-Ddu; some rails survived to the 1940s as rafters in lineside huts and those that are not too wasted measure 2 in. wide at head and are 3½ in. deep.

There is a suggestion that the inclines were laid differently, perhaps to give the track more stability on the slope? In June 1842 incline chairs and materials include 'Lower Incline Plane; . . . oak sleepers, and chairs . . .' – this is likely to be the bottom-most 'A' incline in the quarry.

Finally, keys and treenails; again a suggestion that oak treenails (or chair fixing pins) sufficed, but early on (December 1841) Roodee supplied a pattern for iron, although there is no trace of bulk orders. In April 1842 'temporary tree-nails (oak)' cost 3/6 per 1,000 and there were 23,500 'small keys and wedges' @ 2/6 per 1,000 – packed in wooden casks, and enough to lay the whole new route with temporary track. Later comes 'Best wedges and treenails' and 'Gauging of treenails', and

4,000 treenails	@ 100/-	£20	0s.	0d.
12,519 "	"	62	11	11
350 "	25/-	8		9
Setting best wedges and treenails		153	10	11

and 12,000 small keys cost £36. The wedges must have held the butt joints of the rails.

In summer 1842 'iron' was sent to Roodee Foundry 'to make point rails for sidings @ 4/9 per ton' a total cost of £600; there were several lots.

The evolution that emerges of the Padarn Railway track in 1848 when steam locomotives began regular service, is not entirely clear. The line had been constructed by means of a temporary railway and replaced by a permanent way suited to horse haulage. There is no suggestion that the result was unsuited to the extra weights etc. involved and that new materials were needed, and save for re-aligning of curves and opening out of civil engineering in places, the track sufficed until replaced by chaired rails on wooden cross sleepers – probably in the late 1860s. The Accounts leave doubts on several issues, notably if the Newport-shipped rails of late 1841 served for both temporary and permanent lines . . . which it may be assumed they did as there are no further purchases.

The new railway was complete by 30th April, 1843, and by the inclusion of such domestic items as '3 clocks £6 5s. 0d.' the Account was closed on 31st December following with a final sum of £35,952 12s. 6½d.

Track: late 1860s–October 1961

Long before the end of the nineteenth century the double-headed rail and stone sleepers had been replaced by a conventional track with all the appearance of a main line standard gauge railway. Double-headed steel rail from Cammell of Penistone, in 30 ft lengths and weighing 80 lb. per yard were laid in cast-iron chairs with wooden keys on wooden cross sleepers, with fish-plated joints. Later rails were 84 lb. Considerable lengths of track were (later still) relaid in second-hand main line materials, and many ex-North Eastern Railway pattern chairs were used. In July 1891 the Darlington Iron & Steel Co. Ltd. of Middleborough delivered 200 tons of double-headed rail.

Basically the 4 ft gauge used four consecutive designs of chair: (a) the originals of the 1840s, (b) an 'S'-shaped base type cast at Gilfach-Ddu (a pattern widely used everywhere from about 1865), (c) a development in a heavier chair with three-bolt fixing, and (d) an even heavier type with four bolts, one on each side being of bigger size than its companion . . . a curious feature which would involve using two sizes of fixing-screw. At pointwork some chairs were supplied by 'C.C. & Co. 1895' (Charles Cammell?) but patterns for all purposes kept at Gilfach-Ddu made it unnecessary to buy outside, and chair-casting continued until 1964.

The oiling of points at Pen-Scoins was done by an odd-job man among his other duties; at Gilfach-Ddu the fireman oiled the points. The maintenance of the track was divided into eight sections with two men on each, and a number of p.w. trolleys was available. On Monday mornings the line was walked from Bryn-Pistyll to Pen-Scoins before the Workmen's Train left, to ensure a clear run. Latterly, the gang sections were: Pen-Scoins–Bethel; Bethel–Pen-y-Llyn; Pen-y-Llyn–Gilfach-Ddu.

Operation – Slate traffic: from Horse to Steam

There was a gradual change-over from Dinorwic to Padarn Rail-way and whatever problems this caused, there is no account of them. Contemporary diaries (Wm. Morris) reveal that the 'first run of the rail road from Muriau to the sea' took place on 3rd November, 1842, a 'run' being the vernacular for a rake of slate wagons (locally 'ryn'). This must have been a trial, for only between March and May 1843 were the Roberts paid for carriage on both railways, an average of 56 tons a day passing down both lines, so revealing that the change-over was possibly reducing the traffic flow. Tonnage over 'The Padarn Rail Road' for June was 4,134 tons 20 cwt. @ 4½d. ton showing a remarkable period when 172 tons were being taken down per average day . . . perhaps due to the backlog in transport? At the same time is an entry 'altering and repairing Trucks and Small Waggons', again an indication there may have been a shortage of stock and that some modifications were essential (the original slate wagons, i.e. 'Small Waggons' may have had full length axles which prevented them being loaded onto the 'Trucks', i.e. transporter or host wagons); such alterations feature until the following September.

The pattern of traffic flow is interesting, recalling each wagon was calculated to hold approx. 1 ton of slate – the weight depended on the size of slates in transit – though in later years a basis of 1¾ tons per wagon prevailed.

1843	July	4,974 tons	13 cwt.	av.	207	wagons per day		
	Sept.	7,061	4	"	294	"	"	(rate reduced to 3¾d. ton thereafter)
1844	Sept.	5,967	12	"	248	"	"	
	Oct.	6,038		"	251	"	"	(rate reduced to ½d. ton thereafter)
1846	May	6,332		"	264	"	"	(rate now 3½d. ton)
	June	5,685	9	"	237	"	"	

'Balance due to Richard and Daniel Roberts to 23rd November, 1848 when T. Assheton-Smith took same into his own hands £4 15s. 0d.' is a significant entry as steam haulage began on that day. During autumn 1843 the haulage contract was re-drawn and Hugh Roberts was made responsible for track repairs and incline overhaul based on passing tonnage at ¾d. ton. The next year the Port Incline was 'cleared and repaired' for 1/6d. a day over a period of three weeks – suggesting some heavy wear and tear. The Port Incline chains needed frequent replacement @ £179 17s. 7d. each.

Anticipating the change-over from horse to steam, alterations had begun in November 1847 and continued to August 1848; the entries mainly concern 'altering curves'. The diarist[33] wrote 'first steam engine beginning to work on the Rail Road from Quarry to Port 22nd August, 1848'; another source gives the date as the previous 10th February (an impossible time) but regular running from 23rd November (as just mentioned) was the change-over date. In December 1850 the first entry concerning their reliability reads 'Attending to the Locomotive Engines at Top of the Incline (Wm. Owen & Partners) 4 weeks and 1 day @ 21/6d. per week £10 5s. 0d.'

Casting the net a little wider over the costs of operating the new railway, there had been numerous small entries showing the expense of horses, e.g. 'taxes' and 'rent of land, part of Garreg-y-Gwalch Farm, had for horse used on Railway'; 'Regulating and repairing 3 clocks on Padarn Railway'; stables' timber at Craig-y-Dinas; an amount of 2/6d. for lettering a board at the Port tunnel; 3 new hay cutting machines – these as late as November 1848 showing that horse feed was still required; 2 casks cement to repair Port tunnel; sowing seeds at Port Incline; 'walling and fencing alongside railway', and so on. Small but

significant changes were to take place when the iron horse replaced
nature's animal, and there is ominously 'Attending to Turnouts of the
Rail Road at the top of the Incline on the arrival of the Locomotive
Engine', an entry which recurs at this time and shows all was not well.
(The Port horse needed a lot of medicine too, at the same period!)

Regarding the pattern of traffic; during the horse-hauled period the
line was divided into (level) sections by the positions of the stables
where horses would be changed, viz: Muriau–Craig-y-Dinas, Craig-y-
Dinas–Garreg-y-Walch. 'Pass byes' (previously recorded) at app.
1 mile intervals would allow the runs to pass each other.

In the time of steam, it was usual to have only one engine operating
each day, and thus there was no need for any protection as would be
necessary if two engines were working independently on a single line of
track. The working engine was housed at Pen-Scoins and took the first
run of empties to the Quarry at various early hours of the day
dependent on the time of year (the hours of Quarry working varying
with the season and daylight hours). Throughout the early years, as can
be recalled, four trips each way were worked Monday to Friday by the
slate trains; normally these trains did not run in the dark. A second
engine was used as a stand-by and a third would be available for
overhaul. A petrol tractor obtained in the mid-1920s and kept at
Gilfach-Ddu was not used for train haulage. According to quarry
publicity as business fell away after World War I the average weight of
slate in a train was rarely more than 130 tons.

Though the returning empty slate wagons formed almost all the
return traffic, there were occasionally loads of coal for the mill steam
engine and locomotive use, timber for building, building materials
including sand and cement, lime for fields and the curious traffic in 'salt
stones' for the use of tenant sheep farmers who used it to supplement
other feeds.

Operation – Transport for Workmen

During the 1850–70 period FIRE QUEEN and JENNY LIND sufficed for
Padarn Railway purposes and the system must have been well-main-
tained and efficient, much to the disadvantage of competitive local slate
transport; the more surprising therefore that a cruder form of transport
shared the same metals . . . but *outside* the hours of the first and last
slate train. This was in the form of individual vehicles termed 'Velocipedes' which the quarrymen were permitted to build and use for
bringing them to and from work; they were non-standard (except in
basic design) and dangerous, but so long as they did not interfere with
the running of the railway, were tolerated: they were clumsy but
capable of being lifted from the track onto the Gilfach-Ddu rubbish
apron during the day, and left at any convenient lineside location near
the men's homes overnight. It must be explained that although Llanberis and district had virtually been created by the building of the road

over the Pass and later, by the business of the quarries nearby, there was always a daily entrance and exit of labour from outlying districts, and one natural route was the railway. Eardley-Wilmot wrote of the velocipedes: '. . . as it is now evening, and the works above have all at once become silent, it is curious to watch the quarrymen who live along the line returning home. This they accomplish by the aid of thirty velocipedes, which are placed on the railway and worked by the men themselves, by means of a windlass. Each velocipede contains sixteen persons and, proceeding along the line in the direction of the Port, it deposits the labourer at the nearest point to his respective dwelling. The last man returns back towards the quarry to take up a fresh load, or leaves his velocipede on the line until the next morning . . .' (the 'parking' of velocipedes on the track was, in fact, strictly forbidden, but they were far from 'light' when only one operator remained!) Wilmot mentions that before the railway came, twenty six boats did the same duty on the lower lake.

Other railed systems in North Wales saw variations in vehicles built by the men to ease their daily travelling, and tolerated by their employers. They enjoyed the common euphemism of 'Ceir Gwylltion' or Wild Cars and so Dinorwic, though different, was no exception. Introduced here before 1855, the two main varieties were 'Car Troi' and 'Car Cicio' (being 'Turning Car' and 'Kicking Car'), the former driven by handles and the latter, an earlier pattern, by foot treadles. Either was lethal to arms and legs if the limbs did not keep pace with the rhythm of movement; a 16-man team could be carried in each though not all men could operate at the same time. Overloading was commonplace, exceptional speeds were claimed and derailments frequent; one car leapt into Padarn lake and some men were drowned. Most accidents were due to over-running and collisions; a popular past-time was a version of the river 'Bumping Race'. Some control over the situation was attempted by issuing a set of rules and for a time they were allowed to run after the introduction of a proper workmen's train. Latterly there were 52 vehicles, each carrying exotic and frequently changed names, for which their appearance was quite unsuited, such as JENNY LIND and GARIBALDI. Kicking Cars disappeared first; they created more injuries and were long-remembered for arguments among the pedallers! They were finally driven off the track by the issue of this Notice whose limitations, in contrast with the effortless freedom of having a train provided for them, persuaded the owners that the new system had everything in their favour:

> With a view of avoiding accidents Employees are required to observe the following regulations:–
> No Velocipedes . . . shall be put upon or used on the Railway without the written permit (Caniatad) of the General Manager.
> Employees shall not get into, or out of any such velocipede . . . whilst in motion, and such velocipede . . . shall not travel at such a rate of speed as to endanger the

Plate XXVIII Gilfach-Ddu before 1882 showing one of the Horlock engines in the old platform (*bottom left*), the first Saloon in front of the transporter loading platform, and the west mouth of the Glan-y-Bala tunnel.

Gwynedd Archives

Plate XXIX Loading slate wagons onto transporter at Gilfach-Ddu. Note the locking handle to secure transporter against the loading dock: c 1905.   *from an official brochure*

Plate XXX Various forms of transporter at the loading dock, Gilfach- Ddu. The left hand has handbrake and buffing pads at one end, and will have to be turned at Pen-Scoins to remove the slate wagons. The second wagon has coil springs: c 1931.   *S. Bale Ltd.*

Plate XXXI AMALTHEA with the braked wagon on Plate XXX, with walled coaling yard behind. Gilfach-Ddu.   *Hamson*

Plate XXXII Loaded slate wagon train leaves Gilfach-Ddu with brake van at each end. (The Workmen's Train shelter and platform on extreme left.)   *'Maid Marian' Fund*

Plate XXXIII A well-loaded train skirts the shore of Llyn Padarn en route for Pen-Scoins: May 1952.
J.I.C. Boyd

Plate XXXIV Slowing down at Craig-y-Dinas, the engine makes extensive use of its warning hooter.
Hamson

Plate XXXV AMALTHEA brings down the 4 p.m. train with Saloon used as Pay Carriage, 31 July 1957.
Erw Ffordd.   *I. Higgon*

Plate XXXVI Pen-Scoins, with loaded wagons on high level (*left*) ready to run down to the transfer dock.
Empty wagons (*right*) have run down the slope from the transfer dock and will be picked up from the
other end by the locomotive, and depart for Gilfach-Ddu: 1954.   *D.L. Chatfield*

Plate XXXVII The transfer dock at Pen-Scoins; slate wagons were run off and descended by the Port Incline on the far side of the shed.   *G. Alliez*

Plate XXXVIII Looking up the Port Incline from the tunnel at the foot. At this period wagons were chained individually to the haulage chain. This was replaced by a steel cable in May 1924.

Gwynedd Archives

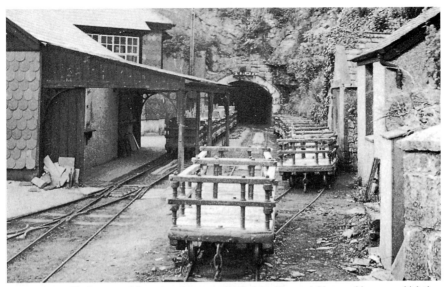

Plate XXXIX The Port tunnel foot opened out onto the dock beside a weighing machine over which the full wagons passed. Empties were formed up on the right. By now worked by cable, the wagons went in 'runs' rather than individually on the Incline: June 1949.   *J.I.C. Boyd*

Plate XL No. 1 hauls the loaded wagons off the Port weighbridge, and is seen crossing the portable rails laid over the standard gauge Port Siding.   *Hamson*

Plate XLI Leaving Pen-Scoins with the empties, DINORWIC chuffs stealthily past under an impressive smoke pall. The signal was little more than a point-indicator.

P. Ward

Plate XLII A few yards further on than the above, VELINHELI passes Pen-Scoins Cottages on the first stage of the journey to the Quarry: 16 April 1946.

R.E. Tustin

Plate XLIII Pulling nicely, AMALTHEA passes Erw Ffordd with the empties. The braked wagon is (as usual), behind the engine. Note the link-and-pin front coupler on the engine, operated from the foot-plate: 6 October 1959. *I. Higgon*

Plate XLIV The story behind the necessity to erect this substantial footbridge at Bethel has not been unearthed. *J.I.C. Boyd*

Plate XLV Pen-y-Llyn, a Workmen's Train station, looking towards Gilfach-Ddu. The corrugated-iron carriage shed was later taken to the Quarry as a brick-making plant shelter; the 1870 bridge beyond was faced with old stone block sleepers and its beams cast by de Winton & Co: June 1949.   *J.I.C. Boyd*

Plate XLVI The signalled crossing at Pont Pen-y-Llyn, the west end of Llyn Padarn, looking east.
Hamson

Plates XLVII & XLVIII Two viewpoints of the earliest track on the Padarn Railway, with double-headed iron rail and stone sleeper blocks.   *Both J.I.C. Boyd*

Plate XLIX Padarn Railway: 'imported' stone sleeper, later replaced by timber. *J.I.C. Boyd*

Plate L Padarn Railway: progression of chairs, earliest form in front. *J.I.C. Boyd*

Plate LI Padarn Railway: the same chairs. Third from left dates c 1870. *J.I.C. Boyd*

Plate LII Inside the former Workmen's Train station shed, transporters are lined up. That with the brake handle would carry a brake van: October 1953. *J.I.C. Boyd*

Plates LIII Close-up views of slate wagon securing mechanism on transporter wagons showing striker in 'clear' position after hitting beam of transfer dock (locking latch thrown clear to right).
J.I.C. Boyd

Overleaf: Plate LIV Striker in 'clear' position and chocks clear of slate wagon running rails and (*Plate LV*) striker hand-pushed back and latch dropped across; chocks now across slate wagon rails to prevent movement in transit. *J.I.C. Boyd*

Plate LVI Blue and white enamelled bi-lingual Trespass Notice (1895) by Imperial Enamel Co., Birmingham.
J.I.C. Boyd

Plate LVII Unused locomotive nameplate patterns from Gilfach-Ddu Pattern Shop, some of racehorses which did not reach the owner's hopes! The window frame behind was also made here. *J.I.C. Boyd*

Plate LVIII Further patterns from Gilfach-Ddu emphasising the variety of castings needed for switches and rail joints of the varying sections in use. *J.I.C. Boyd*

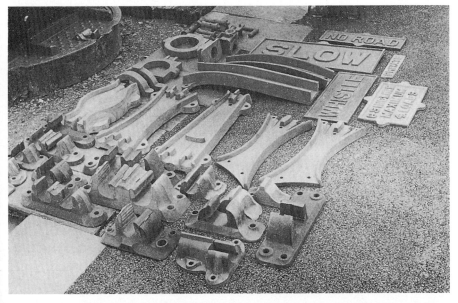

Plate LIX   Posed scene at Gilfach-Ddu showing pedal-operated (*left*) and hand-worked (*right*) Velocipedes. The men in the centre are making slates: c 1894.   *Gwynedd Archives*

Plate LX Another posed scene at Gilfach-Ddu probably taken to mark the end of velocipede usage. The 'Dramatis Personae' appear to be the same! Vehicles on the right have had wheels removed; it was the practice to line them up off the track during the day. (This view was one of a set of lantern slides of North Wales.)   *Gwynedd Archives*

persons riding in them, or any other person travelling on the Railway.
A distance of at least 25 yards shall be maintained between each velocipede . . .
whilst travelling.
No Velocipede or other conveyance shall travel on the Railway whilst a train or
engine is on the road . . .
Dinorwic Quarry Office
April 3rd 1894

One or two survived for the use of permanent way gangs, one being stored on the lineside at Bethel.

At the height of popularity these cars carried 500 men daily, but at Saturday mid-days they were left at Gilfach-Ddu where a local arrangement enabled a degree of maintenance to be carried out. Their owners were required to travel on the last slate train of the Saturday and return by the first empty train on the Monday following. This arrangement persisted until August 1895, when negotiations between the men and the owners resulted in a proper train for workmen being run.

Looking back, it seems that this primitive transport enjoyed permissive existence from earliest times and may date from the building of the Padarn Railway itself. In 1851 the 'CAMBRIAN MIRROR' said '. . . two thousand workmen . . . a large proportion of them live at a distance . . . and it's amusing to watch them . . . returning to their homes . . . to save the labour of walking, skim rapidly along the railway by means of machines which run on the rails, and are propelled by the action of feet upon treadles . . . others descend the lake in boats . . .'.

Their accidents frequently appeared in the press or were recorded by local diarists; on 28th January, 1858 'Hu Griffith, Tai-Newyddion and the son of Jn Pritchard, Cae Glas, Llanrug drowned through the Car Gwyllt running into the Lake by Llechfulfran'; and as to riding on the slate train 'Y Tren Chwarel' we read 29th May, 1867: 'Fatal accident to the son of Dd Hughes, Ebenezer. Falling off the run'; 26th January, 1876: 'Robert Wm Roberts of Brynrefail died suddenly in the Car Gwyllt whilst coming to work. 65 years of age'. Giving deeper insight into some of the more dangerous pranks and practices, especially on the downhill run after work, is this newspaper extract from the 'CARNARVON & DENBIGH HERALD' dated 14th February, 1863:

Llanberis Fatal Railway Accident
An accident of a most distressing nature occurred on the above railway on Tuesday last . . . many of the workmen . . . have velocipedes for the purpose of travelling to and fro upon the line; and very frequently they indulge in the foolish practice of attempting to overtake a velocipede which happens to be in advance of them. On Tuesday evening between 5 and 6 the deceased, a boy of about 14 years of age named Robert Prichard was returning towards his home at Bryngwyn, Llanrug in one of these carriages with a party who were leaving their work, the unfortunate boy sitting at the back of the carriage with his legs hanging over. They were followed by two other similar vehicles which came up with them near Pont Rhyddallt. The first of

these dashed up against the one in which Prichard sat crushing his legs in a dreadful manner but no sooner had it struck the preceding carriage than the second came behind with fearful momentum and completed this horrid catastrophe. Both the unfortunate poor fellow's legs were smashed almost to pieces and the flesh was torn away from above the right knee down to the middle of the leg. He bled most fearfully and death appears to have been caused by this . . . On Wednesday, Doctors Maugham and W.W. Roberts visited him for the purpose of amputating his right leg, but he was so debilitated that it would have been worse than madness to attempt it. On Wednesday night his sufferings were terminated by the hand of death.

The following newspaper article indicates that the Saturday Workmen's Train (when the velocipedes were retained at Gilfach-Ddu) stopped at certain recognised places only, and that all and sundry made use of it whether they worked in the Quarry or not; it will be noted there was at this early date a regular stop at 'Penllyn' (Pen-y-Llyn) and the train slowed for a road crossing. 'CARNARVON & DENBIGH HERALD' 29th April, 1865:

Pontrhythallt, Llanrug. Inquest
On Thursday last an Inquest was held at Pontrhythallt, Llanrug on the body of William Williams, Stonemason . . . "I went to Penllyn to meet the slate train from the Dinorwic Quarries . . . as it approached Pontrhythallt I saw my father (the deceased) standing on the road. The train then was going a little slower. My father attempted to catch hold of one of the leading carriages. He managed to catch hold of one and tried to jump on the side of the carriage. He lost his hold and fell and the carriages went over one of his legs and hurt the other foot very much . . . I jumped down and got to him before anyone else. The train stopped as soon as it could. The deceased appeared very much injured but spoke a little. Assistance was given and we carried him here". (Deceased died the following Thursday).

This Saturday and Monday transport on the slate train, together with the dangers of the velocipedes and the improvements in quarrymen's travel being afforded on the nearby Penrhyn Railway, became an increasing concern to the management. Their legal responsibilities were investigated and in February 1892 they issued the following Notice:

EACH MONDAY MORNING THE FIRST TRAIN LEAVING "THE PORT END" WILL STOP TO PICK UP PERSONS EMPLOYED IN THE DINORWIC QUARRIES AT BETHEL & PONTRHYTHALLT . . . LAST TRAIN WILL STOP TO DROP MEN ON SATURDAY & PAY DAYS [last Friday in each month] . . . ALL PERSONS . . . TRAVELLING AT OWN RISK

At the same time steps were taken to regularise the use of velocipedes and licence them for six month periods; green card permits on which the names of the Velocipede, 'Breaksman', the date of issue and card number were hand-entered (note there was no entry for 'Owner') read:

THIS PERMIT IS FOR SIX MONTHS, BUT IS SUBJECT TO BE WITH-DRAWN WITHOUT ANY NOTICE.

In April 1894 the screw was given a further turn, an essential step anticipating the introduction of a formal Workmen's Train in August

1895, by the issue of the customary bi-lingual notice, forbidding velocipedes to travel on the 'Railway whilst a train or engine is on the road . . .'.

The final nails in the velocipede 'coffin' were driven in by the management with such circulars as 'Notice to Breaksmen of Velocipedes running on the Quarry Railway – the Quarry Engine will be running on the line between the Quarry and the top of Port Incline tomorrow morning . . . between 5 and 5.30 a.m.' and there was a large sheet on which the men signed: 52 names of vehicles are listed. Then came the beginning of the break, firstly by this Notice and then by extending its basic conditions to every working day:

ON SATURDAYS AFTER 12 O'CLOCK NO VELOCIPEDES ARE TO RUN ON THE LINE. THE QUARRY TRAIN STARTING 25 MINUTES AFTER THE LAST WHISTLE WILL TAKE ANY DINORWIC QUARRY WORKMEN DESIROUS OF TRAVELLING BY SAME . . . ON MONDAY MORNINGS NO VELOCIPEDES ARE TO RUN . . . THE QUARRY TRAIN WILL LEAVE PENSCOINS 1 HOUR BEFORE THE FIRST WHISTLE SOUNDS

As the official Workmen's Train proved itself and the exhausting labour of the velocipede could be exchanged for a more attractive mode, it fell out of use. It had enjoyed half a century of singularly unusual life, and its extinction was foreshadowed by steps among its own users for an up-to-date system. But that is to anticipate.

The introduction of steam locomotion has had previous mention and a full description of these engines and their successors, together with that of the velocipedes, workmen's carriages, saloons, slate train wagons and other stock follows; it remains the present purpose to relate this equipment to the operation of the railway. To begin with the steam locomotion; the somewhat primitive pair of original engines was nearing the end of useful life by 1880 and JENNY LIND was ultimately dismantled, some parts going to repair FIRE QUEEN, others to contrive a pump for the Quarry whilst some of the brasswork survived in the stores to be sold in the auction of 1969! To replace these engines a series of six-coupled side tank engines was bought individually in 1882, 1886 and, to assist with the running of the recently-introduced Workmen's Train, a third was delivered in 1895.

Details of slate tonnages passing over the Railway are rare but an average run at this period was 15 host wagons, with 22 a well-remembered record – in calculating the length for a proposed Workmen's Train, different figures were used: lengths were limited to 32 host wagons due to the track layouts (133 yards 1 foot exactly was allowed per train(!) equivalent to 19 workmen's carriages each 24 ft long, a total of 152 yards in the calculations).

It was in September 1892 following two meetings of Bethel-based employees, that Isaac Parry and Hugh Griffiths first wrote to the Hon. W.W. Vivian the Quarry Manager asking for better transport for those men living in Bethel 'existing velocipedes are both dangerous to limb and laborious to propel' and the correspondence was extended to include Assheton-Smith the same month. Parry and Griffiths, influenced by what Lord Penrhyn was providing for his own workmen, wanted nothing less than that the Quarry should provide them with a special train to meet the needs of both weekly and daily-travelling employees. Vivian passed his own interpretation of the enquiry to Assheton-Smith in terms typical of himself: '. . . I cannot see my way to say that I consider it advisable for you to comply with this request . . .' including in his objections:

a) that the matter had been raised four years earlier and put aside
b) the extra labour costs of such a train, plus coal and oil would be considerable
c) the extra wear and tear 'for engine, about 30 Main Line Trucks & about 120 small trucks' and on the Main Line itself. (Clearly the use of existing wagons was envisaged)
d) the additional responsibility of operating the train
e) that though Penrhyn 'have for some years run the men to and from work, but by Narrow Gauge; here we are different'
f) that many employees living near the quarry were tenants of the Estate. If a train was provided they might 'migrate to such places as Bethel, Capel Sion or Llanrug . . .' outside the Vaynol Estate, with consequent loss of income to the owner

Like most of Vivian's letters to his employer (to whom he was related by marriage), the impression of servility and sycophancy is inescapable.

In reply, Assheton-Smith – showing to his credit a trace of humour – wrote '. . . I do not know why Bethel is to be singularly favoured' and pointing out that if a service was begun and found not to work, it could be stopped again with due notice, but he was more concerned with his responsibility if an accident was to occur. The men, meanwhile, had submitted more detailed proposals to offset Vivian's comments; these included the appreciation that the line was a private one and not a statutory company, and enquiring of Assheton-Smith's legal position as regards 'powers to convey us for a fixed monthly payment'. If not it was suggested he might 'build the carriages and charge us a moderate rate of interest on the capital or advance the capital to the men in exchange for adequate security'. In order to cater for men working irregular hours, it was proposed that certain velocipedes be retained, 'a few for each station' (confirming that recognised if informal 'stations' then existed).

· Deliberations tended to drag on, as they do when legal issues are involved; correspondence from the men's representative in early 1895 asks if transport was available for men going home at noon, or for some men who now broke their week's stay by going home for the night on Wednesdays, if boys under 16 would pay full fees for the service, and would the train stop at Craig-y-Dinas, 'Capel Seion and Crawia Bridge'? The men also wished to sit in the same places, in the same carriage 'to save a rush and over-crowding'.

Ultimately the details were settled. Those using the train would sign an Agreement (a form of indemnity) – those travelling without having signed would be dealt with as trespassers. Payment would be a contribution given by the man himself from his monthly wages (for which a receipt would be given), related to the journeys made in the previous month: if a man refused to pay his contribution he might be refused conveyance, then if, due to walking, he was late for work, he might be dismissed. All these conditions were framed by R. Mostyn Roberts (solicitor) who was engaged for the purpose. Roberts added two other leading comments: (a) he presumed the Railway was free of the conditions of the Gauge Act of 1846, as it was constructed before that date and, (b) who gave the Railway leave to 'cross highroads'? The answer to the latter would seem to be that it was an arrangement with other landowners where necessary, and in any case, would there be much other opposition from other local parties? All in all, in Roberts's opinion he had covered all issues and left Assheton-Smith free of liability on any count. It was envisaged that the men's contributions would go towards the capital cost of the management providing a train and the engine and rolling stock in it, and interest on that capital towards the running costs of the train.

In passing, Roberts also pointed out to Vivian that the Railway was in default of the Act (2 & 3 Vic. Cap. 45: Gates at Level Crossings) for not having gated its road crossings and must do so without delay and provide persons to operate them. Also that as under the Gauge Act it was unlawful to carry passengers on a railway of less than 4 ft 8½ in. gauge, even if the line had been built before the passing of that Act and had been a mineral railway until then, it was now proposed to convert it into a passenger railway. Roberts ends by recommending the management to take the advice of 'a good Railway Counsel' for an opinion on some of these points; later in 1895 suitable legal forms to meet the situation had been printed. One Agreement said that W.W. Vivian and 'the proprietor for the time being of the said Railway' shall 'not be liable in any way . . . (for) accident, injury or damage . . .'. The Receipt was to be worded '. . . contribution towards the expenses of providing maintaining and running carriages on the Railway . . .'. The basis of the Rules was similar to those already applying to the week-end trains, which ended '. . . must not overcrowd the wagons or trucks and they must not attempt to ride on the engine'. By now all these Notices were headed DINORWIC QUARRY RAILWAY and the term Padarn Railway had almost been dropped.

It was quickly established that special vehicles would be needed; the management approached The Gloucester Railway Carriage & Wagon Co. for prices, and after some bargaining bought closed carriages very competitively as Gloucester needed orders badly; there were to be 15 @ £105 6s. 0d. and 4 @ £113 (presumably braked vehicles), a total of £2,031 10s. 0d., the makers squealing that this would show them no profit. The quarry workshop was to provide 'Train Labels' and these would slot into brackets and hang as headboards on the platform side of the carriage only (black characters on a white ground); they were painted with the 'District' name, and would be affixed to each of the nineteen carriages, each of which would carry the letter 'A' to 'S', viz: (the spelling is taken from the records)

Penscoins	A B C	3	Boards
Penscoins & Bethel	P	1	"
Bethel	D E	2	"
Bethel & Pontrht	Q	1	"
Pontrhytallt	F G H I J K L M	8	"
Pontrht & Penllyn	R	1	"
Penllyn	N O S	3	"

the object being to concentrate the men into vehicles which might be detached in groups (or singly) in each district.

Station or District*	No. of men expected to use train	Men left over from last station	Total Men	No. of Carrs.	(Ordinary)	(Brake)	Men left over
Penllyn	230	Nil	230	3	2	1	52
Stabla	101	52	153	2	1	1	35
Pontrhythallt	420	35	455	7	6	1	37
Bethel	184	37					
Penscoins	196	Nil	417	7	5	2	1
Totals	1,131 passengers			19	(14)	(5)	Carriages

*vernacular spellings

To keep the men of the same district together the seats were allocated by token, each seat being numbered. The Register of tokens was to read e.g.

Name	Orig. No.	Check (or Token No.)	Carriage	Seat No.	Department
John Jones	64	1	A	1	Garret

The cost of providing the service was based on purchasing carriages (£2,300), an extra locomotive (£1,400), building carriage sheds and for land (£600) and 'obtaining certain rails' (£200); a total of £4,500. Annual running costs were estimated at £1,040; the monthly passenger numbers and fares for 23rd February, 1895 survive – takings were £107. At this rate the cost of the carriages would be covered in about two years and all capital expense within five: the service must have been a profitable venture for some time after that, but no figures have survived. Fares were based on mileages (an assumed 6½ miles Pen-Scoins to Gilfach-Ddu); the number of carriages per station and the numbers travelling occasionally produced curious anomalies. The position for 1915 with spellings as then used was:

Gilfach-Ddu to	Penscoins	(return: for 4 week period)	1/-	('Anglesey Men' travelling once weekly only).
"	Penscoins	"	2/2d.	(daily journey)
"	Bethel	"	2/-	" "
"	Pontrhythallt	"	1/8d. – later 1/10d.	" "
"	Penllyn	"	1/1d.	(daily journey)

In due time the carriage sheds had regular residents, which for 1915 were: Pen-Scoins 'A', 'B', 'C', 'P', 'U' (5): Bethel 'D', 'E', 'F', 'Q' (4): Pont-Rhythallt 'G', 'H', 'I', 'J', 'K', 'L', 'R' (7): Pen-y-Llyn 'M', 'N', 'O', 'S' (4).

At this date, vehicles 'C', 'H', 'L' were kept in the Works, and 'T' and 'W' were not allocated. By June 1926 (takings now being much reduced at £72 for 4 weeks) carriages in service and their loadings were: 'A' 46; 'D' 54; 'F' 57; 'G' 57; 'H' 59; 'J' 59; 'K' 57; 'M' 55; 'N' 55; 'O' 50; 'Q' 56; 'R' 56; 'S' 51; 'T' 51¾ [sic]; 'U' 54 = 817¾ persons in 15 vehicles. Significantly by June 1944 only 'K', 'Q', 'V' (these may, by then, not have been their original letters) were usable and monthly takings were down to £18 but this was wartime. Records of carriage capacity were discontinued in December 1928. (Final comment on survivors is made on page 84.)

To each carriage the Quarry Manager allotted a foreman who was responsible for discipline, collection of the monthly levy and naming the gang of men required to shunt the carriages in and out of the sheds each day. Certain but not all carriages had a handbrake and at least one braked vehicle was included in each station rake; when the train first ran the braked vehicles had a brakesman allocated to each and besides this duty, together with coupling to and uncoupling from the train, he had to examine the ticket (or check) and refuse admittance to anyone without one on pain of dismissal. Over the years the duties of brakesman and foreman became fused into the latter person and a man employed as a guard worked from Pen-Scoins on every train.[34] Foremen received free travel and from 2/- per month[35] for their services. After each monthly pay day the foreman would receive a list of passengers and fares due and the sum would be delivered to the office at Port Dinorwic next month when the next list was ready for collection.

The method of train operation was that the Pen-Scoins-bound train would stop beyond the carriage siding points at each stopping place and the men would uncouple the carriages to be stabled there and push them into the shed; in the morning the shunt was reversed, the engine running off the train it had brought to enable the last carriage rake to be inserted into the train in the order for detachment in the evening run.

A guard, who also did duty on the slate trains, had to travel in the last vehicle so that on the evening run he was constantly changing his carriage! It was he who kept the neat leatherbound register of 'Workmen's Trains' (similar to those bound up for 'Slate Train' with gilded letters on the spine) showing loadings and timings. The latter-day three-coach train is entered for its last run when the monthly takings up to 8th November, 1947 were £21 5s. 2d.; 2/6d. monthly was charged for travelling in 'U' and only 2/- for the other two!

Bi-lingual signs in white enamel, framed, were hung in appropriate places and were headed DINORWIC QUARRIES RAILWAY Dinorwic Quarrymen's Train and dated August 1895. They left no opening for abuse of the passenger service (!) and the notice began: 'For the convenience of persons employed at the Dinorwic Quarries whose homes are adjacent to the Dinorwic Quarries Railway, arrangements have been made whereby such persons can travel along the Railway to and from the Quarries . . .'

The conditions included:

1) licence to use the service would only be given to those employed and subject to observance of certain Rules and Regulations
2) use of the line would be at user's risk
3) licence to use would take the form of a ticket or 'check' which would be shown to the brakesman as required; tickets were not transferable
4) each person to travel in the carriage and the numbered seat allotted to him
5) no one to enter into or alight from the train whilst in motion
6) everyone to prevent damage, the use of offensive language, to be free of infectious diseases and not to be in possession of explosives 'or other articles of a dangerous nature'

The men were required to be at their appropriate stations five minutes before the train and assist with shunting as required; the loss of a ticket would cost 6d. for its replacement; contributions for the preceding month towards the expenses of the train to be given to the foreman on the Tuesday following every Quarry pay day.

The Workmen's Train operation produced some statistics which had not been necessary previously:

Mileage from Pen-Scoins	Station (or) name	Height above sea level	Platform length	Siding	Carr. sdg.	Carriage Shed details
0 m. 0 ch.	Pen-Scoins	296 ft	'causeway'	Yes	Yes	Built 1895, part of loco shed. Stone/Slab; 4 carrs.
0 7	Cefn-Gwyn[a]	302 ft	30 ft	No	No	—
1 68	Bethel	315 ft	164 ft	No	Yes	Built 1895. Stone/Slab;4 carrs.
2 40	*Pen-Sarn	315 ft	30 ft	Yes[b]	No	—
2 45	Pont-Rhythallt Mill (West)		None	Yes	No	—
2 62	" (East)		None	No	No	—
3 48	Pont-Rhythallt		450 ft[c]	No	Yes	Built 1895. Stone/Slab;7 carrs.
4 40	Pen-y-Llyn[d]	345 ft	184 ft	No	Yes	Corrugated iron; 4 carrs.
(4 58	Pen-y-Llyn Crossing)					
(5 46	Boundary Quarry)					
6 42	Gilfach-Ddu	346 ft	Extensive	Yes	Yes	Recent building in steelwork etc. to shelter all stock

*classified as a Halt
(a)   or Bryn-Pistyll
(b)   Siding for p.w. trolley only
(c)   Platform extension of narrow width
(d)   or Pen-Llyn or Bryn-Erfel

The first morning train to leave Pen-Scoins did so 1 hr 30 mins before the first quarry whistle, Cefn-Gwyn 5 mins, Bethel 13 mins, Pen-Sarn 18 mins, Pont-Rhythallt 27 mins, Pen-y-Llyn 31 mins, after leaving Pen-Scoins, being allowed 45 minutes for the whole journey. Except on Saturdays when 35 mins were allowed, the train left the Quarry 30 minutes after the last quarry whistle. The size of Pont-Rhythallt was due to the large number of men from Waen-Fawr who used it daily.

The carriage foremen's task was not all milk and honey! Perhaps the most difficult was the prevention of men entering and leaving when the train was moving and much ill-feeling is still recalled by those who were too late and for whom the train would not stop again after it had left a station. The foremen kept a record book of payments, but there are regular entries like 'Men left owing Train Money'. All concerned with the operation of the train were given a 10 in. × 7 in. card timetable each month; and each month the users of the train were bound to sign the Workmen's Train Book 'I certify that I have been made acquainted with the terms & conditions printed on the Dinorwic Quarry "Padarn Railway" Ticket' after which was entered, name, address and date. Staff not directly employed in the Quarry also signed e.g. females working in the Quarry hospital, and quarrymen's wives might also use the train. By law, those under 21 might not sign; signing was done on their behalf. Some who were illiterate signed with a 'X' but after 31st December, 1946 regular users were no longer required to sign, this being reserved solely for casual visitors, and there are only seven of these thereafter, the formality being honoured in the breach.

The tickets took the form of metal tokens having the following shapes: square (with bevelled corners), circular, oval. It may have been the intention to distinguish by outline alone – with the probability that most might not read English – this aim was however, lost. The station common to all was Gilfach-Ddu and a typical specimen (oval) reads:

DINORWIC QUARRY   WORKMENS TRAIN   AVAILABLE BETWEEN
GILFACH DDU AND PEN LLYN   ANY PERSON TRANSFERRING THIS
CHECK WILL BE LIABLE TO DISMISSAL

whilst the other face had

Check No.   Carriage No.   Seat No.   HOLDER TRAVELS ENTIRELY
AT HIS OWN RISK. Issued subject and to be used under the conditions and rules
and regulations in force.

The metal check-tickets were supplanted by a simple yellow-coloured card (3 in. × 2¼ in.) to incorporate other classes of traveller entitled to use the train; with name and address on one side, date of issue and issuers signature, the other side summarized thus;

'. . . they must not attempt to enter or leave the train when in motion . . . they must not overcrowd the wagons or trucks, and they must not attempt to ride on the engine.' (Compared with the somewhat pedantic phrasing of other official notices, certain inaccuracies are surprising!)

Between the wars the train carried an average of 1,200 daily (20 carriages). On Mondays and Saturdays about 450 – later about 120 – 'Anglesey' men, with their white carrier bags containing food or clothes distinguishing them, were carried in 2–4 extra carriages next to the engine added to the rake on those days. These men crossed the Straits at Moel-y-Don Ferry (closed 1935) and lodged in the Quarry Barracks by the week; they were a 'race apart' and distrusted by some of the mainlanders who considered them inferior and poor working colleagues, but by others to be hard working and full of humour. When the morning train arrived, those who worked in the bottom of the Quarry could slumber on in the carriages at Gilfach-Ddu until nearer the time for work!

The Workmen's Train was discontinued on 8th November, 1947 and apart from when Crosville bus strikes re-instated it briefly, the end had come. The carriages – many of which were already in poor shape – were left in the Yard and the weather took its toll. Ultimately they were broken up or burned.

Operation and Signalling

In 1906 14 men found employment on the Railway: as to the working of it (and the underlying influence of the Assheton-Smiths on its daily routine,) the instructions of the Manager reflect the atmosphere of those times.

For instance, in relation to its size there can hardly have been another railway where trespassers, users of level crossing or stiles, quarrymen travelling on the train, enginemen, guards . . . indeed anyone likely to come within audible distance of the Railway was not made aware of some dictatorial presence; large enamelled notices – bi-lingual to avoid doubt – were liberally posted in any position where employees and public would see them: it was as if the Company was aware that being a private undertaking, it had not always carried out such preventative measures as the Board of Trade would impose on a Public Undertaking, and was anxious to avoid any accident which might result in an embarrassing Enquiry! If some of the legally-phrased directions confused the English reader, what of the unfortunate Welsh?!

When the Staff System was introduced – and subsequently – employees signed the Staff System Book after reading (or had read to them): 'We clearly understand that when working two of the main line engines are ordered to be worked, or are working that we, two engine drivers, two stokers and two guards are to work same upon the Main Line on a Staff system, that is to say, the Engine which takes the Run down to the Port is to wait at the Port without moving until the arrival of the Workmens Train with Engine. And the Driver of Workmens Train is to hand the Staff to the Driver of the Engine waiting with the Run'. Every day the Staff System was in operation, the book was to be signed on pain of dismissal or 'no wages'.

Small entries of the late 1890s include (July 1896) places where the whistle must be blown, especially Bethel level crossing. In December the last slate 'run' left the Quarry at 3.20 p.m. and if two engines were in use, it remained at Pen-Scoins until the Workmen's Train arrived, the empty slate train and engine then returning to the Quarry. By January the last slate train was leaving at 4.30 p.m. This is the earliest reference to the Workmen's Train.

Assheton-Smith was also requiring an evening Special (9th December, 1896) to leave Pen-Scoins 6.55 p.m. with engine and Saloon, needing 25 minutes for the journey and leaving again at 9.45 this time cutting the journey time to 20 minutes. Lamps were to be lit in the Saloon also tail lamps on both vehicles; all level crossings to be manned and two men were to patrol the line from 6.45 p.m. and again after the train had gone.

That same dictatorial message underlines that no one may travel on the engine (of 'Padarn Railway or Tram line') without permission 'and no one is allowed to drive the same without written permission'. However, there are six names added who might mount the footplate.

One of the greatest dangers lay in the level crossings: flagmen or gatekeepers were latterly connected by telephone and would open gates five minutes before the train was due – there were no gates before the 1926 accident but after this flagmen were employed continuously; some gatemen doubled up duties as platelayers. Drivers were expected to traverse level crossings so as to be capable of stopping within two yards! (1926).

Some risk was attached to passing trains by the slaty nature of cuttings; there was usually something of a 'special effort' made to bring down and clear away any unsafe rocks when Royal or similar trains were expected, but there was a monthly examination of 'rocks and bridges' in addition; and a daily inspection of points and padlocks, by platelayers, before the Workmen's Train passed.

In August 1897 so great was the demand for accommodation in the Workmen's Train that on Saturdays when the train left the Quarry at 12.30 there were to be '4 Padarn Railway empty trucks, for Anglesea men, coupled behind all the carriages'.

A typical Royal day in 1899 involved engine and carriage 'U' leaving the Quarry at 11.55 for Pen-Scoins. It returned with the Saloon attached and the engine was uncoupled from the coaches 'below the Hospital . . . Loco, after shunting run to draw same to Special Platform'. However, Royalty was not always especially favoured; in September 1899 an engine and workmen's carriage left Gilfach-Ddu at 6.30 p.m. to take 30 men to Pen-Scoins; these were the Committee and competitors for the Sheepdog Trials at Vaynol. Another day with a difference ended when VELINHELI, then only five years old, failed at Pen-Scoins and PANDORA had to be steamed belatedly to go to the rescue, leaving the Quarry after 6 p.m.

The absence of intermediate sidings (save at carriage sheds) gave some operating difficulties; it might be necessary to detach wagons – for trackwork – en route for Pen-Scoins and on return to Gilfach-Ddu the management allowed such wagons to be propelled in front of the engine 'and shunted before pulling in the Empty Run with the Chain'.[36] It was customary to post flagmen 1,000 yards each side of work on the track (but this figure seems unnecessarily excessive!) Precautions concerning ballast wagons left on the line required a man with red flag to be with it at all times, and no wagons to be taken on to the line without a written order from the office.

The hand-shunting of carriages in the dark had led to some accidents involving the shed doors, so in December 1912 it was ruled that 'Brakesman in charge of carriages is to put his brake on after the Train is uncoupled, and is not to move until he receives a signal from the man at the Shed that the doors are properly open'.

The book from which these extracts is taken ends immediately following the Bethel collision, however from an earlier date some loose sheets have survived and a little evidence of the years when velocipedes came under some management control confirms that the line was divided into two sections at Bethel. The rules did not always give the engine preference over a velocipede – for reasons unclear – but in most cases if an engine was working in either of the two sections, velocipedes were to wait at the terminii or Bethel.

In October 1891, before the last Saloon was built – and perhaps the original one was either too small or by then withdrawn – reference is made to a special train to carry 35–40 persons from 'top of Port Incline . . . W. Davies (Guard) to see Bus is put on, and as many seats provided in trucks as possible; Driver to run extra cautiously'.

As to the early days of the Workmen's Train, its precursor was instructed, from 11th February, 1892, as being the first train from Pen-Scoins, to pick up at Bethel and Pont-Rhythallt, as would also the last train leaving the Quarry (also on Saturdays and pay days). From February 1894 any loaded slate train to Pen-Scoins which also carried workmen was to consist of '23 full cars and 5 empty cars'.

Only one reference is made to the signalling near 'Crawia' (March 1894) – 'Signal near Factory – arm will be up for danger, down for safety. Engine to go slowly on approaching signal when going down from Quarry, and to whistle when sighting the signal'.

MOTIVE POWER AND LOCOMOTIVE WORKING

Assheton-Smith had a close connection with steam power at sea, and recalling his 12 ton coke-burning stationary steam engine for pumping in the Quarry supplied by Davy Bros. of Sheffield for £300 in November 1847, it comes as no surprise that by then a decision to use locomotives had been made, and in October there begins a long list of expenses to 'Altering Line of Railway'.

The existing railway contained some sharp curves, portions of limited clearance and an intermediate tunnel, all of which had to go; £1000 was spent in wages alone during the first four months of 1848. The reconstruction had been surveyed and drawn out by Richard Roberts who was paid £45 1s. 6d. for his trouble. In June Alfred Horlock & Co. were paid £733 for FIRE QUEEN the first locomotive; it was shipped from Gravesend to Caernarvon, and £7 12s. 8d. spent on cartage by Robert Roberts and Robert Morris, from thence to the Quarry (possibly in semi-dismantled state and by teams of horses). The second engine JENNY LIND cost £40 for shipment in September following and FIRE QUEEN was put to trial from 23rd November: in the same month Horlock was paid £564 2s. 10d. as balance on the two engines plus extras, and it may be concluded that as a separate amount is not entered for JENNY LIND, the two engines and tenders (including extras) cost about £1,300 each ex works.

Improvements to the line continued from November 1847 to August 1848 and though both engines were available by the end of 1848 and a test run was recorded on 22nd August, 1848 it was to be December 1849 before both started regular work. Some hint of the delay may be read into the accounts – somewhat peremptorily the operating contractors had been dismissed whilst at the same time William Owen & Others were contracted 'to attend the locomotive engines at top of incline' (were they both stabled there?) from November 1849, a duty they performed until at least 1850 when the accounts cease. The pointwork at Pen-Scoins too must have required modification, and we learn of problems on the engines due to their long coupling rods which frequently bent, the shifting of the original set-screwed eccentric sheaves which upset the valve timing and a succession of accidents which were attributed to having no brakes on the engine.[37]

In time these difficulties were overcome and both engines gave good service – being used alternately – until mid-1880s when probably they were due for new fireboxes/boilers and their curious Crampton-like design was unfitted for the heavier tonnages then offering.

STEAM LOCOMOTIVES

Name	Maker	Date	Notes
FIRE QUEEN	Alfred Horlock & Co., North Fleet Ironworks, Kent.	1848	Withdrawn 1886, and preserved
JENNY LIND	ditto	1848	Withdrawn 188X?, and scrapped

According to C.R. Weaver,[38] Horlock's were engineers whose products went mainly to ship-building yards on the south side of the Thames and for reasons so far unexplained may have become suppliers of shipping or quarrying machinery to Dinorwic during the 1840s. They may have been unfamiliar with railway locomotive design and manufacture and so consulted Messrs. G. & J. Rennie, then the nearest builders, whose designer was Thomas Russell Crampton, then aged 32, who had been associated with Gooch on the design of some of the first Great Western Railway broad gauge engines. In this connection he designed a type with single driving axle behind the firebox and patented it, the arrangement including scope for a large-diameter boiler with a low centre of gravity, the latter feature being then considered highly desirable. In 1844 he had left Gooch to work with Rennie.

The Dinorwic engine design was based on Crampton's fourth patent of 1847, a conception which included having one driving axle at each end of the chassis with the valve motion derived from eccentrics fixed on the leading axle; the cylinders were placed, considerably inclined, on the boiler and reminiscent of George Stephenson's ROCKET; in fact the Dinorwic engines' appearance smacked of a throw-back in design. Other features of the patent were not evident in the Dinorwic product, and they are believed to be the only locomotives built by Horlock.

The engines were in some respects similar to later road engine practice, and had no main frames whatsoever: the pull from the drawbars is taken on the barrel by appropriate joints, the cylinders are soundly seated to the barrel to ensure rigidity; two sub-frames, one under the smokebox to carry the leading axle – mounted on spiral coil springs to give 1¼ in. vertical movement – and the other to take the rear axle, are attached to the firebox wrapper as in road engine design. The extremely long coupled wheelbase explains why so much alteration had to be made to the original curves on the line, and the height of the chimney to the removal of the intermediate tunnel. The wheels were linked by an extremely long coupling rod which if removed, would disable the engine, as the valve gear – as in the later Fletcher Patent No. 327 of February 1864 – was driven from the leading axle. The expansion links hung in front of the firebox and drove the steam chest slide valves through rocker arms; the cylinders received steam from a dome on top of the boiler through an exterior lagged pipe and exhausted along the boilerside into the smokebox through a cast pipe of rare outline: the boiler, firebox and cylinders were lagged by wooden strips. At some date FIRE QUEEN was given a sandbox between chimney and dome, but the delivery pipes are now missing. The wrought-iron boiler has a copper firebox and brass tubes; Weaver suggests the boiler was a standard product of that time. Two safety valves are fitted, one Salter and one lock-up, the former being taken down the left-hand side of the firebox top; the water-gauge includes three test-cocks in the one fitting and the regulator is similar to road engine style, its rod taken outside the boiler top to the round brass-topped dome. Stephenson valve gear is reversed from the driver's (right hand) side and is of screw-type rather than lever – anticipating wider use by Ramsbottom and Stroudley in 1859 and 1871; indeed the firebox, its inner wrapper flanged outwardly and rivetted to the outer and having no foundation ring, is usually credited to Francis Webb at Crewe in 1877! Also on each side of the firebox may be seen a boiler feed pump, connected directly to the crosshead; these being the only method of filling the boiler, the engine could not stand stationary indefinitely but would have to run to and fro to fill the boiler when necessary. As built the engines burned coke, but in the early 1860s they were turned over to coal and a brick arch fitted in the firebox. Among other features may be noted: the Bradley's Patent leather and rubber clad buffers and hooked coupling chains; smokebox door; wooden buffer beams each end; blowdown valve on side firebox. Uncoupling was by foot-treadle.

The tenders (or there may have been only *one*!) were also four-wheeled, each fitted with wooden brake blocks – but now on right hand side only – the engine having no brake as was common in those times; there was a large water tank surmounted by wooden tool boxes, and small pockets at the footplate end to hold a small quantity of sand (presumably sufficient for reverse running?) The frames are of cast-iron but the beams are wooden; the wheels have cast centres with iron spokes of + section, and there is a lamp bracket on the rear (but none on the engine itself).

The painting and lining out of the engine as presently displayed in the Industrial Railway Museum at Penrhyn Castle (the property of the National Trust) is given elsewhere but though the lining agrees with the rare picture of these engines in traffic, their contemporary colour is not recorded – presumably FIRE QUEEN was never repainted but after withdrawal in 1886 it was a ritual for the Dinorwic apprentices to clean the engine once a week – later this was but once a year!! This practice, and indeed the survival of the engine itself, has been attributed to an affection for it felt by one of Assheton-Smith's daughters!

Some minor facts may be noted: that the two engines were placed in traffic facing in opposite directions (FIRE QUEEN led chimney first from Pen-Scoins); the engines were not quite identical and JENNY LIND had no leading dome and its maker's plates were on the leading splashers; JENNY LIND had a cab with name-plates on the side of it (FIRE QUEEN seems never to have owned one); the cover plates on the footplate to protect the enginemen from the coil springs; only one fitting on the boiler backhead; there is a slight difference of less than one inch in the back-to-back dimensions of wheels between engine and tender; the concave tread of the driving wheel tyres due to usage.

JENNY LIND's brass dome and safety valve covers were listed in the 1969 sale (as was the chimney base) despite – as mentioned – the absence of a dome in illustrations!

Snowdonia was long an unexplored territory to the majority, and to write of its vastness, wildness and beauty became almost a prescription for early Victorian travellers; the 'CAMBRIAN MIRROR' (though clearly confused about certain matters of situation), found the existence of the steam locomotive hereabouts in 1851 as worthy of comment '. . . A railroad winds along the side of the lake, and down the valley of the Seiont, to the wharf under Caernarvon Castle. Only at intervals is anything seen of this railway, unless you are close to it; but it is not a little curious, while you are gazing over the seemingly solitary land-scape, to hear the puffing of a locomotive engine, and then to behold it, with its train of heavily laden wagons, emerge from behind some huge crag, and come panting along the edge of the lake . . .'. And it may be said that the present writer found this to be equally true, ninety years later!

The leading dimensions of the Horlock engines are:

Engine

Coupled Wheels	4 ft 6 in. diam.
Driving Wheelbase	12 ft 0½ in.
Cylinders	13 in. × 22 in. stroke
Valve travel	5¾ in.

Boiler barrel	8 ft 3½ in. long
Boiler barrel	3 ft diam.
Boiler pressure	60 lb. sq. in.

Boiler 86 brass tubes (2 in. outside diam.)	= 386¼ sq. ft Heating Surface
Firebox	= 50½ sq. ft Heating Surface

436¾ sq. ft Total Heating Surface

Grate Area	9¾ sq. ft
Height from rail to top chimney	11 ft 6 in.
Chimney height	5 ft
Chimney diameter	1 ft 1 in.
Length front beam to rear of cab floor	18 ft 2 in.
Width loco over cab floor	6 ft
Width loco over cylinder covers	6 ft 6½ in.
Height boiler C/L from rail	4 ft 8 in.
Height top boiler from rail	6 ft 3 in.
Height buffer C/L from rail	2 ft 9 in.
Buffers C/L	4 ft 6 in. apart
Width over faces sub-frames	3 ft 8 in.
Cylinders project from mounting	1 ft 5¼ in.
Width loco front beam (length across)	5 ft 4¾ in.

Tender

Wheels	3 ft 6 in. diam.
Wheelbase	7 ft 9¼ in.
Width over footplating	5 ft 11¾ in.
Height footplate from rail	3 ft 5 in.
Height top side from rail	6 ft 0½ in.
Length over footplate	14 ft 6½ in.

Painting in 1905

Wooden lagging: green
Undergear, tender frame etc: brown
Beams: vermilion
Remainder: black
Lining out: not given

FIRE QUEEN and JENNY LIND, being life- and design-expired, were replaced by two six-coupled tank engines based on a standard gauge design of The Hunslet Engine Co. Ltd. with whom the Quarry Company must by now have been well satisfied in terms of the narrow

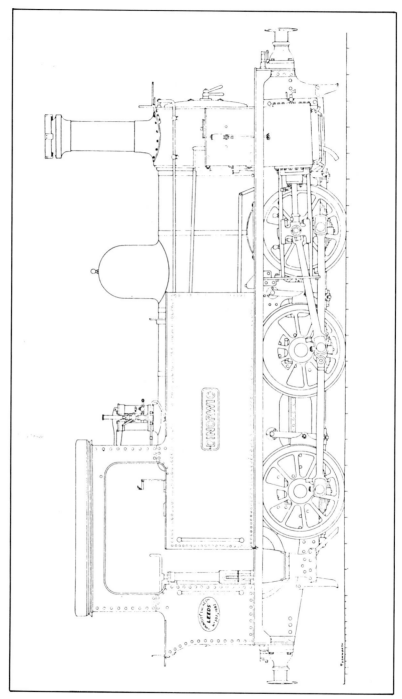

The first of three Hunslet-built engines for the 4 ft gauge.
Drawing: T.F. Rushworth

gauge engines they had had in service since 1870. The new engines emphasised all the locomotive development which had taken place in under thirty-five years and it would be hard to under-estimate fully their impact on the operating and maintenance staff. DINORWIC (Works No. 302) was the first in 1882 and evidently carried out the traffic needs (with one of the Horlocks as stand-by,) for almost four years, when PANDORA arrived (Works No. 410) in 1886. Together these would have been sufficient, but the introduction of the Workmen's Train made it essential to have another engine available, and this was financed from the same fund as found the carriages and operators for this service. VELINHELI (Works No. 631) came in 1895. No particular engine was reserved for any one purpose, but it was possible to run the daily service with one engine in traffic, one stand-by, and one undergoing overhaul in the Works. The traffic engine would be shedded at Pen-Scoins, and the stand-by at Gilfach-Ddu: this arrangement survived until the fatal accident between the slate train and a road lorry in 1926 when the lack of secondary motive power was severely criticised; it would have taken some hours to raise steam in the stand-by locomotive and the authorities took note of this and purchased a petrol tractor for such emergencies; a description of it follows.

The three Hunslet engines were identical, having right-hand drive, screw reverse, inside frames, outside cylinders, side tanks and inside Stephenson link motion – in fact at first glance they might be taken for a conventional standard gauge product. However, there were small differences other than the main one of track gauge; noticeable were the side wings to the smokebox with sandboxes alongside, the closely centred buffers (4 ft 2½ in.), the jaw-and-link couplings which could be released from the footplate by a treadle (one on each side of the cab applying to each end of the engine), the bracket yoke linking the side tank tops and looped over the boiler top, the large brass dome cover and the brass hooter. Nameplates were applied by Gilfach-Ddu and PANDORA was changed to AMALTHAEA in May 1909; differences in style between the nameplates will be noted.[39] (This latter engine also received new wheels in 1930; both it and DINORWIC had been supplied with wrought-iron wheel centres but by the time VELINHELI was built, cast-steel was the standard).

Principal dimensions were:

Cylinders	12½ in. × 20 in.
Wheel diam.	3 ft 6 in.
Wheelbase	10 ft
Height to top chimney	11 ft 8¼ in. (new)
Length overall	25 ft 1 in.
Width overall	7 ft 10¼ in.
Tractive Effort at 75% b.p.	7,812 lb.

Grate Area	8 sq. ft
Total Heating Surface	507 sq. ft
Boiler Pressure	140 lb.
Water Capacity	600 galls
Coal	1 ton
Weight in working order	26 tons

The engines were supplied in Midland Red, with black lining out edged yellow; beneath the footplate all was black, save for the side rods which were polished; buffer beams were vermilion, as were nameplate grounds: when new, domes were painted over. Latterly the engines were black with white side rods and certain steelwork polished; the dome was scraped bright and the brass spectacle frames and hooter polished – no lining-out survived but cleanliness was commendable.

It will be noted that one engine carried a chimney of slightly different outline to the other two. The men soon found the ample cab side openings over-generous in the winter, and wooden screens were supplied by the workshops which would close off two-thirds of the opening; the Works also fitted spark arrestors. To assist with coupling the workmen's carriages in the dark, VELINHELI was fitted with a large carbide lamp beneath chimney and cab rear sheet – the large brackets remained long after the lamps had gone. This same engine also sported additional side chains on the beams and could always be identified by this feature.

Apart from a few spare items which survived, the complete destruction of these three engines in 1963 was in direct contrast to the survival of the smaller quarry and port units. VELINHELI was in the Works for major overhaul in 1953 and lay in pieces until it and the Hardy tractor were scrapped in April 1963; the other engines were cut up in the summer. As with the smaller engines, consideration was given to convert to oil firing in the early 1920s, using a Hunslet-supplied Kermode 'Onchan' burner.

Name	*New firebox*	*New boiler*
DINORWIC	1912	1923 (Hunslet)
PANDORA (AMALTHAEA)	1910 1922 1947	1930 (Port Dinorwic)
VELINHELI	1916	{ 1927 (Port Dinorwic) { 1942 (Port Dinorwic)

(Port Dinorwic = built and fitted at Dry Dock Co.)

Maker's Works Nos. transferred to the boilers as reference numbers when locos were given names.

The Hunslet engines were fitted with a mellifluous hooter rather than a whistle; its sound was colloquially known as 'The Cuckoo' and so reliable was the running of the trains that the local people regulated their lives to it – they would say to each other, 'The Cuckoo is coming'. Returning to the Quarry with the empties one day the hooter stuck open and such was the cloud of steam coming from it that the driver,

Bob Williams, could not see ahead; he drove cautiously with his fireman Eric Jones, hanging half out of the cab and urging him to drive faster as the escaping steam was rapidly dropping the boiler water-level and the side tanks were almost empty . . . the nearest water tank was at Gilfach-Ddu. The sound of the hooter brought folks from far and wide to the lineside to see what was afoot, and luckily all the gate-keepers – expecting a runaway at least – had their gates open. The train was greeted at the Quarry by a large crowd of workmen and Mr. Morris, the Engineer, who soon ended the affair by muffling the offending organ with one of his long socks! Operation of the line was most efficient and only one serious accident ever took place.

It has been explained elsewhere that the working engine was shedded nightly and at weekends at Pen-Scoins: in the evening it was the driver who banked down the fire and at 5 a.m. would be back again to draw it up and raise working pressure. On Friday nights (there being latterly no train on Saturdays) he drew the fire completely; after evening Chapel on Sunday he prepared the fire once more and was up on the engine at 4.30 a.m. on Monday mornings to light up before going home for breakfast. Needless to say, he lived hard by the shed and his first working would be the Workmen's Train, which would leave at varying times from 6 a.m. onwards according to season. The generous use of the whistle at level crossings was always the rule. After a sharp blast before the train left Pen-Scoins, the men blew the whistle for long periods when approaching level crossings and stations. Station starts were made after the guard had shown a green flag (or green lamp) – these lamps were of traditional pattern and could be used to show a red light when required; they burned oil, not paraffin.[40]

4-WHEEL PETROL TRACTOR

To ensure there was a stand-by motive power for emergency or breakdown, the Company purchased a four-wheeled, petrol-engined rail tractor from Hardy Motors Ltd., Slough, Bucks (formerly the Four-Wheel Drive Lorry Co. Ltd.). It was their Works No. 954, built in 1925. The use of chains and coupling rods was avoided by cardan-shaft drive to all wheels. The engine was four-cylinder cooled by radiators fitted at each end of the body; there was a near-central cab in which the operator sat sideways – as usual on this type of unit; the capacity was 55 h.p. and four speeds from 2½ to 16 m.p.h. in either direction were available. There was a transmission brake (as on the modern Land Rover, for instance) worked by the foot, and conventional shoe railway brakes on the wheels operated by hand screw. The cab, (off-centre) was flanked by bonnets concealing the engine unit and additional ballast bringing the basic weight up from 6¼ to 12 tons. There was a multi-disc Hele-Shaw clutch and the gearwheels were in constant mesh, engagement being through a sliding dog-jaw clutch.

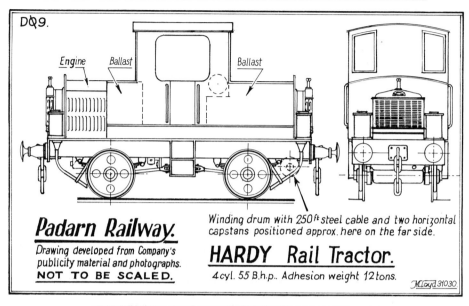

DQ9.

Engine   Ballast   Ballast

Padarn Railway.

Drawing developed from Company's
publicity material and photographs.
NOT TO BE SCALED.

Winding drum with 250 ft steel cable and two horizontal
capstans positioned approx. here on the far side.

HARDY   Rail Tractor.

4 cyl. 55 B.h.p.. Adhesion weight 12 tons.

M.Lloyd 31030

A front end view of the Petrol Locomotive of the type used in the Dinorwic
Quarries. This shows well the capstans and winding drum.

Railway Gazette

The length was 19 ft 2 in. (16 ft 2 in. over beams); wheelbase 8 ft 5 in.; wheel diameter 2 ft 6 in.; cylinders 4¾ in. × 5½ in. and the normal load was rated as 70–80 tons. However, under one end was fitted a horizontal winch with a cable drum at each end, to this 250 ft of ⅝ in. diameter wire rope could be hauled in either direction. Sandboxes were fitted each end. Because each wheel was independently driven, slipping, it was claimed, could be eliminated. Painting was as for the steam locomotives. When no buyer could be found for it after closure of the Quarry, it was brought out of its small shed at Gilfach-Ddu, petrol was poured over and it was set alight . . . the scrap man finished off the work in April 1963.

On investigation, the whole saga of this tractor is strange. It appears to have been purchased to assuage the criticism of those who felt that had such a unit been available, the aftermath of accidents would be less fraught with risk; in practice this was not so, for it is doubtful if the tractor ever saw use . . . indeed, no one living recalls it in service. When delivered, a representative from Hardy demonstrated its starting and operation, but the starting procedure (electric) was never fully understood by the Dinorwic men who maintained the 'tractor is a poor starter' as they hated using it; someone removed and hid away part of the starting gear so effectively immobilising it! The tradition that during the 1930s 'it was used regularly as the Gilfach-Ddu shunter' is based on information supplied to the management, which thought its instructions were being carried out!

All motive power had been scrapped by Pittrail Ltd. of Aldridge, Staffs. (who also dismantled the Padarn Railway) by Autumn 1963. The last train of 27th October, 1961 had been hauled by AMALTHAEA, Gilfach-Ddu to Pen-Scoins and back again. DINORWIC worked the wrecking train, (starting duty from Pen-Scoins) between 16th May, 1962 and February 1963.

CARRIAGE & WAGON STOCK

Host Wagons (orientation refers to wagons assembled from the Quarry to Pen-Scoins direction)

There is no visible indication that the pattern of the eighty-four host wagons has changed over the years, being a simple iron frame secured by cast-iron spacing pieces carried on four unsprung wheels. These heavy load-carrying frames continued from horse-worked days and with four loaded slate wagons on the back of each, the carried weight would be scarcely less than ten tons. The 'rails' to carry the slate wagons were simply cast bars incorporated into the wagon frame: certain wagons were later given the luxury of springs, and though intended to be those for carrying a brake van, (indeed not all had brakes anyway!) they were not reserved for that purpose; a few had band brakes fitted to all wheels and even fewer had these replaced by the more modern shoe brakes. Those wagons which carried the brake van were, of course, all braked – the object of braked wagons carried within the train was to serve as a substitute for the sprags which were normally used to control moving wagons especially at Pen-Scoins. No. 45 was an oddity with no springs, shoe brakes worked from a side lever for which a footstep was fitted and buffing pads at the west end; it was often therefore, found next to the locomotive on loaded trains. Nos. 24, 28 and 54 had coiled springs but no brakes: No. ? (no number) had side lever brakes, underhung laminated springs and a south-east chain hook – it was seen carrying a van though it had no suitable brake handle!

Apart from those wagons specially fitted with buffing pads at one end, the remainder had a simple curved pad at each end; also there was a single hook facing outwards at one end and a linking chain at the other of each wagon. Alongside these a bracket carried a projecting pin which, when it struck the dock wall, released chocks which prevented the smaller wagons running off *en route*; these latter wagons were however, additionally secured by engaging their own couplings hooks through eyes in the frame of the host wagon. The small brake vans were permanently coupled to similar eyes and could be released only with the aid of a large spanner!

The iron sideframes were actually a channel which acted as a rail and had a higher flange on the outside to prevent the wheels of the smaller wagons jumping off; the host wagon wheels projected up through the floorless top, and their rims ran between the slate wagon wheels (which due to this, could not carry the conventional two-wheels-per-axle). The 'H'-spoked wheels had iron centres and separate tyres; some wheels were disc type and others were solid but had the spokes embossed on the face.

The striker pin above-mentioned was connected to a curved link which, besides carrying out the release of the chocks, also disconnected the coupling gear allowing the hook to fall and release the coupling link; from the upper extremity of the curved link a connection was taken to a vertical pin – which could be locked in the 'safe' position to secure the chocks and the wagon couplings when on the move – whereby the couplings could be released by hand without unchocking the load. The whole assembly was robust and ingenious; fortunately No. 70, complete with brake van and slate wagons, has survived and is in The Narrow Gauge Railway Museum at Tywyn.

Among the wagons individually noted were: No. 68 with shoe brakes on both sides, carrying a brake van and with chain-shunting hooks on the south-east corner only and having open-spoked wheels; No. 46? for carrying brake van with band brake on north side wheels only; Nos. 15, 16, 51, 54, 55, 56, 72 and 75 were among the simple carriers, without brake, springs or other embellishments.

It will be noted that the 'official' van-carrying wagons had their brake handles brought up diagonally and centrally so that the handle-end lay beside the van and within reach of its door. Some handles were plain, and others looped like a shepherd's crook.

The wagons were usually painted red oxide with black running gear. Numbers (if carried) were in white, stencilled in the centre of the side channel. The bearings were plain grease boxes and later the thick oil which replaced the grease was liberally applied to such effect that to walk along the trackside at Gilfach-Ddu or Pen-Scoins was to tread a solidified causeway of oil droppings!

Principal dimensions were:

Frames	12 ft long × 5 ft 11 in. wide
Wheelbase	6 ft
Wheel diameter	3 ft
Distance between slate wagon tracks	1 ft 8 in.
Gauge slate wagon track over centres	2 ft 0¼ in.

When the wagons arrived at the end dock they were locked to it by means of a lever-operated latch; at Pen-Scoins the men unloading used a long-handled hook to pull the slate wagons from the transporter. Trains averaged fifteen transporters and the trainmen gave them the English names of 'Big Cars' or 'Large Trolleys'.

If there was any additional stock on the Padarn Railway in times past, it is long forgotten, but clearly the life of the host wagons was very long indeed; their most robust construction must have contributed to this. In August 1841, in connection with the building of the Railway, there is a note of the first wagons provided for the 4 ft gauge. There were four, costing '70/6d. each' and they were taken 'to Pen-Llyn, Cefn-Gwyn and Carreg-y-Walch' by Owen Jones for £23 3s. 9d. . . . which seems expensive. Elias Parry made the axles for £8 3s. 1d. and the joiner assembled the whole. They would be in use by the August.

The creation of such wagons first appears in the accounts towards the beginning of 1841 'Castings for trucks £199 5s. 3d.' and in December 'Evan Williams; building large trucks for slates for £10 10s. 0d. each . . . 12 trucks per bill . . . £126 0s. 0d.'. Between January and August 1842 is entered 'Elias Parry (Blacksmith) Caernarvon; ironwork for large trucks @ 3½d. per lb.' and '12 trucks ironwork £130 18s. 0d.'. In March of that year Lewis Williams, Pentir – also a blacksmith – received £139 5s. 5d. for 'Iron & Smithwork for building 13 large trucks' at the same poundage rate; William Pritchard of Pentir and Daniel Roberts of Bethel each also built another 13 and we may ask why the fondness for the 'baker's dozen'?! A few months afterwards the entries show that men were 'altering and repairing trucks and small waggons', perhaps by removing full axles from existing slate wagons to make them suitable for the transporters? In September 1843 Robert & William Jones, who had been the carriage contractors and maintained the 'Trucks and small waggons in repair' were put onto contract for the latter work. The period-names for the transporters were 'Large Trucks' and the slate wagons 'Small Waggons' to distinguish their costs; the books suggest there were 50 transporters[41] available by June 1842 at an average chassis cost of £21 each and as the carpenter's work on each was £1 15s. 0d. their woodwork content was minimal.

In mid-1843 the making of castings for trucks was let out to contract, as was the supplying of oil, but contracts were not being handed out liberally, for in October 1843 a lathe was built for use in the carpenter's yard at Port Dinorwic 'to turn axles for the trucks' when the wagon building contracts terminated; from then onwards wagons were assembled there. Before that date the indefatigable Robert and William Jones built the wagons too – they would have a special work-force for that contract. If the terminology of the accounts remained consistent, then further 'Truck wheels' were needed in the late 1840s (1848–9) and were supplied by Smith & Willey, shipped from Liverpool to Port Dinorwic and carted to the Quarry; the wheels cost £207 10s. 0d. but the quantity is not given; a second similar lot followed. Clearly, erection had by now passed from the carpenter's yard to the Quarry premises.

There is practically no written record of these wagons down the years, save for a stock valuation list of 1877 which, like most descriptions, lacks precise definition, but by taking other entries as a means of elimination, lists 72 wagons @ £50 each and 26 pairs of wheels (presumably for the same as other wagons did not use 'pairs of wheels') @ £10 pair. A further entry uses the expression 'transporter' and costs them as 'Timber/labour/wheels etc. £51 19s. 9d. each'.

Open Wagons

Abandoned outside the doors of the Hardy tractor shed in 1946 were two low dropside single plank open wagons of clear origin – each had been contrived from a host wagon chassis, one without alteration to the chassis, the remains of a shoe brake on one wheel (the wagon was spragged) and with a plank fastened to the outside of the original side frame, on which was mounted a hinged side. The second wagon had arisen from some butchery of similar parts, but was so foreshortened that the adjacent wheels' rims were only about one foot apart. A shoe brake had been fitted to one wheel and the sides and ends built up on the frame parts as for the other wagon. Due to the high frame of the original materials, the floors had to be laid above the level of the outer side members of the chassis concealed behind the side planks, and a design wherein the floor was placed so high above track level could hardly be efficient! Consequently the single plank height of the side was only sufficient for a very shallow load. These wagons carried no markings; the woodwork was red oxide and the ironwork black – large wooden blocks sufficed for 'buffers'. They were used by the track gangs for chairs, sleepers, ballast of slate waste etc., and were reputed to have originated in the writing slate traffic from Crawia Mill.

Maintenance Vehicles

A few small flat trolleys were available for maintenance gangs and one survives at Gilfach-Ddu. One hand-worked velocipede stood on the trackside near Bethel for many years, for use of such gangs and it must have been a relief *not* to use it! There was also a quadricycle built by New Howe Co. Ltd.[42] using cycle parts (tubular frame, spoked wheels, handlebars, single saddle etc.) with conventional pedals and chain drive which might be used by an individual as an 'Inspection Trolley': the Hon. W.W. Vivian obtained it for personal use but found it too heavy – it was passed to the P.W. Dept. who liked it no more than he!

Saloon Carriages

Assheton-Smith was not a man to hide his light under a bushel and with good reason he encouraged visitors to his Quarry. Most found their way from Glan-y-Bala into the workings, but the privileged, amongst whom were guests at Vaynol Park, travelled over the Padarn Railway from Pen-Scoins.

It has already been noted that a suitable building was begun in August 1845 – long before steam power was contemplated – 'stone Coach House for the Railway Carriage at the top of the Incline at the Port – £4 19s. 0d.' and it was roofed and ready within four weeks. That there is no mention of purchase of materials to build or an account for a complete carriage at this period might suggest that Assheton-Smith funded it from his own pocket. It was four-wheeled, had a verandah at the west end (if not at both ends) and features minutely in a pre-1885 scene at Gilfach-Ddu – in which a Horlock engine also appears – and was a smaller version (but with a balcony only at one end) of the Saloon which survives today. We read: 'Mr. Smith was very fond of taking parties from Vaenol to see the quarries, and always had his joke with the young ladies who inquired if it was dangerous to ascend the inclines, by asking his agent who frequently accompanied him, how long it was since the last accident. His favourite spot of such occasions was the Braich Quarry ('Arm of the Mountain') which commanded a magnificent prospect of the Llanberris [*sic*] Pass. A signal was hoisted on the house when he intended going from the port by train. This was responded to from the top of the first incline, and a comfortable omnibus with as much glass about it as could enable those within to see most of the view, there awaited the arrival of his guests, and conveyed them along the edge of the lake, until they were obliged to dismount for the purpose of commencing the steeper part of the ascent . . .'. At first this carriage must have been horse-hauled.

Lest it should be thought that the 'omnibus' was used invariably for the purpose, the idea must be corrected. In 'ROYAL VISITS & PROGRESS TO WALES' (Edward Parry: 1850) is found 'In the month of September 1849, His Royal Highness the late Duke of Cambridge and suite, paid a

friendly visit to the principality and made some stay at Plas Newydd
. . . early on Wednesday (the 19th) the Dutchess [*sic*] of Cambridge and
Princess Mary . . .' (and several other titled persons) '. . . crossed over
to Port Dinorwic where they were met by Owen Roberts and Mr. John
Millington (Jnr) – the agents of T. Assheton-Smith Esqr. – and pro-
ceeded to Llanberis by the Padarn Railway, in open slate wagons,
which had been fitted up for the occasion . . . they ascended five steep
inclines to the Raven Rock Quarry . . . returned by the same route in
the evening'. All of which suggests they may have sat in the small
wagons (riding on the transporters in the regular way), and it was
convenient to carry visitors by regular train. The account also confirms
that the main slate mill was already worked by steam power.

After the introduction of workmen's carriages, Assheton-Smith must
have thought about his elderly Saloon, for in June 1895 the Gloucester
Railway Carriage & Wagon Co. Ltd. submitted two sets of drawings for
four-wheeled 'carriages' each mounted on the same underframes as the
workmen's stock then under discussion. The first was for a Saloon
Carriage having a central closed saloon, access to which was by hinged
doors off open verandahs at each end – from a distance the vehicle had
the appearance of a standard gauge goods brake van. If such a mundane
purpose was inferred, it was soon dispelled by the contents of the saloon
portion which included revolving bucket chairs, five each side of a
central aisle, blinds, tinted and stained glass, cork felted floor, carpet,
mirrors, roof baskets in 'crinkled brass wire', the interior lower panels
being of teak battening, upper panels in oak and with white lincrusta
ceiling. The exterior lower panels were to have teak vertical matchboarding with a decorated panel centrally for the Coat of Arms. On one
verandah were four tip-up seats, and three on the other, the fourth
place being used for the handbrake wheel. A figure of £347 has been
added to the specification.

The second (and month-earlier specification) was for a Directors'
Carriage, and a figure of £235 has been added to the drawing. This was
a less luxurious vehicle of the same overall specification as the first, but
having seats for nine persons down each side, the upholstery being
buttoned repp. The drawing gives no details of furnishings, but it was
matchboarded inside and had full-length luggage racks above the seats;
generally, a more spartan style which clearly did not come up to
Assheton-Smith's requirements – in fact the drawing lacks certain
detail. The exterior was finished in large vertically moulded panelling,
of exactly the pattern which was ultimately to be used on the verandah
ends of the one saloon which the Company obtained.

Each of these designs had two oil lamps in the roof, handbrakes,
coupling and buffing gear, wheels and suspension of the type supplied
with the workmen's carriages.

An order was placed for a saloon which differed little from the first-
mentioned, but order details and drawings have not survived; luckily

the coach itself was preserved when the Padarn Railway closed and is part of the National Trust collection at Penrhyn Castle (Railway Museum). It was clearly to succeed the existing saloon which may have been that already noted as obtained about the end of the 1840s (or a replacement of it). Its interior remains very much as specified in June 1895 and it was used for private parties visiting the Quarry, Royal occasions, to carry the monthly pay (extra guards being carried on those journeys) and for any special party; it was a privilege to travel therein, for the sumptuous seating remained to the last! The most notable alteration was in the exterior side panelling (the design of the end panels has been noted) which extended the full side length of the saloon portion and carried a garter ("D.A.S."?). Blinds, stained glass and all the exoticism of the day reflected a desire to create a vehicle second to no other private saloon on any railway! Folding steps were placed at the verandah ends, and on the south side a cord along the cantrail could be pulled to signal to the driver, from either verandah. To please the purchaser it was stated that the 'roof (i.e. ceiling) be identical to the L.N.W.R. 1st Class Carriages (New Type) . . .' – this was added in December 1895.

So from an initial specification in May for a Directors' vehicle, to a saloon the following month, to an actual order for a saloon which was at detail stage by the end of the year, the Padarn Railway acquired its only surviving passenger vehicle.

The main dimensions of the Saloon are those used on the workmen's stock (see below) the body having a central compartment 13 ft 4 in. long inside on its 22 ft underframe; interior height from floor to top of side is 6 ft and 6 ft 6 in. at the centreline; body width is 7 ft 6 in. Lamp irons were omitted.

The original paint specification lacks confirmation, but was likely to be 'Midland Red' to match the locomotives. The colour survived as a cherry red in the 1940s, when the mouldings were picked out in black and roof and frames etc. were in dark grey. By 1952 the carriage panels had become yellow and the grey portions black and an amusing account of how this came about is recalled. The red and black livery had already attracted the nickname 'The Black Maria'; one day Sir Michael Duff was about the Railway when he saw the Saloon; he considered it and then walked over to the engine driver (who did not recognise him) saying 'Where did you get that colour scheme?' at which he was told it had been painted in the Works' Yard.

Sir Michael: 'What d'you think of it?

Driver: 'Bloody awful'.

Sir Michael: 'I will send down some yellow paint – the family colour – and they can do it again.'

(The driver's re-action is not recorded!)

For years the Saloon carried out a secondary duty of bringing up the pay from the Port; the wages were made up in Lloyds Bank there and

Padarn Railway.

Workmen's Coach.

Height (approx.)

2'0"

Wheels 2'4" dia.

9'6" wheel base

22'0" underframe & body

5'6" centres of journals

4'0" Gauge

7'9"

NC(2)/DØ5.

taken down to the Quay. Two leather bags were used for the weekly Pay Train and three for the monthly; the cashier from the Company's office at the Port would travel with the weekly bags but for the monthly the General Manager too would accompany him. The weekly train ran on Fridays, when the Saloon was attached to the rear of the empty slate train; the monthly ran on whatever day the pay-month ended – originally this was the only Pay Train, and occasionally a special light engine working would fetch the Saloon from Pen-Scoins. During the hard times of the early 1930s men were often heard to boast they would hold up the Pay Train and rob it, but it never occurred. Latterly, Pay Train duties were the only occasions when the Saloon was put to use.

The outward-opening doors from the balcony were something of a nuisance and tended to be wrenched off if inadvertently striking an obstruction at Gilfach-Ddu platform!

Workmen's Carriages

It is clear from surviving correspondence that the Company intended to spend no more on this provision than was absolutely necessary; their first intention was a design based on the open carriages on the Penrhyn Railway (q.v.) and they shopped around for a set of such vehicles at the keenest price. Up to March 1895 exchanges with The Gloucester Railway Carriage & Wagon Co. Ltd. showed that equally Gloucester would not be brow-beaten, hungry for orders though they were; more than once Gloucester squealed that the price demanded by Dinorwic would show them no profit, and the matter of open stock was dropped. Presumably no other supplier proved as competitive as Gloucester (no other correspondence exists) and Dinorwic returned to the quest, this time for covered coaches of basic style. Costings began on the hint of an order for 15 vehicles to hold 60 persons each, plus a further 4 to hold 58, to be delivered within 12 weeks of order at either Llanberis or Crawia Siding. In March 1895 Gloucester produced a drawing for a matchboarded 4-wheeled coach 22 ft long over underframes, 7 ft 9 in. wide over beams, with a 9 ft 6 in. wheelbase and 2 ft 4 in. diameter 6-spoked wheels with steel tyres on wrought-iron centres. There were six 'compartments' though the interior, which was plain, was open above the slatted seats; there were no windows but glazed droplights in the six doors each side; there was a footboard on one side only though door furniture on both; screw couplings and side chains; a handbrake and blocks on all wheels; laminated springing and conventional buffers with footsteps cast on them. Height was 9 ft 6 in.; solebars were steel channel 9¼ in. × 3½ in. – the remainder of the underframe in oak.

The design was considered and agreed; at delivery (to Llanberis on Midland Railway 4-wheeled well wagons) each carriage had two oil lamps – by Ridsdales' Railway Lamp & Lighting Co. Ltd. A train made up and lettered with carriages alphabetically 'A' to 'S' was running by the year end, a second couple, 'T' and 'U', added by

November 1896, and a solitary carriage 'V' came in February 1904, whilst the last, 'W' – making 23 in all – was added at an unrecorded date before World War I.

In discussion with the author in April 1946 it was suggested the initial carriages had vertical boarded sides and leaf springing, and the later ones matchboarded sides and coil/leaf springing; carriage 'V' however, had vertical boarding, torpedo ventilators in the roof and end-wall lamps instead of roof type when supplied. Latterly only the 6.30 a.m. winter train from Pen-Scoins would be lit, there being only two carriages still with oil lamps. Such carriages as were inspected in 1946 had been given reversible backrests, and to emphasize the earlier-mentioned seating system, each seat was numbered. Interior painting was then: lower panels chocolate – upper panels stone. Carriage 'L', a typical specimen, was body-painted chocolate (including ends); window frames red oxide; letters white; roof light grey; remainder black. It was represented that only one in four surviving carriages had a hand-brake, but 1890s correspondence suggests all were to be so fitted – and this being found unnecessary the order was amended to save cost. After the platform had been roofed over at Gilfach-Ddu – it being the habit of the men to leap from the train on both sides and run towards the Quarry before it came to a standstill – the doors on the north side were close enough to the roof uprights as to strike them as the occupants jumped down onto the track. Accidents to men and doors were unavoidable, and the management's answer was to close off the doors on that side. However, the 1926 collision between train and lorry was ultimately to make everyone more safety-conscious and the doors were freed again. (It is said that some time before this the fact about doors had been 'leaked' to the Factory Inspector who had condemned the management's action). It will be noted that Gilfach-Ddu had added end steps and tall lamp irons on rooftop at the Quarry end of each coach for shunting purposes. Tom Morris's notebook (the Quarry Engineer) confirms that many carriages had been withdrawn for the need of new springs; these seem to have been a weakness.

It is amusing to compare this dilapidated picture at the end of the service with the specification for the carriages agreed in the 1890s; perhaps Gloucester did after all make some small profit, for on dismant-ling certain vehicles they were found to contain timbers painted TAFF VALE RAILWAY. The Quarry too, made good use of them even in death; the doors were used for certain W.C.s up in the Quarry and retained the warning (in Welsh) on the inner face – DO NOT LEAN OUT.

When new, the train must have been very smart. It was finished in 'colour and finish as Midland Railway', and painted purple-brown inside, but having the upper panels and ends 'light grained'. Ceilings were white. Destination names were to be painted in 6 in. tall white lettering; white numbers of the same size were to appear, but in fact works' drawings show that Gilfach-Ddu produced some removable name boards, and letters in place of numbers were used for identifica-

Plate LXI JENNY LIND at Gilfach-Ddu, with cab and weather board fitted to tender.   *F. Moore*

Plate LXII FIRE QUEEN, stored in the former Tram Line engine shed at Gilfach-Ddu, is brought out into the open for the first time in almost eighty years: December 1969.   *J.I.C. Boyd*

Plates LXIII, LXIV & LXV
Details of FIRE QUEEN and tender, the last showing restoration in process at Penrhyn Castle.   *J.I.C. Boyd*

Plate LXVI DINORWIC with Saloon at Gilfach-Ddu; the uncoupling arrangement on the engine was a feature of the Padarn Railway and also the Tram Line. *F. Moore*

Plate LXVII AMALTHEA. with 'winter' protection boards in the cab, takes coal at Gilfach-Ddu. (10 June 1960) Each engine worked about three months at a time. *D.L. Chatfield*

Plate LXVIII Six-thirty on a summer's morning, and AMALTHEA has just rolled out of the Pen-Scoins shed for the first run of the day. (Note smokebox brackets for headlamp): June 1949.   *J.I.C. Boyd*

Plate LXIX VELINHELI, probably as just delivered, outside the Works. VAENOL, on the Tram Line (*left*) is running chimney first to the west . . . a singular occurrence!   *Collection: W.J. Milner*

Plate LXX Saturdays Only: workmen's train with about 30 vehicles and a sheet-iron brake van on the rear, about to leave Gilfach-Ddu. (This method of travel was superceded by the new 'Workmen's Train in 1895.) *Gwynedd Archives*

Plates LXXIA & LXXIB In July 1895 and February 1904 The Gloucester Railway Carriage & Wagon Co. Ltd. built these coaches for the Workmen's Train.
Both Gloucester R. C.& W. Co. Ltd.

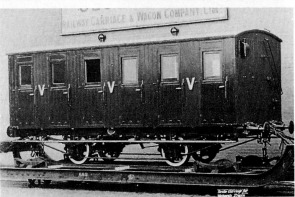

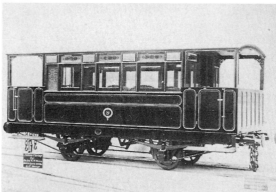

Plate LXXII The new Work Men's Train comprised spartan four-wheeled coaches built for a knock-down price; luxury, however, after the Velocipedes. The engine is piped for the gas-lit headlamp. Gilfach-Ddu c 1931.   *S. Bale Ltd.*

Plate LXXIIIA & LXXIIIB The Saloon for the use of the Assheton-Smiths used a similar underframe to the Workmen's Carriages. The garter reads 'D.Q.R.'
Gloucester R.C. & W. Co. Ltd. and F. Moore

Plate LXXIV Samples of check-tickets, issued to men using the Train; irregular shapes were used to convenience the illiterate among them.   *W.J. Milner*

Plate LXXV The whole sweep of Port Dinorwic is caught by the mo

teamer is the VELINHELI: c 1931.   *S. Bale Ltd.*

Plate LXXVI Loading the ELIDIR at Port Dinorwic about 1925.   *from an official brochure*

Plate LXXVII Port engines (believed to be THE FIRST and THE SECOND) with kidney-shaped buffers, in the early years of the century.   *from an official brochure*

Plate LXXVIII Looking towards the Dry Dock with FAIRFIELD of Chester inside.
S. Bale Ltd.

Plate LXXIX Transferring 'Duchess' size slates from slate wagons to the standard gauge, Port Dinorwic: c 1931.   *S. Bale Ltd.*

Plate LXXX The Dry Dock in the early 1920s. *from an official brochure*

Plate LXXXI By 1949 there was need for only one locomotive down at the Port. (Tracks to the foot of the Port Incline follow round to the right of the picture.) *J.I.C. Boyd*

Plate LXXXII Slate wagons approximating to this pattern have served the Dinorwic Quarries from its earliest days. *J.I.C. Boyd*

Plate LXXXIII Underside of the above, showing separate axles so as to clear the wheels of the transporters. *J.I.C. Boyd*

Plate LXXXIV One of the three 'Yellow Trucks' used for carrying important visitors around the Quarry. The steel 'eyes' each end were for securing the safety chains on inclines: 1969. *J.I.C. Boyd*

Plate LXXXV Flat trolley or sled used for maintenance; it has no drawgear.　　　*J.I.C. Boyd*

Plate LXXXVI Slab truck or sled for gallery use with drawgear and chain rings for securing the load.

J.I.C. Boyd

Plate LXXXVII Used for removal of rubbish banks in conjunction with a Ruston-Bucyrus excavator, there were over 40 of these steel end-tipping wagons. Numbers and tare weights were hand-painted in white, the former thrice - on body sides and end, and twice on chassis.　　　*J.I.C. Boyd*

Plate LXXXVIII 'Spoon Points' were used for temporary switching: 1965.
J.I.C. Boyd

Plate LXXXIX Simple plate-type turntables saved much pointwork: 1954.
J.I.C. Boyd

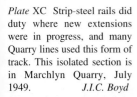*Plate* XC Strip-steel rails did duty where new extensions were in progress, and many Quarry lines used this form of track. This isolated section is in Marchlyn Quarry, July 1949. *J.I.C. Boyd*

Plate XCI (left) An artistic piece of casting, being a crossing for use with double-flanged wheels.   *J.I.C. Boyd*

Plate XCII (below) These channel-shaped castings took double-flanged wheels onto levels connected with inclines: Garrett Incline A8: 1968.   *J.I.C. Boyd*

Plate XCIII (bottom) 'Fothergill' or stub points in their most sophisticated form, using chaired rails, heavy rodding and stout hand levers: Gilfach-Ddu: 1954.   *J.I.C. Boyd*

tion. Seat numbering was in 2 in. white numerals. If hooks and eyes for the communication cord were once fitted, they had long disappeared. The final instructions to the order included 'to carry safely at 30 m.p.h., as many men as can be packed inside (both standing and sitting) . . . a six-month Guarantee must be given . . . delivery on truck to the railway siding at Llanberis, purchaser having to remove from this place'.

The lack of consistency between the carriages listed earlier as surviving in June 1926, and the Quarry Engineer's records at the time the train was discontinued may be explained by the earlier almost total eclipse having to be redressed in part, and some cannibalising and re-lettering done to keep a train available. At the close 'A', 'C', 'D', 'F' to 'P', 'T', 'U' (16) were scrapped – 'C' being only partly so – whilst kept in store in carriage sheds were 'B', 'E', 'Q', 'R', 'S', 'V', 'W' (7) three of which needed running gear repairs; this left an operational train of 'B', 'E', 'V', 'W' and this was the four-coach rake which featured latterly, and ran on Mondays and Saturdays only to accommodate the Anglesey men. At the close of World War II there was a six-coach rake consisting of two vehicles from Pen-Scoins and four from Bethel running daily, and the aforementioned 'Anglesey train' required the four runnable survivors from this!

It has always been a tradition that these carriages came from a colliery in South Wales, but unless they were built from materials intended for such a purpose (and there is no record of this) the story remains unfounded.

Carriage 'U' was usually attached to special trains and the charge for using it was more than the other stock: this suggests it had been fitted with extra comforts, but they are not recalled.

QUARRY TRACKWORK

Inclines apart, there were three main areas of trackwork and each was suited to the nature of that geographical area. Stage 1 was a portable track laid near the working face, which could be moved from time to time, yet strong enough to be buried by rockfalls after blasting. Stage 2 was the system of permanent tracks linking Quarry faces with mills, inclines and main line; this was a more robust form, originally suited to horse haulage but strong enough for the light rail tractors which superceded these animals but not heavy enough for steam locomotives. Stage 3 was the latest form, suited to all types of traffic and being in the heaviest materials, was laid where locomotives operated.

The use of commercially-built light railway material as available from outside manufacturers such as Robert Hudson Ltd. of Leeds, was largely avoided, these Quarries having the ability (apart from rails) to manufacture their own track. Thus for instance, the conventional light

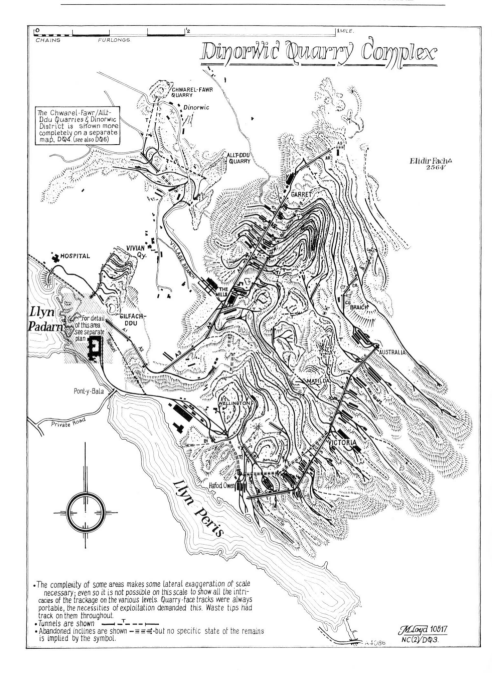

Dinorwic Quarry Complex

CHAINS   FURLONGS   1 MILE.

CHWAREL-FAWR QUARRY

Dinorwic

The Chwarel-Fawr/Allt-Ddu Quarries & Dinorwic District is shown more completely on a separate map, DQ4 (see also DQ6)

ALLT-DDU QUARRY

GARRET

Elidir Fach△ 2564'

HOSPITAL

VIVIAN Qy.

VILLAGE BRANCH

THE MILLS

C7 C8
C6
BRAICH

Llyn
Padarn

for detail of this area See separate plan

GILFACH-DDU
A1
A2
A3

AUSTRALIA

MATILDA

Pont-y-Bala

WELLINGTON

Private Road

B1

VICTORIA

Hafod Owen

Llyn Peris

• The complexity of some areas makes some lateral exaggeration of scale necessary; even so it is not possible on this scale to show all the intricacies of the trackage on the various levels. Quarry-face tracks were always portable, the necessities of exploitation demanded this. Waste tips had track on them throughout.
• Tunnels are shown ⊢—┳—⊣
• Abandoned inclines are shown —≡≡≡⊰-but no specific state of the remains is implied by the symbol.

M.Lloyd 10517
NC(2)/DQ3.

track of 25 lb. flat bottomed rail clipped to pressed steel sleepers as usually found in quarry locations, was seldom seen here.

Stage 1   Rails of bar-iron (later steel) laid vertically; 3½ in. high × ¾ in. thick varying lengths, butt-jointed. Laid at the historic 2 ft 1½ in. centres (approx. 1 ft 11⅝ in. between bar faces). Dropped into (a) one piece casting of sleeper and two chairs, the latter having a plain slot and no keyway; (b) a similar sleeper/chairs casting to (a) but of heavier cross-section having an extra strengthening rib centrally along the upper face.

These bars could also be found (c) dropped into sawn notches in wooden sleepers and butt-jointed in a wider sleeper, or (d) dropped into individual chairs pinned to wooden sleepers (in the oldest workings these individual chairs might be pinned into slab sleepers).

There were several patterns of chair to hold the bar rail on the portable track. None had keys. Although the rail-slot in them remained constant in dimension, the heaviest pattern chairs were much deeper . . . probably the result of tyre wear and flanges striking the shallower pattern chairs which did not hold the rail so high above their cheeks.

Stage 2   Wrought-iron rails were basically of 'T' section, with 2 in. or 1½ in. wide head; width over webs was ½ in. and the bottom flange was formed of a bulbous section to give strength. Two types predominated, the heavier being 2½ in. deep and the lighter 1¾ in. and the section of the former rail was not unlike a 'junior' version of the double-headed rail adopted for the 1843 4 ft gauge.

The historic form was to be found in the Garret Department where the deeper rail was held in equal-sided chairs 3¼ in. high and having a small keyway in each cheek to hold round or square section iron pins 1½ in. long. Chairs at butt-joints had   8½ in. × 6½ in.   base,   and   elsewhere   were 8½ in. × 3 in.

The replacement of this simple material was usually a conventional flat bottomed rail spiked to wooden sleepers, and with fishplated joints.

Stage 3   These were main lines within the Quarry, and built to high standard. Rails were double-headed 42 lb. per yard in steel, held in 2 or 3 pin cast-iron chairs on wooden sleepers, with fishplated joints; conventional outside wooden keys were used. There were at least half a dozen patterns of chair, but the rail slot size remained constant; the earliest chair bases had 'S'-shaped bases (a version first used on British main lines about 1865) but later forms had the more usual rectangular base shape.

Inclines   The most modern track was built up in 3 in. × 1 in. steel bars laid on edge, in plain chairs and having no keys. Butt-joints were used, laid in a much enlarged chair to provide a firm seating.

From place to place there would be a need to link, for instance, bar rail with double-head, or flat bottomed with 'T' rails; for this purpose such odd sections would be butt-jointed in special 'compound' chairs as for instance, a chair to link 42 lb. double-head with bar rail would be made in the form of the keyed chair usual to this rail but cast integrally and mated against a plain slotted chair of the pattern used in the bar rail. Though having the appearance of two separate types laid closely together, such chairs were cast as one unit having four-hole fixing.

(It is worth mentioning that Dinorwic quarry-type materials might be found in other Welsh locations, perhaps because they were sold out of use, or Gilfach-Ddu Foundry had had an order for them; one such was at the Lliwedd Copper Works on South Snowdon where Dinorwic incline material (chaired bar rails) was to be seen on an isolated 4 ft gauge tramway on the upper level in the mine.)

Quarry Pointwork

To remove a wagon from one line to another, brute force was often reverted to, and empty wagons moved bodily overground; but having said this, actual pointwork in the Quarry may be divided into categories (though it must be appreciated that this is not an official division of types). Even among these varieties of turn-out, there were considerable differences in detail, and the larger parts were made by castings produced in the foundry which were manifold in style!

Portable tracks at Quarry face (made up in bar rails as for plain track):

(a)   Two loose bars, one for each rail, connected at one end to the track onto which wagons were to be diverted: the loose ends of each rail were dropped over the rails of the track from which divergence was to be made, the portion which lay over the 'permanent' rails having a 'spoon' or inverted channel-shaped end to keep it on the lower 'permanent' rail. When not in use, the loose ends were literally thrown aside. This type was known as jumper-bar, spoon, lay-over or climbing.

(b)   Pointwork wherein all rails except the actual switch and point of crossing were 'permanent'. Switches were made up in channel (cast in the foundry) which in simplest form had no switch, the wagon being pushed to the side required. In other forms there might be a loose switch which was held in notches cast therein for the purpose, having 'V'-shaped ends. An improved type was of proper switch design, with one end pivotted; in some cases a switch was only fitted to one rail, with a plain channel without switch on the other – as in street-tram practice. Some of the more sophisticated were operated by point lever. The crossings were either plain, or had lifting short lengths of 'rail' which fitted into notches in the crossing channel. In all forms of crossing (and switch) the quarry wagons wheels – at these two locations – would be running on their flanges in the bottom of the channel.

(c)   Turntables, of either plain type where wagons were simply manhandled on a plain plate, or of revolving pattern with or without rails thereon.

Permanent tracks: as all pointwork had to accommodate double-flanged wheel wagons, conventional switches were unacceptable; therefore, (although made up in varying materials) all points of Fothergill type (see Vol. 2 'THE PENRHYN QUARRY RAILWAYS' p. 89 for detail) with stub switches and centrally pivotted crossing pieces, all worked from a single lever. The heaviest type was laid in chaired 42 lb. rail for steam locomotive working.

Inclines: The use of cast channel troughs to divert wagons off inclines (in some instances no blades or switches being used) was peculiar to this Quarry. Wagons were brought on and off the main line incline by means of a method devised for the purpose; a suitable number of loaded wagons (any load would suffice) was drawn up the incline to a position where the other free end of the cable could be manhandled across the tracks of the incline and hooked round the front of the leading wagon of the train to be lowered. The drum at the summit would then draw the loaded wagons upwards a little further and men would push the train due to descend out onto the main incline until the slight slackness of the cable (caused by drawing up the loaded train slightly), was taken up. The down-going train would then be eased completely onto the incline until the cable round the leading wagon was taking all the strain of it; then, the brake being released from the summit drum, the descending train would move off, drawing the loaded wagons upwards as it did so. This manoeuvre was a tricky operation, and the initial movement of the downgoing train from its level out onto the incline when the cable was angled across the incline rails, had to be judged expertly.

Tree trunks laid between the tracks were sometimes used to keep the cable off the ground and prevent its near-diagonal movement from catching on any fittings such as the rollers which carried the cable in its normal position between the rails.

The extracted rock might be (a) split there and then and carried to the mill as slabs on a slab truck or (b) carried from the working face in open-ended rubbish wagons. Any unsuitable material was taken to the tip and shot over the end; the clatter and tinkle of ever-falling stone from this source was a perpetual background sound. Suitable material was taken by trainload to the Dressing Mill and converted into commercial products which, when loaded into slate wagons, was dropped by incline to the Padarn-Peris Tram Line thence brought to Gilfach-Ddu where the individual wagons were pushed onto the host wagons at the two-level loading dock. In certain pits, extracted rock was loaded onto wagons to be lifted bodily by aerial ropeways ('Blondins') to an adjacent gallery and dropped onto a steel plate: here they ran off onto the gallery tramway. This cumbersome arrangement was avoided by providing tunnels at suitable pits where tramways were run out at pit floor level onto a gallery of suitable level without; some considerable tunnelling resulted from this method.

Inclines formed a major feature of the internal Quarry system and fell mainly into two types; the more common used loaded wagons descending to haul up the empties on a parallel track; each rake of wagons was fastened to its own rope and these wound round a common horizontal above-ground drum at the summit. In the Big Quarry some novel pointwork was to be found where junctions were made part-way up such inclines to give access to intermediate galleries; among inclines of this pattern were some having four tracks carried up the mountainside on very substantial slab embankments.

The less evident type resembled a near-vertical lift which was slightly inclined and was reserved for places where the longer balanced incline was unsuited. Single wagons rose and fell on a tracked platform in the manner of a cliff lift; the two-cable system and a drum was used (the drums were sometimes below ground) and though the method of using water in a tank under the 'lift' to provide movement was not used, the native name for this type was Tank Incline. Considerable detail variation was to be found, for instance there might be colliery-type winding gear in place of a drum. This latter type required a wharf at the summit and a pit at the foot to bring the platform level with the surrounding ground.

Most of the cable drums were of wood, housed in a substantial open-sided and roofed summit building. The rotation of the drum was controlled by a handbrake and to prevent wagons descending unbe-sought, a chain was thrown over the rails at the summit, or in certain cases a sophisticated chock could be brought up from ground level to sprag the wheels. A 'run' of wagons would consist of up to half a dozen vehicles, and a cast-iron plate fixed to the wall of each drumhouse stated the maximum load for that incline; the plate also gave the incline its identity number. To link the operators above and below, a system of beats on electric bells was used.

TRAVELLING RULES
for persons riding on inclines

(1) No more than 8 persons shall ride in one waggon.

(2) No more than 3 waggons shall be coupled together to form a 'Pass' or set.

(3) The maximum speed at which waggons carrying men may travel is 5 m.p.h.

(4) The man appointed as Hooker shall use the following code of bell signals for controlling of Passes on inclines . . .

    1 Ring: stop winding

    2 Rings: start winding

(5) In the event of a derailment or for some other reason any person riding in a waggon may indicate to the Brakesman or Hooker that he wished the Pass to be stopped by raising his arm.

(6) Before the Pass be hauled up the incline the Hooker shall do the following:

(a) make sure that each waggon in the Pass is securely hooked onto the next and that the safety chains are in position between each waggon.

(b) make sure that the Pass is securely coupled to the hauling rope by means of both the main hook and the safety chains.

etc.   etc.

STEAM LOCOMOTIVE POWER *(including the Port)* 1 ft 10¾ in. gauge

With the exception of a number of vertical-boilered engines from the local firm of de Winton & Co., Caernarvon, much of the remainder of the locomotive fleet was made up of four-wheeled tank engines having outside cylinders; most of these came from the Leeds firm of The Hunslet Engine Co. Ltd. and the bulk to one basic design. The Leeds engines were of three main classes, 'Alice' class, 'Port' class and 'Tram' or 'Mills' class. Besides the foregoing there were a few engines either of different type or purchased second-hand though, unlike the authorities at Penrhyn, Dinorwic did not purchase many used engines. The Company policy was to buy additional boilers from the makers and when engines required heavy repairs, the next available boiler was put on the chassis if the existing boiler also needed heavy repair. This reduced the time the engine was out of service in the Gilfach-Ddu workshops, and more importantly, once an engine had been hauled up to its working gallery by inclines, it allowed it to remain there unless needing heavy overhaul; the process of bringing engines up and down the mountain face required some dismantling to pass them under the winding drums, a chore which was carried out as infrequently as possible.

The engines were identified immediately by their names, or (in past times) by a plate carrying a number instead of a name. These names came from members of the Assheton-Smith family, their homes, their racehorses or their ships (the two last-mentioned often exchanging names!) or geographical locations. However, the workshop definition was different, the frames being numbered in a separate series from the boilers: the frames, complete with wheels, cylinders etc. would tend to remain as one chassis, together with bunker and cab (if fitted); but boilers and saddle tanks thereon, plus any other smaller fittings, were interchangeable. This system was not rigorously followed however and recently in 1962 parts of CLOISTER were carried on the frames of WILD ASTER and again, DOLBADARN, a 'Port' class engine, was modified to accept an 'Alice' class boiler and the one removed used for stationary work at Gilfach-Ddu. When new, sand boxes were fitted on each side of the tanks, but these soon disappeared.

At first, engines went to their locations of work and stayed there for many years but as galleries became life-expired and the output of the Quarry ran down, they were moved where production was greatest. After 1898 when engines were first used at the Port, certain of them (and not always of the 'Port' class) spent long years working there; and here too, the need for so many units fell away and latterly only one steam engine remained there, and 'Port' class engines moved to the Quarry. It will also be noted from the Tables which follow, that certain 'Alice' class engines were allocated to the Village Line. In general there was an outward appearance that engines had remained in one place of work for many years, but close enquiry showed this was not so. If the Company kept notes of earlier years, these no longer survive; the period before 1923 is difficult to explore whilst, some little time before the Quarry closed, instructions were given to the workshops to destroy all documents, and only those rescued by the staff for sentimental reasons, have survived.

Summarising the suppliers of locomotives emphasises the Company's allegiance to one manufacturer:

	New	Secondhand
de Winton & Co., Caernarvon	5	
The Hunslet Engine Co. Ltd., Leeds	22	1
W.G. Bagnall Ltd., Stafford	1	
Avonside Engine Co. Ltd., Bristol		1
Andrew Barclay Sons & Co. Ltd., Kilmarnock		1

and of the above, only the Barclay (a standard product of their Light Engine Class 'E') carried a small plate from its previous owner, reading 'No. 70'; this was not disturbed during its life in North Wales, mostly down at the Port.

The engines from de Winton are somewhat wrapped in mystery, as are most engines of the 1870s from this firm, which supplied many to quarries which were turning from horses to steam power. At Dinorwic their simplicity seems to have been quite basic; they were reputed to have had only a single cylinder and unlike elsewhere, double-flanged wheels (as with the wagons) were fitted. They first appear on a Stock List of 1877 but not on another list of 1895, when perhaps there would be sufficient Hunslet engines to replace the weaker de Wintons. Their varying cost may reflect market factors; PADARN and WELLINGTON were in a sale and went to Glynrhonwy slate quarries (on the other shore of Llyn Padarn) about 1898. Something of WELLINGTON is known; it had a short chimney with pronounced flare to the lip, a double-ended straight regulator handle (not seen on other de Winton engines), outside frames and rodding, 'WELLINGTON' in gilt lettering shaded vermilion on the bunker rear and a chain attached to the coupling hook at the bunker end to assist uncoupling without leaving the footplate! The location of steam at the Quarry may at first have been to place de Wintons in Departments (of their name?) and the later incoming Hunslet engines on the bottom Tram Line; however, it will be noted that the need to replace horses on the Tram Line was the most pressing requirement and Hunslet No. 51 of 1870 (DINORWIC) – the first narrow gauge engine to appear from that maker – was in service before the bulk of the de Wintons was envisaged. This engine cost £750 and perhaps the siting of de Winton products (at half the price) for lighter work on galleries was a natural decision. Seven years later another Hunslet was bought for the Tram Line, GEORGE. When the heavier 'Tramway' class was delivered in the late 1890s, both these early engines went up to New York until 1916, when the former was withdrawn (but not cut up until 1936) and the latter went to S. Fletcher of Haley Mill, Halifax before it found another owner in Cothercott Mining Co., Pulverbatch. These Hunslet engines were good value! The next engine also came from Hunslet, LOUISA, but the reason for acquiring such a small unit is not clear, unless it was to match it against de Winton engines for light Quarry work. LOUISA found its way to Glynrhonwy and was working there in 1898. None of the foregoing found a place in the classified system.

VELINHELI of 1886 was the first 'Alice' class engine – the class could negotiate a 21 ft radius curve; the frame was 11 ft 6 in. long with front and rear overhang of 4 ft; the overall length was 13 ft, height 7 ft 3 in. and width 5 ft 4 in. The firebox was longest across the frame, being 2 ft 8 in. across the width but only 1 ft 7 in. front to back: the box was raised 6 in. above the boiler and steam taken from the highest point in

Dinorwic Quarry tried this Hunslet engine in the workings but no further purchases of the type were made.

Drawing: T.F. Rushworth

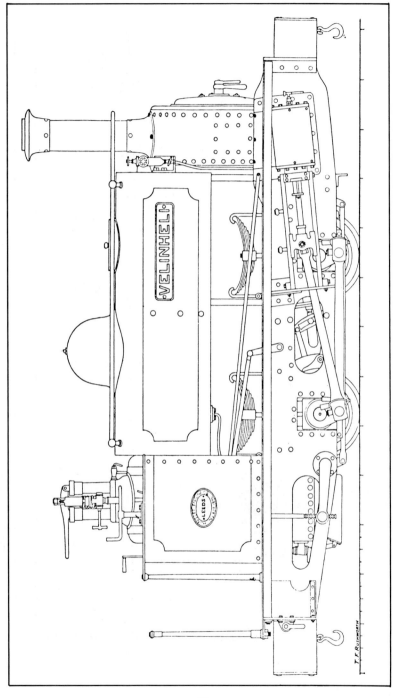

The answer to the Dinorwic Quarry requirements was found in this design, and first supplied in 1886.

Drawing: T.F. Rushworth

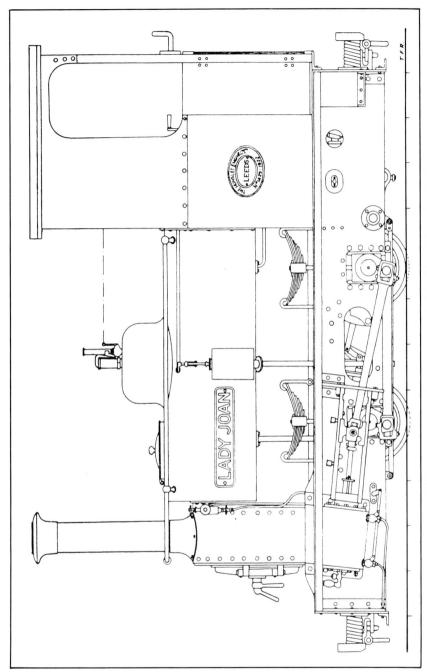

In the early 1920s, two new engines were supplied for Port Dinorwic of this type.

Drawing: T.F. Rushworth

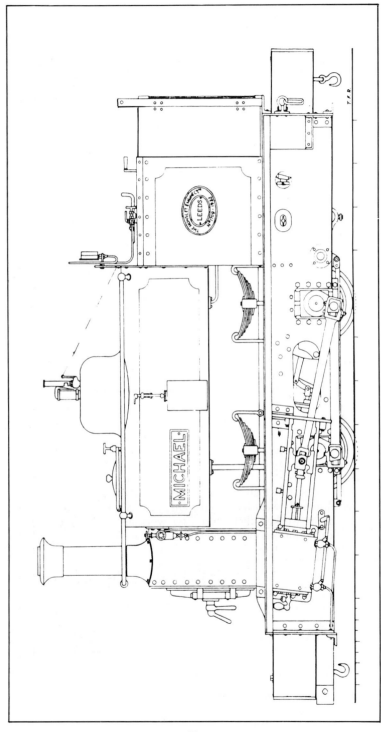

MICHAEL was the sole example of its type, shown here with cab removed.
Drawing: T.F. Rushworth

it. There were domes on the 'Alice' class boilers as fitted on Port class boilers: later, some 'Alice' class engines which had lost their domed boilers used tanks with dome covers, but this was simply a matter of fitting the next available tank in the workshop. Two engines were only 6 ft 6 in. tall to the top of the chimney (KING OF THE SCARLETS and RED DAMSEL) but the remainder had taller chimneys and stood 7 ft 3 in. above the rails; here again, the shorter chimneys might be found on other engines in due course.

LADY MADCAP was another unclassified Hunslet engine bought secondhand ex-The Groby Granite Co. Ltd. (their SEXTUS) from the makers at Leeds. It was distinguished from the other Hunslet engines by its dropped rear frame. Hunslet modified it at the time of purchase to increase the wheelbase by 7 in. and allow the frame to carry a 'Port' class boiler supplied for £900. In 1931 Gilfach-Ddu made further alterations to carry an 'Alice' class boiler but the dome cover on the tank was retained. This engine began life in Victoria (1910) but found itself more suited to the Village Line where it worked in isolation from 1931 when a new firebox was fitted.

'Port' class engines had cabs when new (and were 8 ft 3 in. high), and some 'Alice' class had them (IRISH MAIL for example); apart from Lernion level, cabs were unsuited to the narrow clearances elsewhere and if fitted, were removed. 'Tramway' class engines carried cabs as the Tram Line had no restrictions.

'Alice' class engines had shackle-and-hook couplers and carried large wooden buffers sheeted in steel plate: one face was flat, the other rounded. During rope or chain shunting these large wooden protrusions became in essence 'bollards' to take the rope.

'Port' class engines had deep full buffer beams, sandboxes, higher-pitched boiler (with safety valves and hooter on the dome) than the 'Alice' class; the first 'Port' engine moved to the Quarry in 1922. BERNSTEIN, COVERTCOAT and perhaps GEORGE B began their lives at the Port but ultimately went back to the Quarry.[43] MICHAEL, though of 'Port' class, never worked there and after working on Lernion until 1950, had its cab removed when taken down to Dyffryn. Nos. 1 and 2 of the class had sprung central buffers when working at Port Dinorwic.

The last of the 'Alice' class, WILD ASTER brought an end to regular buying of engines, but a document suggesting a 'duplicate of No. 7' for 1 December 1905 from Hunslet confirms another purchase was con-templated. At that time Ernest Neale was Manager and he may have considered W.G. Bagnall to offer a suitable engine at a keener price for SYBIL was then bought, and delivered in his name.

The two engines of the 'Tramway' class had kidney-shaped sprung central buffers when delivered and from their names it is often sug-gested they were intended for work at the Port. They could uncouple the train by a treadle on the footplate, and had a device for watering the flanges on sharp curves; they had dropped frames at the rear and like

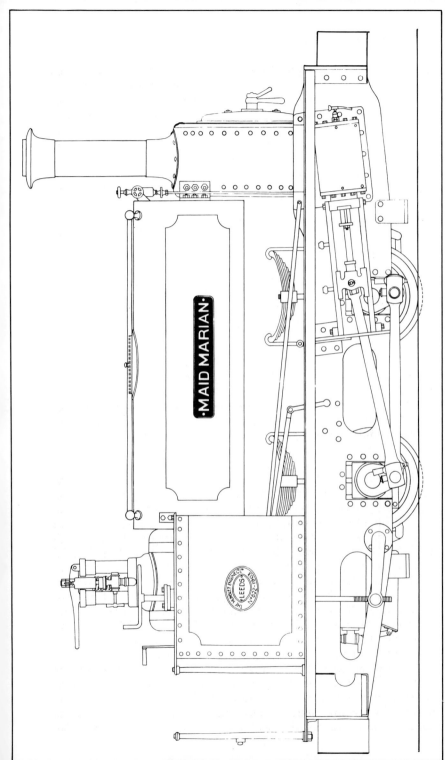

A 1903-built engine of a type to be found scattered up the mountainside above the lakes, busily engaged on gallery haulage.

Drawing: T.F. Rushworth

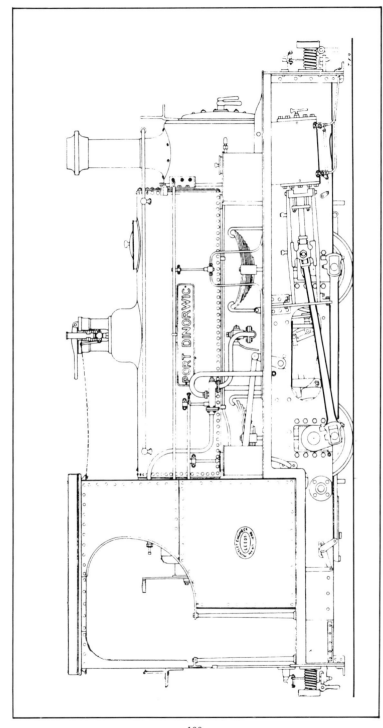

'Tramway' class engines worked the Tram Line rail link between Peris shore and the Gilfach-Ddu interchange.

Drawing: T.F. Rushworth

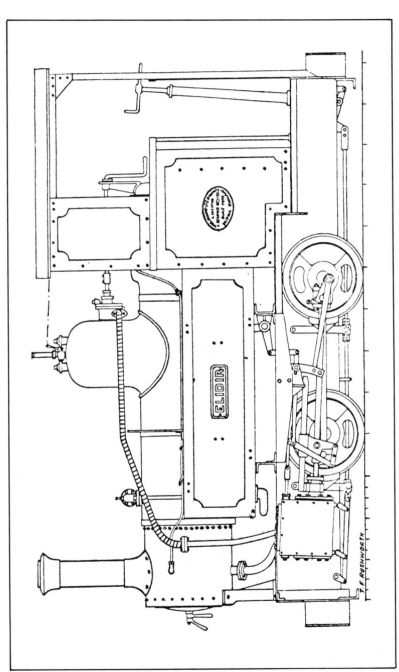

One of a small number of second-hand locomotives purchased by Dinorwic Quarries; this one spent its life on the Tram Line.

Drawing: T.F. Rushworth

the 'Port' class, safety valves on the dome – also a steam hooter. They were 17 ft 5¼ in. long; 7 ft 10 in. high and 6 ft wide.

As to the remainder of the fleet; SYBIL (though liked by some men) was never popular as its marine boiler would not make nor maintain steam – it certainly required more careful firing than a Hunslet. No. 70 came from Raisby Hill Limestone Co. in County Durham in 1948[44] and was a useful light engine for the Port; although lacking the quality of a Hunslet product of the same tonnage it was simpler and cheaper. ELIDIR came from Blythe & Sons (The Birtley Brick Co.) County Durham through R. Dunn (a dealer) of Bishop Auckland. Like SYBIL, it spent most of its working life on the Tramway.[45] SYBIL, ELIDIR and No. 70 were the only engines with inside frames on the system, whilst the side tanks and Belpaire boiler on ELIDIR, and the well tank on No. 70 made them different from the remainder which carried saddle tanks. As to valve gear, all the classified Hunslets had Stephenson Link Motion between the frames; the Barclay and Avonside had outside Walschaerts Motion and the Bagnall was – as customary – fitted with Bagnall & Price Patent Motion. The second-hand engines required gauge modification as they were built for the two-foot gauge.

Such was the quality of the workmanship and the method of maintenance that despite the fact that they worked in rough conditions, these engines soon found buyers when they were put up for sale; a number of them found new life in their old parish . . . on the newly-formed Llanberis Lake Railway (see p.219).

Conversion of Steam Engines to Oil Firing

Some consideration was given to adapting all main line and Quarry engines to burn oil in place of coal in 1920, using the Kermode 'Galva' oil burner at a cost of £120 10s. 0d. per locomotive. The idea seems to have been confined to the 'Alice' class but was never developed.

Un-used Engine Names

At some juncture, and following the success of several of Sir Charles Assheton-Smith's racehorses (one or two became household names) a change in naming was begun before World War I. Probably Sir Charles preferred horses' names to those of his relations! 'Numbered names' were also involved in the name-changes: CLOISTER, COVERTCOAT and JERRY M were chosen, being winners of the Grand National.[46] When the business closed, a number of wooden patterns survived in the Pattern Shop and were presumably of horses which did not take first place and so were never carried on the quarry engines. Five patterns – and does the existence of three of them suggest that on delivery no engine was already named? – varying considerably in size of lettering, were noted in 1958; these were GEORGE, PANDORA, CHARLIE, FLAX-SEED, INDIAN RUNNER. The last-mentioned had a curious diamond between the words in the form of a hyphen. Two other patterns which never came off the 'waiting list' have survived – FLAXEN and BRASS-LOCK.

Livery of Steam Locomotives

The colour of the first steam engines is not known; de Wintons are likely to have been black. The preferred colour of the management at the turn of the century was Midland Railway red, lined in black and edged each side of black with Naples yellow (the same colours were applied to the 4 ft gauge engines). Gilfach-Ddu had its own interpretation and the shade would vary between deep crimson to chocolate brown. Lining out became rarer and in certain cases, non-existent; the black lining gave way to a bright red, sometimes edged with narrow yellow but often not so: green and also grey have been seen for narrow lines. COVERTCOAT and BERNSTEIN were black when they ended their duties at the Port whilst MICHAEL was delivered in a shade of green. Side rods might be black, vermilion or white: frames appear to have been black originally; beams were vermilion; smokeboxes, chimneys, boiler backplates and cab interiors black; wheels black or Midland red; nameplates and makers plates polished brass, as were some domes; handrails – sometimes extending round the chimney – were once bright.

Movements of Engines to and from, and within the Quarry

The lengthy stays which engines made on certain galleries was remarkable; in one instance BERNSTEIN worked on Pen Garret for thirty three years. It was possible in some of the small gallery sheds to carry out some heavy and sophisticated work as most sheds had the means of suspending a block and tackle, and all had inspection pits. Roving fitters and blacksmiths had special wagons provided for them and they would take their gear to the site; there were numerous smithies within the Quarry, and where possible these were used rather than return parts to Gilfach-Ddu – where questions might be asked as to why damage had been suffered! It is on record that RED DAMSEL and BERNSTEIN had replacement boilers fitted on the gallery.

In certain locations engines could not be moved on inclines without thorough dismantling; the parts would then be moved in wagons. Over the years alterations had been made to certain inclines to avoid this, and by removing the side rods and boiler mountings, in many cases an engine could be brought down on its own wheels – in earlier times complete wheel sets were removed and a set of double-flanged wheels on an axle substituted. It was necessary to provide ample balancing, and empty rubbish wagons were filled with metal scrap for the purpose,

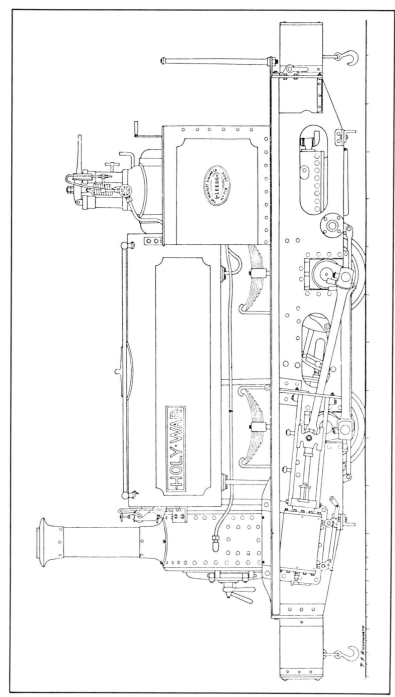

The pronounced wooden buffers with sheet-metal plated faces also did duty as stanchions for the wire haulage ropes used to drag trains alongside a parallel track to the engine!

Drawing: T.F. Rushworth

this being easier to handle than lumps of rock. Certain engines had rectangular side-frames and in consequence, their buffer beams were lower than the rest which had the frames cut away fore and aft. Such full-framed engines gave additional problems as their buffer beams fouled the rails when they ran off the incline bottoms. In more recent times engines have been moved by road lorry; HOLY WAR was dismembered and carried elsewhere by overhead 'Blondin' ropeway.

It will have been previously noted that rolling stock purchases for both gauges of railway were delivered to Llanberis station, the terminus of the L.N.W.R. branch from Caernarvon; special portable lengths of track were once available for running stock along the intervening road surface, the lengths being put down and taken up during progress.

Lighter equipment was simply run in the web of double-headed rail laid on its side. To reduce the time involved, horses were used to tow the rails into position. Carrington[47] recalls that at one time a traction engine had delivered some materials at Gilfach-Ddu, on an occasion when a temporary track of some length had been laid to enable GEORGE to travel under its own steam to the L.N.W.R. station. The road engine driver offered to tow, and GEORGE's side rods were removed and its springs packed up with wooden blocks. It is said the journey was made with some speed and in taking the corner onto the main road in Llanberis the traction engine turned sharply right and canted the now rigid GEORGE – moving smartly as it did so – into the position of an embanked turn!

DINORWIC was dragged into Gilfach-Ddu along the road on its own flanges 'without any rails or planks, and without the slightest accident' ('THE ENGINEER' 13th January, 1871).

To encourage good maintenance of locomotives, drivers were 'cautioned' if they kept them in poor condition, and management encouraged them by giving a cash bonus for cleanliness.

Finally, if an engine required turning, the triangle of tracks at Dyffryn was used.

UNCLASSIFIED

First Name/No.	Second Name	Builder	Works No.	Year	Location (where known)	Notes	Disposal
WELLINGTON	—	de Winton & Co.	—	c1870?	Wellington? Vivian 1895	1	Sold c1898
HARRIET	—	"	—	1874	Harriet?	2	
PERIS*	—	"	—	1875	Peris shore?	3	pre 1895
VICTORIA	—	"	—	1876	Victoria?	4	
PADARN	—	"	—	?	Padarn shore?	5	Sold c1898
DINORWIC	CHARLIE	Hunslet Engine Co. Ltd.	51	1870	Padarn-Peris Tram Line	6	Sold by 1919
GEORGE	MINSTREL PARK	Hunslet Engine Co. Ltd.	184	1877	Padarn-Peris Tram Line	7	Sold by 1919
LOUISA	—	Hunslet Engine Co. Ltd.	195	1877	Quarry	8	Sold by 1898
ELIDIR	LADY MADCAP	Hunslet Engine Co. Ltd.	652	1896	Victoria 1910 Village Line 1931	9	Parts sold 1963
SYBIL	—	W.G. Bagnall Ltd.	1760	1906	Anglesey 1906 Padarn-Peris Tram Line (latterly)	10	Sold
('No. 70')	—	A. Barclay Sons & Co. Ltd.	1995	1931	The Port	11	Sold 1962
ELIDIR	—	Avonside Engine Co. Ltd.	2071	1933	Padarn-Peris Tram Line	12	Sold 1966

Notes

1. Reputed to have a single cylinder and double-flanged wheels?
2. Cost £350. Reputed to have a single cylinder and double-flanged wheels?
3. Cost £360. Reputed to have a single cylinder and double-flanged wheels?
4. Cost £220. Reputed to have a single cylinder and double-flanged wheels?
5. Reputed to have a single cylinder and double-flanged wheels?
6. Low position of outside cylinders unsuited to Quarry locations: built for working on 1 in 50 in Glan-y-Bala tunnel.
7. —
8. To Glynrhonwy Quarry who auctioned it in 1916.
9. Dismantled after damage in an accident 1952: remains sold to John Hughes, Conway, 1963 for scrap.
10. Said to be un-named on delivery. New boiler ex Port Dinorwic 1925.
11. —
12. Probably had 7 inch cylinders when new.
*but see under Penrhyn Quarry for alternative supplier of this engine, and also p.112.

'ALICE' CLASS –

Builders   The Hunslet Engine Co. Ltd., Leeds

No records pre-1923

First Name/No.	Second Name	Notes	Works No.	Year	Fire-boxes	Boilers	Location in Quarry (where known)	Disposal
VELINHELI	—	At one period carried tank with dome (but boiler domeless)	409	1886	1904 1928	1935	Ponc-Fawr 1928 Dyffryn 1935 Village Line 1958	Sold
ALICE	KING OF THE SCARLETS	Damaged by rock fall 1962 – withdrawn	492	1889	1912 19—	1924 1935 1947 19—	Dyffryn 1947	Sold 1965
ENID	RED DAMSEL	Brought down and dismantled	493	1889	1905 1923 19—	19— 1932 19—	New York Gilfach-Ddu 1931* ? (out of use 1942–6)	Parts sold 1969
No. 1	ROUGH PUP	Withdrawn 1960	541	1891	1920 19—	1904 1930 1938 19— 19—	Dyffryn (latterly)	To Narrow Gauge Railway Museum Tywyn 1968
No. 2	CLOISTER	Brought down 1961	542	1892	?	1908 1924 1933 1947	New York 1932 Gilfach-Ddu 1933* Dyffryn 1934 Ponc-Fawr	Sold 1962
THE FIRST	BERNSTEIN		678	1898	1904	1932	The Port 1898 New York 1923 Victoria 1932 Pen-Garret 1933	Sold 1967

		Notes						Locations	Disposal
THE SECOND	COVERTCOAT		679	1898	1923	1932 1935 1947		The Port 1898 / Village Line 1910–14 / Victoria 1923 / California	Sold 1964
WELLINGTON	GEORGE B		680	1898	1929	1935 19—		?The Port 1898 / Dyffryn 1929 / Gilfach-Ddu 1935★ / Wellington	Sold 1965
No. 3	HOLY WAR	Last steam engine in service – ceased work 1967 – stored on Level	779	1902	?	1924 1931 1939 19—		Penrhydd-Bach (latterly)	Sold 1968
No. 4	ALICE		780	1902	1923	1925 1931		Australia (latterly)	'Remains' sold 1972
No. 5	MAID MARIAN (COVERTCOAT 1912–13?)	Out of use by 1964.	822	1903	?	1927 1936 19—		Village Line 1903–14 / Gilfach-Ddu 1931★ / Padarn-Peris Tram Line (1956) / Pen-Garret (latterly)	Sold 1966
No. 6	IRISH MAIL	Fitted with cab on delivery. Dismantled 1959	823	1903	1925	1936		Pen-Garret 1903 / Sinc-Fawr 1929 / Australia 1936	Parts sold 1969
No. 7	WILD ASTER	Brought down and withdrawn 1961	849	1904	1926	1919 1931 1935		Pen-Garret 1904 / Gilfach-Ddu 1934★ / Ponc-Fawr 1935 / Penrhydd-Bach 1950	Sold 1969

★In Yard for overhaul.

'PORT' CLASS – Builders The Hunslet Engine Co. Ltd., Leeds

First Name/No.	Second Name	Notes	Works No.	Year	Fire-boxes	Boilers	Location in Quarry (where known)	Disposal
					No records pre-1923			
No. 1	LADY JOAN (later reverted to No. 1)	Ceased work by 1967	1429	1922	?	?	The Port Quarry pre 1966 (less cab)	Sold 1967
No. 2	DOLBADARN	Received Alice class boiler 1950. Withdrawn 1968	1430	1922	1930	19—	The Port (to Quarry 1935 and cab removed) Penrhydd-Bach 1936 Sinc-Fawr (latterly)	Sold 1969
MICHAEL	—	Out of use by 1963	1709	1932	?	19—	(Delivered to Quarry) Lernion 1932 Dyffryn 1950 Australia (latterly)	Sold 1965

'TRAM' ('TRAMWAY') or 'MILLS' CLASS – Builders The Hunslet Engine Co. Ltd., Leeds

First Name/No.	Second Name	Notes	Works No.	Year	Fire-boxes	Boilers	Location in Quarry (where known)	Disposal
VAENOL	JERRY M		638	1895	?	?	Padarn-Peris Tram Line	Sold 1967
PORT DINORWIC	CACKLER		671	1898	?	?	Padarn-Peris Tram Line	Sold 1966

HORIZONTAL-BOILERED LOCOMOTIVES: PRINCIPAL DIMENSIONS

	Wheel Arrangement	Cylinders Bore (in.)	Cylinders Stroke (in.)	Driving Wheel Diameter (ft)	(in.)	Wheel Base (ft)	(in.)	Boiler Pressure (lb.)	Tractive Effort at 75% B.P. (lb.)	Grate Area (sq. ft)	Total Heating Surface (sq. ft)	Weight Working Order (Tons)	(cwt)	Water Capacity (galls)	Minimum Curve Radius (ft)
(UN-CLASSIFIED) (7 LOCOS)															
DINORWIC	0-4-0ST	7½	14	2	0	4	3	150	3690		160	9	0	200	
GEORGE	0-4-0ST	7½	14	2	0										
LOUISA	0-4-0ST	5*	8	1	6	3	0		1250	1¾	56	3	18	60	
LADY MADCAP	0-4-0ST	7	10	1	8¼	4	0	160	2900					100	
SYBIL	0-4-0ST	7	12	1	9½	3	6	140	2870		80	7	0	150	45
'No. 70'	0-4-0WT	7	11	1	10	3	11½	180	3305			7	0	120	44
ELIDIR	0-4-0T	7½	12	2	0	3	9	180	3795	3½	136	7	10		
'ALICE' CLASS (13 LOCOS)	0-4-0ST	7	10	1	8	3	3	140	2578	2½	100	6	0	100	21
'PORT' CLASS (3 LOCOS)	0-4-0ST	7	10	1	8	3	3	160	2940	2½	100	6	14	100	21
'TRAM' or 'MILLS' CLASS (2 LOCOS)	0-4-0ST	8½	14	2	2	4	6	140	4085	3½	193	11	15	220	

*Described as 6 in. × 8 in. in Glynrhonwy sale list of 1916

Other Locomotive Power

The Dinorwic Quarries must rank as one of few locations where the internal combustion rail tractor never made its mark; traditionally this was for two reasons – firstly the steam engines' work was heavy and rough, and consequently the Company owned no tractors which could be used turn-about with the steam units, so that tractors had to be used on locations where lighter work was performed – a situation seldom offering in the Quarry: so the tractor would therefore be of limited application. Secondly, the age-old problem of maintaining motive power of different type with men whose lifetime experience was on steam, together with the attempt by tractor drivers to put them to work which only resulted in heavy depreciation, gave poor financial benefits compared with the cost of keeping the more robust steam engines at work. Tractors were first introduced in 1935 and by 1957 twenty diesel and one petrol (some secondhand) had found their way to Quarry, Yard and Port; at first they carried the number of the Level on which they worked and though they never usurped the steam engine, as roadways were built with modern earthmoving equipment it was lorries which took their place. The twenty-one units of 1957 were reduced to five ten years later, many having been cannibalised to keep the others running. One survived to the end, and found a new sphere of activity on the Llanberis Lake Railway.

INTERNAL COMBUSTION RAIL TRACTORS

Ruston & Hornsby Ltd, Lincoln, fitted diesel engines. All four-wheeled: mechanical transmission.

No. first allocated	Works No.	Class	Date			Out of Service*
A2	175987	27/32 HP	1935	New		1967
A1	181807	"	1936	"		1964
E3	186322	16/20 HP	1937	Secondhand	1950	
E4	186342	"	1937	"	1950	1967
E6	191645	"	1938	"	1950	
E5	191661	"	1938	"	1950	
E10	202979	20 DL	1940	"	1956	
E8	203009	"	1941	"	1952	
E1	211598	"	1941	"	1947	1967
E2	211620	"	1941	"	1947	
E7	221605	"	1943	"	1952	
E11	222081	"	1943	"	1957	
E9	235704	"	1945	"	1956	
B2	246809	30 DL	1947	New		
B1	252799	"	1947	"		1967
D2	273854	"	1949	"		
D1	277265	"	1949	"		
D3	277269	"	1949	"		

No. first allocated	Works No.	Class	Date		Out of Service*
F.C. Hibberd & Co. Ltd., Park Royal; four-wheeled: diesel-mechanical.					
C1	2782		1945	New	1960
C3	2791		1945	"	1961
C2	2792		1945	"	1962
R.A. Lister & Co. Ltd., Dursley; four-wheeled: petrol.					
—	28608		1946	New	1954

*By 1969 D1, E2 and E6 (as E5) survived: D1 passed to Llanberis Lake Railway.

As a postscript to the locomotive story must be added a typical example of their mystery in these quarry locations where only oral evidence and memory are available: the engine PERIS which on the scantiest basis is assumed to have been a de Winton product, may have quite different origins.[48] The James Beatson correspondence (the Derby contractor) includes a letter of 15th June, 1875 referring to their delivery of an engine to Dinorwic Quarry. This was about the same period when Beatson had sold GEORGE SHOLTO (1) to Penrhyn Quarry; GEORGE SHOLTO (1) may have been similar to the engine supplied to Dinorwic (i.e. both were Lewin-built well tanks?) and a later letter of 21st December, 1875 says of GEORGE SHOLTO (1) 'I find the chimney is 2 feet higher than the Dinorwic Engine'. The only engine at Dinorwic which fits the date is PERIS, but one cannot conclude that all previous accounts are valueless. Indeed, all this time Dinorwic was understand- ably experimenting with small horizontal-boilered engines for the galleries, and had not until 1875 tried one. If PERIS proved to be a Lewin rather than a de Winton, then the diminutive LOUISA by Hunslet would be the second small engine, not the first, under trial.[49]

1 ft 10¾ in. Gauge Stock – General Note

The largest stock of wagons was the type used for carrying slates, and which could be run onto the transporters of the Padarn Railway. These, and the four small guard's vans, one of which ran on the end of each 'slate run' (train) on the P.R. were specially fitted with an individual axle to each wheel to enable them to ride on the transporters (see p.116). The remainder of the stock was almost all fitted with full axles, although those wagons converted from slate wagons might retain their four axles.

All stock had double-flanged wheels of 11 in. nominal tyre diameter, with link and hook for coupling at each end. Certain Quarry-confined stock was given lifting rings to enable them to be lifted from the pits by overhead wire ropeways ('Blondins'). Many of the Quarry wagons had wheels loosely mounted on axles; these wheels could shift laterally and were bounded by the wagon frame at the back and a cotter-pin at the axle end: such stock with its double-flanged wheels was ideal for the roughly-gauged lines in the working area but did not run too easily in trains as the bodies tended to twist when pushed against other wagons; mechanically of low efficiency, they were simple and robust, well-suited to the work.

Summing up the complete '2 ft gauge' stock picture:

a) Wagons and vans used within the Quarry and on the transporter train
b) Wagons used within the Quarry area only but exchanged between the galleries
c) Wagons used within the Quarry area only and confined to their own gallery
d) Wagons for special purposes
e) Wagons based on Gilfach-Ddu Yard and used temporarily in the Quarry
f) Passenger trucks used for visitors

It will be convenient to describe (f) first and so dispose of them, but an explanation of the terms used by the men is called-for: the expression 'wagon, truck or car' was used indiscriminately, the names in Welsh 'Wagan' or 'Car' being the most common; thus 'Yellow Trucks' or 'Yr Tryciau Melyn' (the Passenger Trucks) and 'Slate Wagons' or 'Waganau Llwythwr' (the omnipresent slate wagons). Whatever the 21 'Crowds Cars' of the 1877 inventory were, is long forgotten!

Iron wagons were usually unpainted, or either grey or black. Wagons with wooden portions had them painted purple brown – the Quarry standard colour. Lettering where extant was white. Metal portions on wooden wagons were black.

Personnel Stock: 'The Yellow Trucks' – universal availability

Not all visitors were special guests or came from Vaynol houseparties. It was the continuing custom of the management to encourage visits to the Quarry from all walks of life, and accordingly guides were available and proper provision made to conduct them through the workings. Many parties were conveniently carried along galleries and by inclines in trains of empty slate wagons having planks inserted through their side frames to make simple seats; the more important parties would have steam haulage and perhaps a special detonation of rock would be arranged and trains of visitors would lurk in the linking tunnels as the explosion took place.

Pride of place was taken by a special rake of three vehicles which survived to the last – known as the Yellow Trucks from their daffodil yellow colour of the Assheton-Smith family, there were two similar (and one individual) four-wheel open coaches, of varying appearance. They were not unlike the wagons used on a fairground roller-coaster but had angled seats to make them more comfortable on inclines, for which they were also fitted with iron 'eyes' to which chains would be fastened to secure them to each other. The two similar ones with central entrance and opposing seating were built up from slate wagon running gear, the smaller with 2 ft 2 in. wheelbase, the larger with 2 ft 8 in.; handrails, footsteps and quarry wagon wheels were used. The largest, with seats facing one way in the form of a motor vehicle, also had sloping seats, handrails, footsteps and a 3 ft 4 in. wheelbase on larger 1 ft 5 in. diameter wheels. None had brakes. The two smaller coaches had no springs, but the larger had an iron underframe and springs; it was a more stylish vehicle than its colleagues. Royal visitors were frequent passengers in this yellow-painted rake.

The procedure for using them is first noted in a visit of the Duke and Duchess of York on 27th April, 1899, when the instructions to the men refer confusingly to both 'three carriages' and 'four carriages and two trucks' which were to be run along the Tramway (i.e. Padarn-Peris Tramway) 'through to Wellington with the Tram Engine'. Two tram engines were each decorated. Later the instructions are more helpful and explain something of the mystery, 'the Tram Engine to be at Glan-y-Bala with two new trucks, two carriages and two temporary carriages'. Visitors qualifying for the use of this rake often arrived from Llanberis village by horse carriage and dismounted opposite Glan-y-Bala garden gate: here the management would place a 'platform' of three risers, standing temporarily beside the tramroad there; it was made up of two wooden sections and long enough to take the three carriages. If the workmen and schoolchildren had been given the time off, they would be marshalled into a square around this transient boarding point and from here the train would disappear westwards. Triumphal arches of evergreens with appropriate slogans would greet the little train and its occupants as it puffed underneath them. After a break to see the Works, it would, with its engine at the east end now, disappear into Glan-y-Bala tunnel en route for an extended tour of the Quarry, the tunnel itself lit by '30 lamps' hung there for such occasions. The sequential tour would frequently ascend by the 'A' incline (still in the Yellow Trucks) to the Mills; whilst the party was perhaps trying its hand at splitting slate, the carriages might be furtively pushed to another part of the Quarry by a gang of men hidden away for just that purpose, and perhaps make its way along a gallery to see a blast. It was not unknown, whilst the passengers were viewing elsewhere, for the whole train to be dragged along some part of the ground where there was no rail, and appear ready and waiting in another adjacent area without rail link to the first! Such was all part of life for the Yellow Trucks . . . and they have survived to this day!

Some of the instructions which preceded such tours are worth quoting: '3 Carriages . . . Lines to be smoothed on Inclines . . . Special platform at Gilfach . . . Main tram engine 4 carriages 2 trucks to run

through to Wellington . . . passes of 2 trucks each (not above 18 &
10^{50}) at each drum . . . engine to be decorated . . . lamps in tunnel
. . .'. Passing through tunnels from pit to pit was a wet business due to
water falling from the roofs, and waterproof aprons were available in
the Trucks. The tram line engine driver and stoker [sic] received 2/6d.
extra for their pains. Finally, the instructions for the non-railway
journey of the Trucks reads (for 27th April, 1899) – '. . . Engine to be
detached at points near Matilda, and 2 men appointed to push each
carriage to the end of road by Sinc Twll Clawdd, whence a good path
will lead to Mills. While inspecting Mills, the carriages can be pushed
down path past Mills to Incline 'A' . . .'. All of which was carried out
without the Royal knowledge and demonstrated the flexibility of the
narrow gauge railway!

The age of these vehicles is not known; it is believed their original
purpose was simply to carry visitors from the Dock, up Port incline and
so transfer them to the Saloon on the Padarn Railway. For many years
they were kept in a shed at the foot of Port Incline. Perhaps because
some visitors wished to continue in these open trucks and to save
bringing out the Saloon, a transporter was furnished with springs on it
and these trucks were carried to the Quarry with their human load,
(along with the empty slate wagons). They were then off-loaded and
could continue a tour of the Quarry. As time went by, they were used
almost solely for Quarry visits and were normally stored above the
Pattern Shop in the yard, and an awkward handling assignment this
was!

Personnel Stock: Guard's Vans – used on Transporter Wagons only

These were the small 'sentry-box-like' shelters, mounted on wheels,
carried on the last transporter in the train. Although fitted with wheels
they were not usually run off the host wagons; they were simply
travelling shelters for the brakesman who operated the transporter's
long brake handle; the method was to stand between the van body and
the adjacent slate wagon, and then stand on the brake-lever end – an
exterior grab-handle fitted to the outside of the van side supported him.

There were two vans in each of two eras, one for each 'slate run'. The
earlier vans were made in sheet iron; mounted on iron frames, they had
inner wooden frames to carry the inner axle bearings. There was a small
window on the outer side; in the van made up of three iron sheets, the
window was in the centre; in the van of two sheets it was at the end of
the side furthest from the end door. Access to the end doors (opening
inwards) was gained by standing on the end of the transporter itself. A
smaller door diagonally opposite this window opened inwards and
allowed the brakesman to operate the brake lever without going outside, and a grab handle just inside the door made life more secure! One
van ended its days as an air raid shelter in a garden at Cwm-y-Glo, the

other (which survives) became a garden tool shed at the hospital. The iron vans were later replaced by wooden-bodied ones mounted on slate wagon frames, built in tongue and groove matchboarding; their upper outer sides were fully glazed, as was the inwards-opening door, but there was no additional door for the brake. Each type had small lockers within, topped by a seat, and they were secured to the transporters by bolts and shackles. A wooden specimen survives at the Narrow Gauge Railway Museum, Tywyn.

It has been explained previously that to load or unload the slate wagons carried on the transporter alongside the guard's van, the transporter must be turned at the end of each journey . . . in fact, it was an offence not to do so; equally so was to fail to run three loaded slate wagons alongside the van for the Pen-Scoins journey. However, such was the time and effort required to do this that it was sometimes 'overlooked' on the first east- or last west-bound journeys of the day! For instance, if the last arrival of the day at the Quarry was late, time spent in assembling a loaded train for the last Pen-Scoins run (the engine having to coal and water and couple up) was saved if the guard's van transporter was attached straight off the rear of the empty train. It was a simple matter, but to find oneself short of something over 5 tons of braking adhesion, and when the time came to check the speed of the train as the engine accelerated away in the 'first act' of the Pen-Scoins fly shunting scene it might be embarrassing!! There were some unfortunate consequences and not all 'final curtains' were worthy of applause, for the guard's van brake efficiency was utterly dependent on the weight of its fellow-travellers.

It should be mentioned that among the men on the Estate (including gamekeepers on the land, Quarry-ships' captains at sea) it was the railway guards alone who were provided with uniforms, double-breasted in dark blue melton finished with brass buttons, embossed "D.Q.R."

Non-personnel Stock: Slate Wagons – universal availability

There were once over 700 frame-sided open wagons for carrying slate, and most of them were built at Gilfach-Ddu. The bodies were mainly of wood and each held c.1¾ tons[51] and each carried its tare weight on the solebar to assist weighing of finished slate. The frame was in timber members and each double-flanged wheel was carried on a separate axle (see p.112); the frame ends were rounded for buffing purposes, and there were link and hook couplers at each end. None had brakes. The side frames were separated by cast-iron bobbin-shaped spacers cast in the foundry; the floors were of heavy planking which was more serviceable in the wet climate than sheet iron.

The earliest surviving reference to slate wagons is found in the accounts for 1841–2 and the problem arising from the terms then used

Plate XCIV Probably the first Quarry locomotive at Dinorwic, WELLINGTON by de Winton & Co. about 1870. Presumably the engine worked through a low tunnel, hence the short chimney. The picture does not confirm there was but one cylinder, but the double-flanged wheels are evident.

Gwynedd Archives

Plate XCV DINORWIC was acquired to replace horse-power on the Tram Line in 1870. The builder's familiar outlines are evident but the type was not perpetuated.   *The Hunslet Engine Co. Ltd.*

Plate XCVI LOUISA of 1877 went into the Quarry, following a batch of de Winton engines there. It was not powerful enough to encourage further orders of this type.   *The Hunslet Engine Co. Ltd.*

Plate XCVII In 1886 the first of what became thirteen similar engines for work in the Quarry, was delivered, VELINHELI: c 1930.   *per D.C. Carrington*

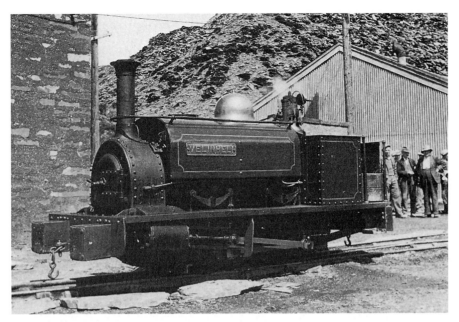

Plate XCVIII VELINHELI in late guise, at The Mills in 1964. The brass dome was part of the replacement saddle-tank, the boiler itself being domeless! *J.I.C. Boyd*

Plate XCIX KING OF THE SCARLETS (ex ALICE), firstly named after Laura Alice Duff - L.A.D.A.S. of the Snowdon Mountain Tramway - and secondly, after a racehorse: 1952. *J.I.C. Boyd*

Plate C The last descent, KING OF THE SCARLETS being brought down for the last time: May 1965.

T.H. Morris

Plate CI RED DAMSEL of 1889, formerly ENID, (the daughter of Alice Duff) also lost its original name to a racehorse.

per J.I.C. Boyd

Plate CII ROUGH PUP was indeed 'rough' by 1960; the smoke-box was heavily patched and the platework dented by collisions. The large slab on the footplate keeps coal in place! 1960.

D.L. Chatfield

Plate CIII CLOISTER is typical of the usual appearance of the Quarry engines - clean, almost unscathed and nicely lined-out.

per J.I.C. Boyd

Plate CIV BERNSTEIN began life at the Port as THE FIRST but spent most of its life in the Quarry.
per J.I.C. Boyd

Plate CV COVERTCOAT was BERNSTEIN'S partner at the Port but was on the Village Line by 1910.
per J.I.C. Boyd

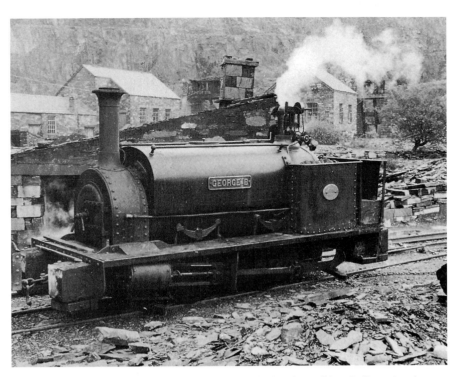

Plate CVI GEORGE B, the third of the 1898 engines, may also have begun life at the Port, where horses were quickly replaced: Hafod Owen, 1960. *D.L. Chatfield*

Plate CVII HOLY WAR (looking as if just returned from same!) was the last steam locomotive at work in the Quarry. It ceased in 1967. *J.I.C. Boyd*

Plate CVIII With Snowdon for a backdrop, IRISH MAIL returns with a train of empty rubbish wagons on Australia level: 23 September 1953.   *H.D. Bowtell*

Plate CIX Men and machine, probably in the early 1920s. The lad would fire, change points, couple up, attach the hawser chain and light up when necessary the equivalent of the Office Tea Boy. The engine is MAID MARIAN.   *per D.C. Carrington*

Plate CX MAID MARIAN about 1931 (still with sandboxes and brass dome, but handrail missing), on Australia level . . . *per D.C. Carrington*

Plate CXI . . . and on Pen-Garrett in June 1960, fitted with domeless boiler. *D.L. Chatfield*

Plate CXII WILD ASTER on Penrhydd-Bach, 1960, has detail differences, including the cut-outs on the front beam. The engine was withdrawn and brought down the next year.   *D.L. Chatfield*

Plate CXIII Down at the Port No. 1 had the whole operation to itself: 1947.   *G. Alliez*

Plate CXIV DOLBADARN, formerly No. 2 down at the Port, was taken to the Quarry in 1935 and lost its cab. *P. Ward*

Plate CXV MICHAEL, probably on Lernion level in the early 1930s, the largest engine to work there. *per C.C. Green*

Plate CXVI MICHAEL is now on Dyffryn level, employed on the customary rubbish trains.

per T.H. Morris

Plate CXVII With a larger boiler and tank, 'pop' valves and hooter on dome, MICHAEL was evident anywhere. There was a cab when new.

D.L. Chatfield

Plate CXVIII SYBIL was the only Bagnall-built engine in the Quarry, seen here at Hafod Owen in 1960.

D.L. Chatfield

Plate CXIX A dinner-hour comparison between SYBIL and MAID MARIAN at Gilfach-Ddu in 1956.

J.I.C. Boyd

Plate CXX The rebuilt LADY MADCAP at work on the Village Line, 1935.   *G.H. Platt*

Plate CXXI 'No. 70', a Barclay 'E' Class, spent all its working life down at the Port: 1954.

J.B. Snell

Plate CXXII ELIDIR passed its working life on the Padarn-Peris Tram Line.   *J.I.C. Boyd*

Plate CXXIII JERRY M (another racehorse name), specially designed for the Tram Line, about to leave Hafod Owen for Gilfach-Ddu, transfer dock: c 1931.   *S. Bale Ltd.*

Plate CXXIV PORT DINORWIC was the second engine supplied for the Tram Line; the right-hand gadget on the tank side is for watering the wheel flanges: Gilfach-Ddu: c 1900.   *F. Moore*

Plate CXXV CACKLER about to leave Gilfach-Ddu for Hafod Owen with an impressive train. Padarn-Peris Tram Line: c 1928.   *W.H. Whitworth*

Plate CXXVI The Top Bank, West Quarry eats into Penmaemnawr Mountain; sett-making sidings serve every working face: 1903.   *Brundrit & Co. Ltd.*

Plate CXXVII The Penmaen Pier with incline crossing the North Wales main line looking east; Wright's Siding holds three sett-filled wagons.   *Nat. Library of Wales*

Plate CXXVIII A later stage in the life of the Penmaen Pier, showing storage hoppers, and enlarged interchange sidings with rows of 'Brundrit & Co. Limited' privately-owned ballast wagons: 1903.

Brundrit & Co. Ltd.

PlateCXXIX The foot of Penmaen Incline, showing staithes: 1910. *I.E. Davies*

Plate CXXX The PUFFIN (registered Liverpool) the last steamship of Brundrit & Co. Ltd., awaits the tide at Penmaen Pier.
Nat. Library of Wales

Plate CXXXI Penmaen Incline (dismantled 1960) and Pier in 1903 looking down from Bonc Jolly; note Sailing Flats.
Brundrit & Co. Ltd.

Plate CXXXII   Penmaen Macadam Mill, workshops, powerhouse and loco shed of Brundrit's undertaking: 1903.
                                                                    Brundrit & Co. Ltd.

Plate CXXXIII As the previous Plate, but looking eastwards towards Darbishire's Quarries: 1903.
                                                                    Brundrit & Co. Ltd.

Plate CXXXIV Braich-LIwyd, Mill of Darbishire's Quarry with workshops and loco sheds below, and de Winton engine and train on right. At this time Brundrit's and Darbishire's were not connected: c 1905.   *Darbishire & Co. Ltd.*

Plate CXXXV Bell Yard, Darbishire's offices, staff houses and intermediary stage on the Graiglwyd Inclines: c 1905.   *Darbishire & Co. Ltd.*

Plate CXXXVI Darbishire's interchange sidings at the Graiglwyd Pier with L.N.W.R. Penmaenmawr station beyond: c 1905. *Darbishire & Co. Ltd.*

Plate CXXVII An unidentified engine by de Winton & Co. in Darbishire's Quarry. *per P.V. Davies*

Plate CXXXVIII LLANFAIR of 1895 fossilises in the Old Quarry: February 1951.   *J.I.C. Boyd*

Plate CXXXIX Putatively LOUISA, cannibalised at Penmaen: February 1951.   *J.I.C. Boyd*

Plate CXL LLANFAIR, showing smokebox door-cum-chimney hinged bracket, Ramsbottom valves (less easing lever), cylinder and valve block with Stephenson valve gear. Obviously things were too horrible inside the boiler to warrant replacing the inspection cover! *J.I.C. Boyd*

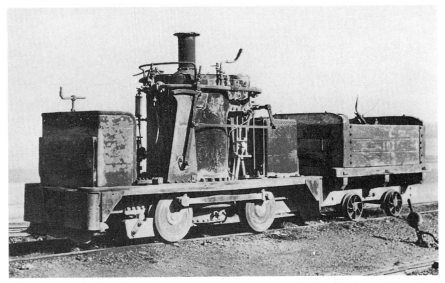

Plate CXLI WATKIN was for many years the shunting engine on Graiglwyd exchange sidings, later being stand-by to a diesel tractor: 1951.   *F. Jones*

Plate CXLII In the Old Quarry in 1908, with (*left to right*) James McClement, Bryn-Helig (under-Manager); Robert Davies, Celyn-Du; John Surion; Arthur Owen, Springfield; Thompson Jones - who had been a driver in South America.   *I.E. Davies*

Plate CXLIII William Thomas (Will Tan Gwalia) on his engine HUGHIE (ex DONALD) on Pen-y-Coed Level. Importantly, when Hunslet sent a specification for this engine in 1905, a gauge of 2 ft 10¼ in. is recorded. *F. Moore*

Plate CXLIV TIGER was built specially with inside cylinders to allow the engine to work where clearances were slender. *The Hunslet Engine Co. Ltd.*

Plate CXLV Diesel fuel tank wagon, gunpowder van and various forms of sett and crushed stone wagons: January 1967.   *J.I.C. Boyd*

Plate CXLVI Visiting parties of County Surveyors were taken round the Quarries in both open and special incline wagons fitted with sharply-tilted seats. Headgear included straw boaters and bowlers; other scenes of this event prove these occasions were a 'jolly day out with the lads'.   *I.E. Davies*

Plate CXLVII Motor-Rail tractor, believed to be NANT ex 2 ft gauge Trevor Quarry, converted to 3 ft gauge and fitted with diesel engine: April 1934.   *I.E. Davies*

Plate CXLVIII The North Wales Power & Traction Company's pole route materials were brought up Ceunant Mawr from Cwm Dyli by machinery somewhat open to the elements!   *Gwynedd Archives*

Plate CXLIX Westward-facing view of Llyn Padarn from the top of A2 Incline after building of Llanberis Lake Railway on site of former Padarn Railway; Gilfach-Ddu terminus below: 1981.

J.I.C. Boyd

Plate CL Eastward view of Llanberis Lake Railway Gilfach-Ddu terminus with former Workmen's Train Shed converted to Carriage Shed (*left*), and Works (*right*): 1984. *J.I.C. Boyd*

Plates CLI, CLII & CLIII Three scenes at Gilfach-Ddu during the period when the C.E.G.B. was using the Llanberis Lake Railway. Bottom view shows single-slip pointwork to 2 ft gauge in heavy materials, an uncommon feature but not now in existence: March 1978.

J.I.C. Boyd

Plate CLIV ELIDIR on a westbound train, skirts the lake boundary: July 1983. *V.J. Bradley*

Plate CLV UNA and ELIDIR encounter on the lake shore loop at Cei Llydan. The former was attached to a train of preserved vehicles: July 1983. *V.J. Bradley*

Plate CLVI A spotless ELIDIR stands outside Gilfach-Ddu Works; the Lake Railway uses the same historic workshop premises as its predecessor: March 1978. *J.I.C. Boyd*

Plate CLVII Although never used locally, UNA is a typical Hunslet-built engine used in Welsh slate quarries, and one of several still available for the Llanberis Lake Railway: July 1983. *V.J. Bradley*

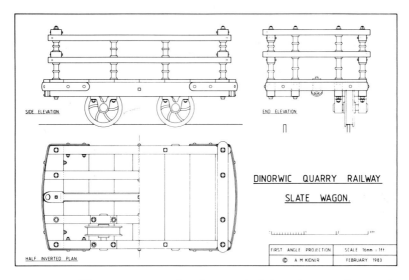

DINORWIC QUARRY RAILWAY

SLATE WAGON.

re-appears. However, as previously recorded there is a consistency in the use of 'Large Trucks for Slates' and 'Slate Waggons', i.e. host wagons and their load 'Slate Waggons'. In October 1841 there was a change in design of slate wagon, presumably due to the necessity of abandoning the customary full axle for the individually mounted wheels, a requirement of the host wagon principle. The carpenters built models to assess the new prototype, being paid £3 12s. 0d. and £1 6s. 0d. on 29th October. A new wheel pattern was produced, turning expenses being 9/3d. Our old friends, William and Robert Jones contracted to build 110 wagons for £3 17s. 9d. each during 1844 and the accounts suggest that the work was put out to various parties (ironwork to blacksmiths etc.) locally and the wagons assembled (perhaps at Port Dinorwic yard in company with the transporters?). Smith & Willey of Liverpool (Windsor Foundry) supplied iron wheels and cast iron pedestals whilst Richard Davies & Son of Menai Bridge provided the timber and paint. In short, the 1840s were good years for the craftsmen of the district, a business which must have declined sharply when the Quarry began to be self-supporting.

The stock-taking of 1877 revealed 724 slate wagons valued at £4 each.

In the latter part of the last century there was a need for additional wagons (or replacements) and enquiries were sent out. There being a sawmill on the Vaynol Estate, the Agent was asked to quote, but replied 'cannot make 34 mortices in a wagon for less than the price quoted – it would be better that the machine stood idle than to lose money' (October 1886). Later documents reveal that the following were among the firms approached to supply wooden bodies (only) and they quoted:

Date	No.		Cost	Details	Builder
February 1897	50	bodies for	£3 17 0 each	with oak frames[52]	Metropolitan Rly. Car. & Wagon Co. Ltd.
February 1900	?	" "	£6 10 0 each	with elm frames ('free of cracks')	Darlington Wagon & Eng. Co. Ltd.
February 1900	24	" "	£6 5 0 each		Metropolitan Rly. Car. & Wagon Co. Ltd.[a]
May 1901	50	" "	£5 15 0 each		" "
May 1901	50	" "	£8 10 0 each		P. & W. McLellan Ltd., Glasgow
May 1901	50	" "	£5 2 6 each		Hurst Nelson & Co. Ltd., Motherwell
May 1901	50	" "	£5 15 0 each		Midland Car. & Wagon Abbey Works, Shrewsbury[b]
May 1901	50	" "	£5 10 0 each	in American rock elm	Darlington Wagon & Eng. Co. Ltd.
May 1901	50	" "	£6 10 0 each	in pitch pine	Bristol Wagon & Car. Works Co. Ltd.

(a) An order was confirmed for this quantity.
(b) £5 if in English pine.

The Wigan Wagon Co. (Springs Branch) were 'Too busy to quote'; John Fowler & Co. (Leeds) Ltd. were 'Too busy in Tractor Wagon Dept. – could have quoted in iron but not wood'; Oldbury Rly. Carriage & Wagon Co. Ltd. also 'Too busy to deliver'. The terminology from those declining to tender was very similar. In the event, Metropolitan was given an order for 20 wagons the following month, and complained Dinorwic had ordered at the 'per 50 wagons' price i.e. £5 15s. 0d. each and there was the usual squabble about 'no profit on the work'. Dinorwic required all woodwork in American rock elm and sample timbers for three bodies were to be submitted before bulk delivery was made.

Though this comprises all the remaining references to slate wagons, one characteristic is clear – the Dinorwic Manager drove a hard bargain.

Coal Wagons ('Box' Wagons) – universal availability

Certain slate wagons were given sheet iron sides, fitted by using the frame members as outside ribbing; these then served as coal wagons, mainly for Quarry and locomotive purposes. They were taken up to the various galleries from the coal yard at Gilfach-Ddu but by the time they had reached the upper levels were almost empty! Each level helped itself to coal as the wagon reached it, there being no coal allowance as was permitted, for instance, in the Penrhyn Quarry.

Slab Trucks ('Car Cyrn') – universal availability within Quarry area only

There was a considerable number of one-ended trucks for carrying large slabs from the working face to the mill. The 'body' was a steel frame with one fenced end which was kept on the downhill end of the loaded wagon as it descended the inclines. Heavily built, these ends required no diagonal bracing; the wagons had full axles and the wheels ran outside the frames, being loose on the axle end and prevented from coming off by a cotter-pin driven through the axle's extremity. Chain rings were fitted for lifting from the pit or linking on inclines. These trucks were all built at Port Dinorwic and had their numbers burned into the end upright.

Slab Trucks ('Sleds') – gallery use only

Some slab wagons resembled slate wagons with the sides removed; though unsuited for the inclines, they were used solely on galleries where this was no disadvantage. Gallery names appeared – such as AUSTRALIA – painted on the frame, denoting its home gallery. These could number among them the '6 ft. car frames' supplied in two lots of six by Metropolitan in the Spring of 1900 @ £5 6s. 0d. each.

Sledge Wagons ('Sleds') – gallery use only

Even smaller than the foregoing was a short wheel-based slab-carrying flat wagon constructed on the same principles. It was essentially a vehicle which could be hand-pushed up to the working face and might be seen running along temporary 'track' made of double headed rails laid roughly on the ground on their sides: the double-flanged wheels ran happily with one flange in the web! Unlike the other flats, they often had lifting rings fitted.

Rubbish Wagons – universal availability within Quarry area

In general there was remarkable standardisation in type – as with most other stock. There was a very high proportion of rock waste to finished slate and most of the quarried rock found its way over the edge of the waste tips, whose length increased over the years, and which moved further from the main scene of operations. Short tips would be worked by man or horsepower (there was a horse working on Sinc Bach (Braich) until comparatively late years) but the big tips were worked by steam locomotives. They would haul the wagons to the tip edge and then run aside by either a short siding or by hauling the loaded wagons beside them over a weighing table: this was done by using a wire rope attached to a buffer and hauling the loaded wagons on a parallel line (sometimes unsuited to loco weight) to avoid having to pass the engine over the weighing table. At the tip end the track would be shaped like a

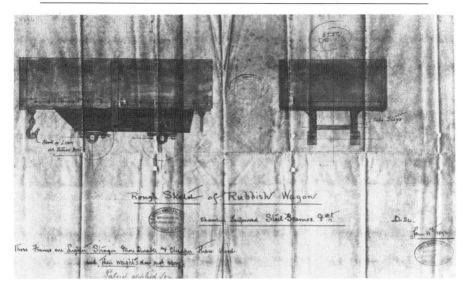

Sketch of Rubbish Wagon; submitted for an order.

Gwynedd Archives

question mark lying on its back ⌣; two men would manhandle each wagon so that it ran, then fell, into the 'crook' in the rails; this shot out the stone through the open end. Handrails were fitted to the back of the wagon to recover it . . . it was heavy work! Now and again a complete wagon or whole train would be lost over the end of the line, but only in cases of several wagons going down did a rescue team go out to recover them; ultimately, falling rubbish would bury the lot. So extensive were these tips that following boundary complaints, tips into the lake were limited by placing marker posts in the water. At the ends of higher exposed tips, a rough stone cabin sheltered the tip-men.

These wagons had channel steel frames, sheet iron sides and wheels loose on the axles: eyes for lifting from pits by 'Blondins' were prominent. If any wagons once had wooden frames (as were found in Penrhyn Quarry) they are gone beyond recall.

The history of the rubbish tipping wagons is obscure and there is no reference at Dinorwic before 1877, when the stocktaking list refers to them as 'Quarrymen's Cars', or '3a-side' indicating the open end: there were 314 valued at £2 each. In a costing of 1891, wooden construction was priced @ £2 13s. 0d and 'iron' @ £3 2s. 2d. each.

In May 1897 the Metropolitan Railway Carriage & Wagon Co. Ltd., quoted £2 14s. 0d. each for 50 bodies in mild steel having angle ribbing round the top edges of the sides/end. There is an undated quarry drawing – probably of this period – of conventional dimensions save that the body was slightly tapered, having a 3 ft wide open end and

2 ft 9 in. at the other; it was built in ¼ in. mild steel plate, with top angle and two handles at the back for the tip men. Like all wagons of the period, paint finish was 'purple brown': it did not last!

Among the surviving papers are drawings for rubbish wagons to their own design by J. Dunnell Garrett & Co. Ltd., Engineers of Festiniog Iron Works, Tan-y-Grisiau, dated January 1893; these had open-ended bodies built up in folded steel sheet, but Dinorwic does not appear to have been tempted – this firm also submitted drawings for slab trolleys.

Open Wagons – restricted to Padarn-Peris Tram Line

These wagons had limited usefulness, their wooden frame carrying a large sheet iron body in the form of a simple open box with an end door, angle iron strengthening rib along the top rim and lifting rings for transport by 'Blondin'. They carried mainly loco coal and all had disappeared soon after the end of the Second War.

Flat Trolleys ('Sleds') – universal availability in the Quarry area

These were small trolleys with light narrow wooden platforms used by the men who kept the quarry tracks in repair, or used to move the portable track sections from place to place; essentially they were maintenance orientated.

End-tipping Wagons – 'American Devil' Wagons – limited availability in the Quarry area

These were large end-tipping skips purchased secondhand (a consignment also went to Penrhyn Quarry) for use with the Ruston-Bucyrus digger/excavator (the 'American Devil') and were used mainly on lake-level clearance where rubbish could be tipped into Llyn Peris.

Yard Cars – universal availability within the Quarry area

A small stock of wagons based on Gilfach-Ddu Yard was used for taking materials such as pipes, cable drums, timber, wire ropes up into the Quarry. They were basically flat wagons but had wooden ends fitted to save the loads slipping off on inclines; these ends were made rigid by means of diagonal iron straps; lifting rings and incline chain rings were fitted. They usually accompanied a fitter sent out from the Yard.

Drum and Tank Wagons – universal availability within the Quarry area or at the Port

Certain slate wagons underwent conversion for carrying oil, creosote or other liquids: some, by a simple alteration were enabled to carry a 40 gallon oil drum horizontally. One or two others, converted into flats, carried rectangular tanks, but they retained their slate wagon's running gear.

Tool Vans – universal availability within the Quarry area

These were built on the chassis of slate wagons in the form of coffin-shaped boxes with outside wooden framing and they had curved roofs which lifted for access. Their purpose was to accompany the old loco boilers mounted on wheels which did duty as mobile air pressure vessels up on the galleries, but they disappeared many years ago.

BASIC DIMENSIONS

Type	Length Overall		Width Overall		Height From Rail Overall		Wheelbase	
	ft	in.	ft	in.	ft	in.	ft	in.
Guard's Van (Iron)	6	0	3	5	6	9	2	3
Guard's Van (Wooden)	6	4	3	7	6	6	2	3
Slate Wagon	6	0	3	0	2	9	2	3
Rubbish Wagon	4	6	3	0	2	8	1	7
Gallery Slab Truck	6	0	3	0		11	2	3

The Village Branch

The closure of the Dinorwic Railway in 1843 reversed the system of working Quarry transport, in that finished products were lowered to the lakeshore instead of being brought uphill to the Dinorwic Railway in the upper part of the Quarry, where it passed through some of the older workings which lay on the western fringe of the Quarry isolated from the Quarry proper as it developed in later years. To link these workings a subsidiary system with an air of independence and its own small 'main line' connected the main 'Steam Mills' with the Allt-Ddu area. It was quite different in character from the remainder of the quarry railway system. Rock was brought out of the old pits, Chwarel-Fawr and Allt-Ddu, by means of tunnels at a low level; these tunnel tracks led to the lower section of the Allt-Ddu incline, an unusual two-stage arrangement (the upper stage had become derelict by 1914) with a gauge of 4 feet and carrying slate wagons laterally on its trolley trans-porter. At the head of the lower section there was formerly a slate mill for local purposes, but for almost a century the Village Branch took all rock from these pits to the Steam Mills for processing (along with the other rock from the main Quarry which was taken there). Working the Branch was a heavy haul, there being a rise of 1 in 60 to the Mills. Near the lip of Allt-Ddu pit at Bryn-Llys there was a shed for two steam

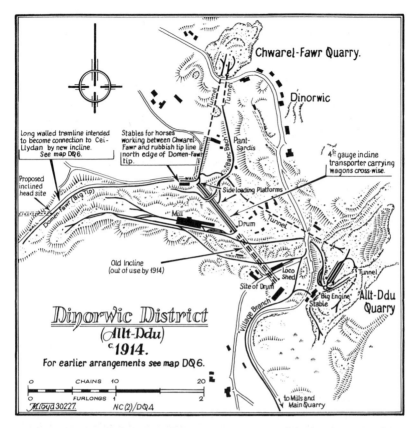

Chwarel-Fawr Quarry.

Dinorwic

Long walled tramline intended to become connection to Cei-Llydan by new incline. See map DQ6.

Stables for horses working between Chwarel-Fawr and rubbish tip line north edge of Domen-Fawr tip.

Pant-Sardis

4ft gauge incline transporter carrying wagons cross-wise.

Proposed inclined head site

Domen-Fawr (Big tip)

Side loading Platforms

Mill

Drum

Tunnel

Old Incline (out of use by 1914)

Loco Shed

Tunnel

Site of Drum

Big Engine Stable

Allt-Ddu Quarry

Village Branch

Dinorwic District
(Allt-Ddu)
c1914.

For earlier arrangements see map DQ6.

CHAINS 10   20

FURLONGS 1   2

J.M.Lloyd 30227.   NC(2)/DQ4

to Mills and Main Quarry

engines, but until the turn of the century, some of the haulage was done additionally by horses, which were better suited to the lower levels.

The Allt-Ddu incline's two trolley transporters, carrying two wagons side by side on each, could be side-loaded at one intermediate position, and in the trackwork at this loading platform was fixed a heavy cast spragging mechanism which prevented transporter movement during load exchange. The transporters had plain inner and double flanged outer wheels – the lower portion of the lower section was a three-rail section without point blades – the plain wheels could negotiate this whereas flanged wheels would not have done. Such was the track layout at the summit, that both trolleys had to be brought up alongside each other and wagons run across both to load/unload. Accordingly, the incline was not a true balanced incline and each track/trolley could be manoeuvred independently.[53] Surviving derelict until 1972, it was a remarkable piece of Industrial Archaeology – it was all swept away in the late 1970s.

The westerly end of the Branch lay along the Assheton-Smith road, but this was more of a headshunt laid in the road surface. Running eastwards the Branch followed this road, but being too steep for locomotives, about 1903 a deviation was made and a better-grade embankment put in for a short distance. Pointwork gave tracks to the west, serving the erstwhile slate mill and the Big Tip (Domen-Fawr) beyond, itself a monument to the vast tonnages of rock extracted from the mountain hereabouts. The line then ran pleasantly through a curve along the hillside and along a narrow defile to emerge below bluffs and with a fine vista of Llanberis with Snowdonia as its backcloth. Maintaining its hillside location and with many of the smaller original dwellings and buildings of the Quarry's earliest days in the woodlands below, the line was built up on vertically walled slab embankment, and wound its way towards a narrow gallery in the hillside just below the main Mills and, passing through a gate, rose sharply for some yards at 1 in 40 to end in a wagon loop beside the Mills. Track connections existed with the remainder of the Quarry complex but the Branch was worked only between Allt-Ddu incline and the Mill, where a local steam engine took over the wagon workings. For much of its life, the Branch was worked by LADY MADCAP, which like the Branch itself, was a unique feature of the locomotive stud. The Branch was laid throughout in double-headed chaired rail, with stub-points. Lifting commenced in January 1968 but the line had been out of use for some years before this.

The Padarn-Peris Tram Line

The origins of this equally 'independent' line have been described already (p.45). The latter-day route stretched from the exchange wharf west of Gilfach-Ddu and alongside the road beside the Works, below the Glan-y-Bala bluff. It passed the head of the road junction giving road connection with Llanberis village and ultimately reached the quarrying premises at Muriau where it continued as a lakeshore system to Hafod-Owen, the full length of the Quarry territory. How impossible here to visualise the pleasant lakeside location of the Muriau demesne and its garden of the 1830s! It was a considerably longer system in its latter days, than when first it replaced the eastern end of the Padarn Railway, becoming in effect a method of collecting the loaded slate wagons from the bottom levels of the Big Quarry and bringing them to the transfer dock at Gilfach-Ddu. The locomotives – some of which were initially built specifically for the tramway – were shedded in the workshop of the Works. As for the Village Branch, the track was laid in double-headed chaired rails, and laid clear and to one side of the roadway.

In 1896 there was a proposal to electrify this 'bottom level system', there being a small hydro-electric plant at Hafod-Owen which might have played a part.

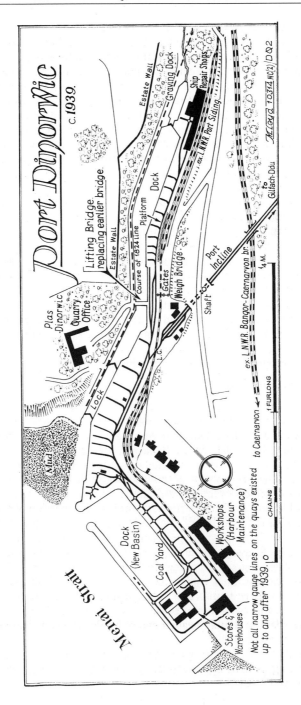

Port Dinorwic
c.1939.

PORT DINORWIC AND SHIPPING

No matter how efficient the railway system, the business of the slate trade could only be done competitively if the complementary shipping point was as competent, but unlike the port for the Penrhyn Railway, Aber-Pwll (soon to become the Port of Dinorwic or Port Dinorwic) lay at the foot of an escarpment so that its railway link with the quarries had perforce to negotiate a rope-worked incline to reach the upper level and the Padarn Railway. Though ingenious methods were devised to overcome the extra handling problems so created, the Port was never as cost-efficient as some other Welsh harbours, but nevertheless, the wharves with their mixed narrow and standard gauge facilities were equipped as effectively – and perhaps better – than most. The intersection of narrow and standard gauge rails was made by a lift-out length of narrow gauge rails which spanned the standard gauge track.

The Port Incline brought Padarn Railway traffic down to the Port-side through the tunnel. The post-1845 complex on the south side of the creek was evolved as business grew; a large basin could contain ships awaiting loading, and upstream there were lock gates and a graving dock for the repair of ships. An engineering, boiler-making and marine business was developed at the head of the creek where at an early date an electric lighting plant supplied port and village; at the south-west end of the harbour were further workshops, stores etc., and in between fans of sidings gave shipside loading direct from the quarries' slate wagons. Consequently the whole system was labour-intensive, for although the idea of carrying slate wagons bodily upon railway wagons was a key feature of the Padarn Railway, an extension of it to transfer them bodily into the holds of ships was not applied. In 1906 117 men were employed here.

The principal developments took place as follows:

1793/	Improved landing facilities at the creek, (with subsequent loss to tonnages
1802	shipped from Caernarvon Harbour.)
1809	Docks and Quays built above High Water Mark, connected to sea by artificial channel from creek (following on Carnarvon Harbour Act 1809).
1812	Slate road to Dinorwic built, commencing from head of creek.
1824	Dinorwic Railway brought down to north side of creek; name 'Port Dinorwic' adopted.
1828	Two sets of lock gates (adjacent-in-line to each other) built to enable creek to take 200 ton ships.
c.1835	An inner dry dock built – appears on Tithe Map c.1840.
1838	Port now able to hold 30 ships.
1843	Horsepower replaces manpower on Port railway system.
1844	Lease of south side creek obtained from Crown for 31 years.
1849	Rees Jones brings shipbuilding business from Barmouth.
1850–2	Extension of sea wall at new Garddfon Quay 'where ballast is deposited'. Old quay demolished.

1852	10 March: 'Private Branch' taken down to the Port. Dinorwic's railway stables demolished in process and rebuilt on new site at expense of C.&H.R.
1853–4	Outer basin begun with lease of southwest foreshore to extend the quays. New ferry slip built in consequence. Quays now lit by gas; lampposts bear 'D.Q. Dinorwic Foundry 1853'.
1856–7	'Private Branch' from 'Policeman's Hut' at Junction, now extended to full length of Port quays, beside 'New Basin' in form of loop.
1858	Premises now comprise New Basin (The Outer Harbour) and two tidal docks. Will hold 120 ships. Basin 480 ft × 156 ft; total length quays 1,060 ft. Patent Slip 220 ft × 18 ft with 74 ft cradle.
1863	Period 1856–63: annual average consigned by rail 11,273 tons: by sea 76,095 tons.
1871	Port extensions now nearing completion (and remain when finished much the same until 1897).[54]
1874	Port Dinorwic main line station moved to south, and opened.
1875	Lease extended for another 31 years; meanwhile a pier built on a sub-lease of the 1844 Agreement (further leases 1906 and 1935).
1877	Standard-gauge branch; extended running-round loop on quay.
1879	Extensions to existing lease in respect of foreshore, landing stage, seawall (mainly minor developments).
1895	339 loaded ships left the Port (c.f. 764 in 1864 when ship capacity would be smaller).
1897–8	Thos. Ayres Ltd. replace tidal river mouth of Port with non-tidal outer lock making whole Inner Harbour independent of tides. Cast-iron intermediate double-span swing bridge replaced by single span liftbridge.
1905	New outer seawalls completed; infilled to form westward extension of quays on southwest between basin and harbour mouth, beyond outer lock gates. Quays widened on south shore and narrowed on north side. New stacking area formed on westward point of harbour. (Rebuilding causes considerable obstruction to loading during period.) Steam locomotives introduced on the quays but some horsework continues for several years. Appeal not to pay Caernarvon Harbour dues dismissed.

From earliest times the Port Pilot was engaged to charter ships to load slates, but in the early 1890s the Company began to build its own fleet of steel-hulled steam screw steamers. There were at first four ships, but VAYNOL was lost in 1902 so three vessels survived throughout the greater part of the steamship period. In more recent times second-hand steamers were obtained cheaply and renamed until ultimately, in the early 1950s (and after some had been laid up at Port Dinorwic out of use) they were sold off. All were steamers save DAWLISH and ALFRED MASON, and all registered at Caernarvon. During a general fall-off in slate business in the early 1920s, the ships went into general coasting. VELINHELI was built to supply the Company's depots at Preston, Runcorn and Liverpool, and Irish ports such as Newry; at Liverpool she could discharge directly into oceangoing ships, and made about three trips weekly from Port Dinorwic. The Company's flagship ELIDIR was built for voyages round the north of Scotland and down the east coast, for which her hull was specially built to prevent twisting in heavy seas. All ship repairs were done at the Port. Funnels were painted stone colour with black tops, hulls and deckworks were grey, and red below the waterline. The Company's totem was the letters DQ (overlapped), one in red and the other in black, on the funnel.

Lighters used at the Port were quarry-owned.

The slate boats' skippers were always renowned for their disregard of bad weather, and when the packet steamers were mid-channel *en route* for Ireland they often might see a small ship plunging about in a wild sea ahead of them on its way to Dublin with a slate cargo; it could well be the only other ship they would see under such conditions. 'There goes a Dinorwic ship!' they would say, admiring the grit of skipper and crew in such foul weather. Little did they know that with the manager's office looking directly down on to vessels in the port at Dinorwic, it was more than the Captain's worth to linger there after loading . . . no matter the weather!

The Dry Dock Co. carried out locomotive repairs for the quarry and local shipowners perhaps from Connah's Quay and Liverpool. The dry dock could accept coasters up to about 160 ft long.

Tradition has it that the non-tidal area was built with the intention of avoiding payment of Carnarvon Harbour Trust dues – but without success!

In earlier times ships ballast was dumped on the foreshore and men with barrows were paid to wheel it down towards the Straits and prevent a build-up at the harbour mouth. Later, coal from Point of Ayr colliery would come in as ballast, be unloaded by the steam crane's bucket into road carts (later lorries) and taken to Gilfach-Ddu coal yard without touching the Padarn Railway at all. It may have been considered too pilferable if carried by open wagon! Coaling Padarn Railway engines was done at Gilfach-Ddu; three box wagons per train would be trundled from the coal yard, along the raised platform behind the transfer dock and so into yet another walled yard where it was kept under lock and key until loaded into engine bunkers.

Ships calling at ports where building materials were available might return with stone as ballast; in this way Terfin Terrace in Bangor Street, Port Dinorwic, was built in Aberdeen granite.

The Union Jack always flew from 'the staff at the Pier Head at the Port'.

As to the Port railway system, it seems that access was at first from the north shore, as early maps show the track there with a branch coming over the creek to the south shore by an intermediate bridge. In May 1848 the accounts refer to 'iron bars for railway at Port' supplied by Richard Davies & Sons, Menai Bridge, probably for extending the system on the south bank. There was no quayside loading of ships at this time, the slates being put into lighters and taken for re-loading into ships lying in the Straits; one horse was then doing duty as motive power; it cost 5/- to 12/- per month to supply oats or bran for it, in addition to hay (£4 18s. 0d. per month) and there were many additional expenses 'for work done at the gear of the Horses at the Port'. Ellis Thomas was paid 2/4d. 'Bill for medicine had for the Horses at the Port'. By 1850 the accounts write of 'horses' and also of troubles when ships left Dinorwic but were blown ashore at Beaumaris and had to have cargoes taken off and re-loaded by 'flats' i.e. broad flat-bottomed craft used in shallow waters, especially in and around the Mersey. The second horse cost £25: 'Owen Roberts – paid by him for a strong Horse purchased for drawing the Waggons at the Port'. The horses were not a cheap form of locomotion and the expenses incurred in vetches, grass, oats, candles for the stable, together with 'gears' (i.e. harness etc.) not to mention paying 'for one of the Quay Horses grazing in the Park' (March 1853) were considerable (the Park would be Vaynol).

These early accounts survive to October 1858, and there is a monthly sum of £371 3s. 5d. paid in Port wages for men shipping and stowing slates, and unloading wagons; also carpenters, sawyers, labourers etc.; in that October 725 tons were 'let down the Port incline' for which the operators were paid ¾d. per ton (£22 13s. 4½d.) Slates that did not leave by sea were carted (by contract) to Bangor station from February 1849 until July 1852 when the Port acquired its own standard gauge siding.

Evidence of prudent management comes in 1850 when 'a wooden cottage' was purchased from the Railway at Bangor 'to be fixed up at the further end of the New Quay . . . for a man to live in to prevent any trespass being done on the Quay'; this cost a lavish £3 16s. 0d.! However, there is evidence of consideration for the workmen when coal is supplied to the quay offices 'and the place where the men have their meals' (this a cottage rented at fifteen shillings a half year).

Such was the attraction of slate tonnages from the Port that the Chester & Holyhead Railway's original intention was to extend a branch from Bangor to Port Dinorwic and terminate on the quay there. However, when the Bangor & Carnarvon Railway Act was passed (20th May, 1851) the line had been extended further to Caernarvon, and the Chester & Holyhead authorised to work it. This alteration may have been due to the influence of the L.N.W.R.'s interest on the Board of the C.&H.R. The Caernarvon extension (9 miles) was opened on 1st July, 1852, but a branch down to the Port ('The Private Branch') had been built at Assheton-Smith's personal expense and began to carry slate traffic from 10th March, 1852.

There was also a wooden auxiliary ketch TRYFAN built by Robert Jones, Rhyl (66 gross tons) launched March 1875 for Robert J. Parry & Others, of Flint. It was acquired on 29th October, 1927 but its period of use is not known. Ultimately broken up; a curious purchase at that date!

Name as operated	Gross tonnage	Period operated	Dimensions (feet)		Builder	Date	Disposal	Note No.
DINORWIC	276	1892–1919	128	× 23 × 10.4	S. McKnight & Co. Ltd., Ayr	Jan. 1892	Sold 1919	1
VELINHELI	126	1894–1941	95	× 18.5 × 7.5	" "	Mar.1892	Sold 1941	2
VAYNOL	233	1892–1902	129	× 22 × 7.7	" "	Dec. 1892	Sunk Oct. 1902	3
ENID	267	1903–1954	131.5	× 22.3 × 7.8	Ailsa Shipbuilding Co. Ltd., Ayr	Aug.1903	Sold July 1954	4
ELIDIR	423	1903–1942	151.6	× 25.1 × 9.9	" "	Oct. 1903	Sold 1942	5
JULIET DUFF	538	1946–1955	163.8	× 25.8 × 10.8	Gebroeder Boot, Liederdorp	1920	Sold 1955	6
DAWLISH	248	1945–1953	130.7	× 23.6 × 8.5	A. Vuijk & Zonen, Capelle	Oct. 1937	Sold 1953	7
VERONICA TENNANT	397	1946–1954	142	× 24.1 × 10.6	Mistley Shipbuilding & Repairing Co., Mistley	Aug.1928	Sold 1954	8
ALFRED MASON	305	1946–1954	127	× 23.6 × 10.4	I.J. Abdela & Mitchell Ltd., Queensferry, N. Wales	Nov.1919	Sold 1954	9
JOSEPH MITCHELL	650	1947–1950	176	× 27.6 × 11.8	C.H. Walker & Co., Sudbrook	Mar. 1918	Sunk Feb. 1950	10

Ships were owned by Duff, Herbert & Mitchell Ltd. (Liverpool & London) from c.1944–1953, thereafter passing to Dinorwic Quarries' ownership. During former time, they were mortgaged to Coutts & Co.

Among other chartered ships using Port Dinorwic and carrying regular cargoes of slate (1920–1930 period) were HARLAW PLAIN and LADY CAROLINE ('Bygone Port Dinorwic' R. W. Roberts: CARNARVON & DENBIGH HERALD 1965–66.)

NOTES

(1) Traditionally reputed to have had double purpose as a private vessel for Assheton-Smith, but this lacks confirmation.
(2) Ordered by Quarry as VELINHELI but reputed to have been rejected as not conforming to specification. Completed for F.M. Allan of Glasgow as DUNLOSSIT, and bought cheaply in 1894 acquiring intended name. Sail-assisted as built;* similar to Scottish 'Pufer' but 30 ft longer.
(3) Sunk in collision off Mull of Galloway whilst returning to Port Dinorwic in ballast. Was among ships to use Manchester Ship Canal on Opening Day, 1st January, 1894.
(4) Lying idle at Port Dinorwic, 1951; uninsured.
(5) Sold due to fall-off in trade: Company's flag-ship.
(6) Purchased as BARANDA; said to have carried the name LADY CAROLINE at Port Dinorwic for short time. Laid off by 1953.
(7) Purchased as DAWLISH and name retained. Reputed to have never traded from Port Dinorwic.
(8) Purchased as IPSWICH TRADER. Hull later lengthened to 161.2 ft: gross tonnage 484 (1935).
(9) Purchased as WARITA.
(10) Purchased as LINCOLNBROOK.

*First five ships probably carried sails to assist.

Ship list and notes based on Lloyd's Registers, Gwynedd Archives' records, and information from W.H. Roberts (Port Dinorwic). Dr. C.V. Waine, and part of a manuscript by Roy Fenton – to be published in due course.

REFERENCES

1. This and other tales may be found in THE REMINISCENCES OF THE LIFE OF THE LATE THOMAS ASSHETON-SMITH *Sir J.E. Eardley-Wilmot* (2nd Edition; 1860) and MEMOIRS OF SIR L.L. TURNER *Edited by J.E. Vincent* (1902).
2. A slate boat has been recovered from Llyn Padarn.
3. See account in CARNARVON & DENBIGH HERALD May 1873.
4. The TRANSACTIONS OF THE CAERNARVONSHIRE HISTORICAL SOCIETY, *J.S. Illsley* (Vol. 40, p.87 on etc.) contains additional evidence of early lake transport, but there is an assumption (which fieldwork does not support) that this early incline fell to the north-east shore of Llyn Padarn – below Allt-Wen – to Cei-Newydd. There is no evidence for this. The same article explains that the boat transport took slate for Caernarvon to Cwm-y-Glo for storage, and to Pen-y-Llyn for Aber-Pwll. (In 1791 Caernarvon shipped 2½ million Dinorwic slates . . . Some researchers maintain boatage was once made down-river right into that town.)
5. TOUR OF NORTH WALES *Rev. W. Bingley* (2nd Edit. 1804).
6. The boat recovered from Llyn Padarn is on display at the North Wales Quarrying Museum, Llanberis: Thomas Wright had boat-crews on his payroll from December 1787.
7. Wire ropes did not become widespread in North Wales before 1860.
8. Horses were bought from Anglesey, the Conway Valley and even Knutsford, Cheshire; average cost £10.
9. CANRIF Y CHWARELWR *Emyr Jones*. (1964.)
10. It is also possible to link this site as belonging to The Dinorwic Slate Co.'s Allt-Ddu to Cei-Newydd system of 1789, whereby a line might have led off their incline along this earthwork, and at this point fell to the water's edge by another incline. The ground is suitable for such an arrangement but the idea is not proven.
11. Such an incline would even then have been an old idea – it was a proposal of 1788 to connect Allt-Ddu with Padarn by an incline down the side of Allt-Ddu (see TRANSACTIONS, CAERNARVONSHIRE HISTORICAL SOCIETY, Vol. 40, p.93). It is often suggested that the 4 ft gauge incline which descended in two stages from Chwarel-Fawr Level (originally a water-balance) formed the first two incline stages of this Allt-Ddu – Bedw-Argoed scheme; its upper stage became disused by September 1904 but the ropes of the lower were then renewed – and again later – the work being electrified before 1935.
12. Documents made available by Gwynedd Archives but not as yet available for general search.
13. A measurement found elsewhere, e.g. The Middleton Railway (or Brandling's Railroad) Leeds – given as 4' or 4' 1" in 1829. (D.C. Carrington suggests this may have been deliberate so as to prevent a 'standard-gauge' link-up!)
14. The first four hearths to build a roundary were installed in 1870 – before then the blacksmiths took portable hearths up into the Quarry.
15. 'Rubbish heap . . . projects far into the lake . . . threatens to reach the opposite shore . . . is terribly destructive of the picturesque . . .' (*Eardley-Wilmot*, p.98).
16. Marchlyn had begun in 1931, but was not continued.
17. U.C.N.W. Bangor Ms 8702.
18. C.C.R.O. Glynllifon 66393.
19. RAILWAY MAGAZINE Vol. 120 p.381 mentions a main stable at Pen-y-Bwlch (near Bigil) but there is no reference to this in the accounts.
20. The Plans suggest the original access to this mill was by a clockwise encircling branch from Allt-Ddu lip.
21. RAILWAYS IN ENGLAND 1826–7 *Carl Von Oeynhausen & Heinrich Von Dechen* (Berlin 1829) p.57–8 etc.
22. PANORAMA OF THE BEAUTIES, CURIOSITIES, AND ANTIQUARIES OF NORTH WALES *J. Hemingway* (1835).
23. The present-day Container Train owes its origins to this system, which was not novel to the Padarn Railway. Early prints of such passenger railways as the Liverpool & Manchester show the carriages of the gentry being carried on flat trucks – their passengers remaining in their own carriages – and The Railway Museum at York displays a model of wagons from the same Railway carrying interchange tubs for the canal, two mounted crosswise per wagon. At this date (1838) the Railway was discontinuing the transport of such canal tubs as uneconomic.
24. Perhaps the 'shaft' shown on the 1888 O.S. 25" survey? There is further reference to sinking a shaft here in 1842 'to expedite work'.
25. *Eardley-Wilmot* describes it 'a small gurgling stream connects the two sheets of water'. (p.96).
26. Latterly 12 ft × 9 ft high.

27. The last chain in use had longer links and only one was cut out annually.
28. This and other information from a portfolio on Port Dinorwic at Gwynedd Archives.
29. Now in The Narrow Gauge Railway Museum, Tywyn.
30. Turntables existed before 1850 and a replacement was put in here in that year, and yet another in 1853!!
31. A proposed standard-gauge railway linking Bangor and Bethesda in both 1863–5 and post-1884 would have crossed the Padarn Railway hereabouts. (C.C.R.O. XG/Maps/14).
32. Latterly the Guard's Van transporter was turned – if required – by lifting on a gantry!
33. COF LYFR. *Gruffydd Ellis.* [U.C.N.W. Bangor 8277].
34. Over the years there were no less than four guards of the name of Roberts – all from the Port Dinorwic area to suit their working base.
35. 7/6d. per month for the full journey to Pen-Scoins.
36. From December, 1891 the empties 'run' was stopped at Gilfach-Ddu gate (under the arch) and chain-hauled therefrom.
37. LOCOMOTIVE MAGAZINE February 1905, p.22: RAILWAY MAGAZINE August 1974, p.383.
38. The Penrhyn Castle Industrial Railway Museum Handbook (Pub. National Trust) has extended technical detail.
39. AMALTHAEA took its name from that of the junior satellite of Jupiter, first discovered in 1892.
40. Of the Hunslet engines, DINORWIC was always preferred by the men; it was the first to be delivered and the last in service. When first delivered it had no steam brake whereas the later engines had a Hunslet fitting. The Workshops designed and fitted a brake of their own to DINORWIC, which was found greatly superior to the Leeds version!
41. Between 30–35 appear in the Saturday train photograph of the early 1890s – not very manoeuvrable!
42. An old-established cycle manufacturing firm in Glasgow (once also making sewing machines) in its fourth title.
43. BERNSTEIN and COVERTCOAT were virtually a class on their own, having fully-squared frames and kidney-shaped buffing plates. Although nominally of 'Alice' class, they foreshadowed the later 'Port' class.
44. It was first noted by the author under repair at the Dry Dock in June 1949 carrying a plate '6. No. 70' but had not then been in use.
45. Noted by the author sheeted-over on Dinorwic Quay in June 1949 – identifiable by 'A 2071' stamped on regulator handle.
46. Rev. Thomas suggests MAID MARION carried the name COVERTCOAT in 1912–13.
47. SLATES TO VELINHELI p.28.
48. I am indebted to Eric Foulkes for this reference.
49. See also THE ENGINEER (advert) 5th November, 1875 concerning an 0–4–2 front and well tank with valve gear worked from the leading axle 'narrow gauge, for mineral traffic, cylinders 9 ins. × 18 ins.'. Also STEPHEN LEWIN & THE POOLE FOUNDRY *Wear & Lees* p.43.
50. Probably referring to the balancing wagon-loads of slates size 18 in. × 10 in.
51. A wagon load of 'Best' slates 24 in. × 14 in. ('Princess' size) would comprise about 500 slates – together with the weight of the wagon this would average 2 tons (wagons tared slightly more than 7 cwt. each).
52. They had supplied a number in October 1896 for £3 10s. 0d. but only made a profit of 7/- on each.
53. Before the incline was electrified, the drum could be manually operated to allow the trolleys to pass over the 'summit'.
54. U.C.N.W. Lligwy Papers p.305–10.

PART 7
THE GREAT ORME TRAMWAY & TRAMROAD

Gauge 3 ft 6 in.

Authorised under Tramways Act 1870 as

THE GREAT ORME TRAMWAYS COMPANY

ACT:	61 V.C. XXVII	(23rd May, 1898)	Incorporation Great Orme Tramway
ORDER:		(24th July, 1933)	Winding up Great Orme Tramway
ORDER:		(13th March, 1935)	Assets to Great Orme Railway Ltd.
ORDER:	to temporarily increase charges in 1934		Ceased 31st December, 1935
ASSIGNMENT:		(30th March, 1935)	Powers G.O.T. to G.O.R.
ORDER:	26 Geo.V. & 1 Edw.VIII	(30th March, 1936)	Rates & Charges

Opening:	Lower Section	31st July, 1902	Length: 872 yds.
Opening:	Upper Section	8th July, 1903	Length: 827 yds.

Total route mileage: 1.05 single + 0.06 double = 1.11. (Total length (originally) was officially 1,706 yards.)

Summit height: 637 ft above sea level

Steepest gradient: 1 in 3.6 (near Black Gate)

Sharpest curve: 75 ft radius (near Black Gate)

Registered Office: Victoria Station, Church Walks, Llandudno

Original Capital: £25,000 in £5 shares and £6,250 borrowing powers (No debentures permitted).

GREAT ORME TRAMWAY

History: Equipment

Llandudno was created out of a village by the late Hon. E.M.L. Mostyn M.P. during the middle of the nineteenth century; it is the newest and best known of the resorts along the north coast of Wales. Northward of it the sea is contained in a large bay flanked each side by prominent sentry-like headlands of carboniferous limestone; the Great Orme (larger and higher) stands to the west, and the Little Orme to the east; the town clusters beneath the landward side of the former and straggles eastwards towards the latter, thinning out as it does so.

Running from west to east through the area was (until 1956) an electric tramway, the Llandudno & Colwyn Bay Electric Railway Co. Ltd., a useful and much-loved transport feature of the district. Such is the nature of things that whilst this conventional electric tramway has disappeared, a cable-operated railway to the top of the Great Orme has survived . . . that it does so is a reflection of the popularity of a headland whose summit (679 ft above sea level) draws thousands in the summer. It is a smaller version of the district's Snowdon Mountain Railway of the same period; both aim to take the tourist 'effortlessly to the top' (in the phrase of their birth time).

The history of the island-like Great Orme precedes that of Llandudno itself by hundreds of years. It was inhabited in the Stone Age and has been mined for copper and lead with their attendant narrow gauge tramways, quarried for stone and was a seat of early religious cults.[1] For years access to its upper levels was by means of 'a long and difficult path' and later by rough trackways, all very steep. As Llandudno was developing there were moves to attract more business by constructing a funicular or cable railway to the summit of the Great Orme; it would encourage new building round the foot of the hill, serve existing residents there and attract tourists in its own right. Fortunately the landowner, Lord Mostyn, was more amenable to such ideas than was Assheton-Smith over the matter of a railway up Snowdon.

In September 1894 H. Enfield Taylor of 15 Newgate Street, Chester, submitted a scheme for an Orme tramway under the Tramways Act 1870 to the Works Committee of Llandudno U.D.C.; this would have run from near the Pier Head and climbed the Orme to a point below and northeast of the summit, but it would have involved a reversing point at about one-quarter of the distance. Again, in December 1895, Taylor submitted an alternative scheme to the Committee, this time avoiding the reversal, and terminating near the quarries some way beyond the existing Halfway station; here it was at some disadvantage, being short of and below the summit. The present course embodies part of both these suggested routes.

(Henry Enfield Taylor deserves more than passing mention, being a small but interesting character in the railway business. By profession a Mining Engineer, he had a small works at 15 Newgate Street, Chester and from 1877 to about 1885 he built four-coupled side tank locomotives for the 3ft 6ins. gauge railway at Swanscombe Works, operated by John Bazley White & Bros. and, for that time, having an antiquated appearance resembling the products of Lewin at Poole. It is a coincidence that the Orme Tramway, the last of his assignments, should be also of this gauge.)

A four-mile carriage road some way above the high tide mark had been made round the foot of the Orme in 1878, superceding Reginald Cust's Path of 1856–8; this work was done under the auspices of the Great Orme's Head Marine Drive Co. Ltd with a capital of £14,000 (an

Act for the purpose was obtained 7th July, 1873) and commenced in 1875. Underlining the local authority's interest in enterprises likely to operate to its benefit, the Urban Council bought the Drive for £10,500 under the Llandudno U.D.C. Act of 6th August, 1897, and in autumn 1901 proposed an electric tramway along its course – this move was defeated by heavy opposition, the ratepayers objecting to the estimated cost of £30,000; in 1930 the pedestrian toll was abolished.[2]

In November 1895 the Works Committee of Llandudno U.D.C. had another proposal put before them by Kincaid, Weller & Manville of London, S.W. for an electric tramway embracing the whole length of the Drive and completing its circuit of the Orme by means of Gloddaeth Avenue along its south flank. From this circling of the headland branches struck out at its southernmost corners to serve Deganwy station on the west and Llandudno station on the east. None of these schemes had come to life when 'THE LONDON GAZETTE' of 23rd November, 1897 gave notice of an intention to apply for an Act of Parliament to build a 'Great Orme Tramway & Tramroad' being:

> A Tramway, work No. 1, from a yard adjoining the Old road at Victoria House to a point in a field adjacent to Pen-y-Mynydd Farm (length 3 furlongs 6 chains)
> . A Tramroad, work No. 2, from the above to a point 110 yards southwest of the building known as the 'Telegraph' Beer House . . . near the summit of Great Ormeshead (length 4 furlongs 0.8 chains)

[The spelling and phraseology are as used in the Notice and the 'Telegraph' referred to the use of the summit as a Semaphore Station for shipping.]

The Notice continued:

> the gauge would be '3 feet six inches . . . and it is not proposed to run thereon carriages or trucks adapted for use on railways'.

There was limited opposition to the Bill and certain apprehensions of Lord Mostyn, Llandudno Urban District Council and the National Telephone Co. were voiced. Douglas H. Coghill (member for Stoke-on-Trent) moved that the Second Reading be deferred for six months, saying 'there is not the least necessity for this tramway . . . which if made must seriously affect the prosperity of the town of Llandudno . . . (which) does not want any such tramway or railway'. He suggested that only a small number of townspeople was interested, and this was true enough but businessmen who used the town as a dormitory and commuted regularly to cities like Liverpool and Manchester brought their energies to bear locally after engaging Messrs Wood & Fowler, Liverpool (Consulting Engineers) to report on the feasibility of a Great Orme cable line. Coghill went on to complain that the tramway, if laid along the road to the summit, would block the only route to the town's cemetery (the sub-section meeting this complaint says: 'The Company shall make provision for the conveyance at a reasonable and fixed charge, and in a decent and seemly manner, of corpses for interment in the St. Tudno Cemetery'); he asked the Commons to reflect "How can an ordinary funeral, where the hearse is drawn by horses, go up a narrow road alongside of which there is a tramway . . .? No horse would face it under such conditions . . . if . . . it is proposed to take corpses . . . by this tramway . . . how unseemly to have a funeral procession mixed up with the ordinary holiday traffic." He concluded by suggesting the line would be the means for speculative builders to convey material for, and cover the slopes of the hill with, new houses. The House permitted a week's deferment, and there were no more objections.

A Private Act was obtained on 23rd May, 1898 (61 Vic. Cap. XXVII) which related the undertaking to the Tramways Act of 1870, and the Railway Clauses Consolidation Act of 1845 relating to mines lying under or near the railway; 'mechanical power' would not include steam or animal power; the Company would be entitled 'The Great Orme Tramways Company' with a capital of £25,000 in £5 shares together with £6,250 in borrowing powers; debentures could not be created. Section 13 foresaw there might be a compulsory sale to the local authority, Section 21 gave the Company two years for the compulsory purchase of land and Section 25 three years for the completion of the work. It was relieved of Section 34 of the Tramways Act 'as limits the extent of the carriage used on any tramway beyond the outer edge of the wheels of such carriage shall not apply to carriages used on the tramways' . . . and might build a hotel at the summit in addition to the customary buildings necessary for the purpose of the undertaking. A fare not exceeding sixpence (single) and ninepence (return) might be levied, nor could fares be raised on Sundays or Public Holidays. (These fares were subsequently increased).

The line might carry goods, minerals and parcels, but not animals; nor could railway vehicles be used. After a period of 28 years the Llandudno U.D.C. might purchase the undertaking on terms, and if dividends reached a certain level the Council could require the Company to maintain a service for eight months in a year if they were not already providing one. Further, if dividends rose higher still, they might be obliged to operate for the full twelve months. Trams were to be run for workmen every day (Christmas Day, Good Friday and Sundays excepted) on days when public services were operating. These must be at times to suit the Council and at a fare of 1/6d. per week for each man. Before Sunday services could be introduced, the Council had to give approval. Alterations were to be made to some roads; the cars to be lit front and rear after sunset, and there were restrictions on carrying advertisements on the cars. In these and other ways the local authority protected itself besides securing a future opportunity to acquire the undertaking. Lord Mostyn was protected in that he had to approve the design of, and materials for, buildings and that no furnace or chimney might be put up near the town. The aforementioned facilities for funerals to the Orme's graveyard were offered. Cuttings and embankments were to be turfed and finished to Mostyn's satisfaction, and the effect of the clause concerning chimneys and buildings was that the winding gear and house had to be situated some distance up the Orme, and in earlier times when the plant was steam driven, fuel had to be taken up to the boiler house by rail.

The idea of a cable tramway is reputed to have been brought to Britain by Job Smith, a townsman of Matlock in Derbyshire who seeing cable trams in San Francisco in 1862, tried to interest his influential fellow townspeople to build such a tramway. Smith had returned home in 1868, but it was 1890 before Mr (later Sir) George Newnes, M.P. – a native of Matlock Bath – was interested in the proposal and when the Matlock Cable Tramway Co. Ltd. was formed, the undertaking was financed largely by Newnes himself. The tramway opened on 28th March, 1893 and closed on 30th September, 1927. For reasons which need not concern us here, Newnes bought out his fellow shareholders by Agreement of 26th June, 1898 and the undertaking was literally handed over as a gift to the local authority in the following November. With its gradient of 1 in 5½ it was described as 'possibly the steepest tramway of any sort in existence'. Matlock became the first municipal authority to operate a cable tramway and Llandudno watched this point with interest. The gauge was 3 ft 6 in. (the same as that proposed for the Orme) and Job Smith was its first Managing Director; it was the first cable tram to operate in England, and also the shortest.[3]

Back in Llandudno, construction began at the foot of the line in April 1901, the intervening time being spent on raising money – a very slow process – and buying land. For a sum of £8,075 Richard White & Sons of Widnes, who had recently been associated with the supply of trackwork for the Snowdon rack railway, were to supply rails, rolling stock, plant and machinery for the Orme line; they were to work under the Company's Engineer, H. Enfield Taylor, who has already been noticed. White's subcontracted for £3,133 12s. 3d. to Thomas and John Owen of Llandudno (builders) for much of the civil engineering work; John Owen was a local councillor and both Owens had always keenly backed the project. They were to work together under A.R. Ellison of Messrs Wood & Fowler, who would have overall supervision. Cables were to be supplied by the St. Helen's Cable Co. Ltd.; they had a working load of 4 tons and breaking load of 62 tons. Although White's were said to be supplying rolling stock, in the event Hurst, Nelson & Co. Ltd. of Motherwell did so; all this was to lead to much bitterness between the interested parties.

At the time Old Road was little more than an alley, and on 10th April had to be closed to other traffic whilst tracklaying went forward. Under the terms of the Act, the alleyway was duly widened and by June 1901 the Owens had reached Ty Gwyn Road, which also had to be widened, and the tram tracks were placed on a raised causeway on the east side of

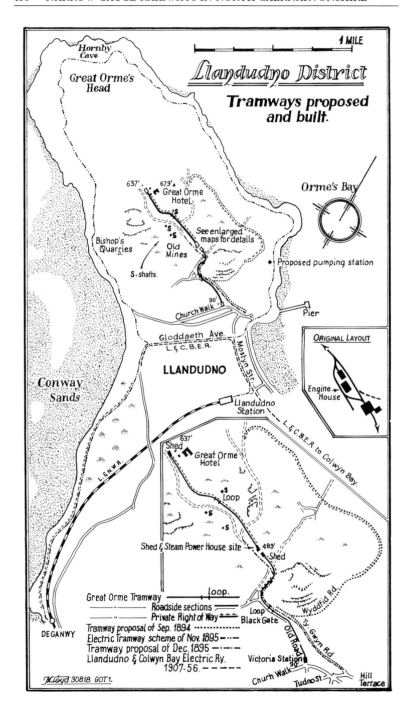

Hornby Cave

Great Orme's Head

1 MILE

Llandudno District

Tramways proposed and built.

637'   679'▲
Great Orme Hotel
·S

·S ·S
See enlarged maps for details

Bishop's Quarries
Old Mines

S·shafts.

Orme's Bay

♦ Proposed pumping station

90'
Church Walk
Pier

Gloddaeth Ave.
L.& C.B.E.R.

LLANDUDNO

Conway Sands

Llandudno Station

Mostyn Str.

L.& C.B.E.R to Colwyn Bay.

ORIGINAL LAYOUT

Engine→ House

637'
Shed
Great Orme Hotel

·S
Loop
·S
·S

L.& N.W.R.

Shed & Steam Power House site
489'
Shed

Great Orme Tramway
———"——— Roadside sections
———"——— Private. Right of Way
Tramway proposal of Sep. 1894 ············
Electric Tramway scheme of Nov. 1895 —··—
Tramway proposal of Dec. 1895 —·—·—
Llandudno & Colwyn Bay Electric Ry.
1907-56. — — — —

DEGANWY

Loop.

Loop
Black Gate

Wyddfid Rd.

Old Road
Gwyn Rd.

Victoria Station
90'
Church Walk
Tudno St.
Hill Terrace

JCLloyd 30818. GOT1.

it; in the intervening weeks it was put about that shortage of funds made it prudent they should suspend work until the following year, but this does not seem to have been upheld, although misleadingly Taylor had told the August 1901 shareholders' meeting that 'all should be ready for running this autumn'. Behind the scenes trouble between Engineer and contractors, mainly concerning rails and rolling stock, prevented the Chairman's forecast of a May 1902 opening taking place. The Chairman had also hoped that with Lord Mostyn's influence, someone notable might perform the ceremony (the Prince of Wales was cited) but it was found that all such persons were more occupied with the forthcoming Coronation and no one could be found.

So rather than dwell on those optimistic hopes, it is prudent to return to affairs as they stood. As early as 29th May, 1901 Taylor and White were 'in difficulty . . . with reference to the rail being used' and the minutes refer to a 'difference of opinion between Mr White (and Mr Taylor) as to the style of rail' . . . 'we again warn our Engineer to take all reasonable steps to have the railway constructed with every provision for safety for which the Directors consider him responsible'. There is reference to White having supplied 'grooved rails' which the Board of Trade supported Taylor in condemning (and among the drawings are some involving them, or a mixture of grooved and flat-bottomed rails) and that they were awaiting instructions from Taylor regarding extra work and payment for 'angle bars' in lieu of the grooved rails. The Directors, in desperation, appointed Mr. Cotterill, Engineer of the Liverpool Overhead Railway, to arbitrate.

August 1901 brought an instruction from the Board for Taylor to test the line 'with trucks', such trucks to 'be useful after', (at this stage in the minutes it is not clear what was meant by a 'truck' but it evolves later that it was the four-wheeled goods tram or jockey car, a creation of Taylor's[4]) but the test was not carried out as there was delay in obtaining rails to lay track beyond Llwyn-Faen. Also, Taylor complained 'the cars were not in as forward state as they should be' and in Tabor Road, the Owens had laid the track over the gas and water mains and given them no access! Later that month the Owens agreed they would ballast the Upper Section . . . at that time little more than a future dream.

Such was the trickle of funds that by October 1901 there were negligible resources to pay White, but at the eleventh hour the National Provincial Bank agreed to an overdraft of £5,000 secured by four Directors and Thomas Owen. There was then another bitter argument between Taylor and White, with the complaint that the latter was using untreated sleepers. Inevitably White fell foul of the local residents for allowing work to be done on Sundays . . . and so 1901 became 1902 and White's men were still at work on 22nd April. So it was May before the first cable was dragged up to the winding house site by a team of twelve horses, and on 12th May this was lowered into the conduit and a single car – presumably one of the small four-wheeled 'trucks' or jockey cars – was pulled up to the top of the section.

Here it had to rest until the second cable was laid on 30th May and tests could take place. There must have been some last minute hitch over the stock, as on 29th April it had been reported that 'two passenger cars and two jockey cars . . . were ready at Motherwell but Mr Taylor declined to go and inspect them'. By 6th May two jockey cars had arrived at Llandudno station 'but White's men had not yet removed them'. Taylor also stated on the same day that 'White's men had not been in a fit condition to go on with the work and hence the delay in getting the cars on the line'.

The Board of Trade sent Colonel Von Donop to inspect the Lower Section on 30th July, 1902, and after conducting emergency brake tests he came away satisfied; the Company, not wishing to lose any chance of income, opened the line for traffic the following day. (The B.O.T. must have had previous knowledge of the line, as their inspector, Colonel Yorke, had written in 1901 'this most dangerous tramway' and in June, 'I confess I regard this tramway with apprehension'.) There was little ceremony, but the Town Band was hurriedly assembled and blew 'God Save the King' as the first tram left the lower terminus. Sir George Newnes, with his close association with cable trams, had been asked to come and 'do the honours', but declined.

Initially, the staff consisted of 1 station master, 6 conductors and 1 stationary-engine driver – the bye-laws of the Liverpool Overhead Railway were used as a model. The necessary power plant had had to be installed before the Lower Section track was complete to the winding house site, and to enable counter-balance working and brake tests to take place before the B.O.T. inspection. Two boilers (which had been delivered by rail to Llandudno station) were taken up to the site on trolleys drawn by steam traction engine; the steepest portion of road-way was of such severity that the engine ran forward and having anchored, drew up each trolley on the traction engine winch by cable. This was some time later than August 1901, at which date no work had begun on the engine house. Von Donop imposed a speed limit of 4 m.p.h.

Fortunately the line was an instant success, and after a first timetable 15 minute-interval service, traffic was kept in being until 3rd January, 1903. Fares were '3d. to the Plateau', 6d. to the Top (not yet open of course) and 9d. return from the Top . . . the names are taken from contemporary spellings. Services might have continued into January 1903, but some repairs were necessary and attention needed to be paid to completing the Upper Section: it was intended to re-open at Easter 1903. As to this upper line, shareholders had been told way back in August 1901 that earthworks 'were in a fair way towards completion', which was ambiguous enough, but it was thirteen months later before work was sufficiently advanced to test it. Trials on 11th September,

1902 had been unsuccessful, and Taylor condemned the rope tension-
ing gear designed by Fowler and Musker, which had failed. On the
Lower Section too the cable pulleys were still inefficient, and White's
men had to adjust them each morning before traffic could begin; they
were considered to be too small with consequent excessive wear on the
rope. On the same section, the rails on the curves were badly worn and
the bogie frames of cars Nos. 4 and 5 were cracked; it was feared a
B.O.T. inspection of the Upper Section might condemn the Lower as
there was also criticism of the 'Zed' [sic] rails near the engine house and
the inefficient governing of the winding engines.

During October 1902 Von Donop was invited to make a statutory
inspection of the upper line, but a condition of his reply was that the
cars had to be worked over the section for three days before his visit –
clearly this was more than could be managed so the matter was allowed
to lapse. Next month there is a reference to delivery of a turntable built
by Warden & Sons; they had been asked to take it back as useless but
Wardens refused, saying it was made specially to the tramway order.

Problems between Engineer and contractors continued, and faulty
operation of the lower portion prompted the Board to ask G.C. Aitchison (then associated with the Snowdon Mountain Tramroad, North
Wales Narrow Gauge Railways and other local lines) to act as
intermediary. Aitchison went to Chester to interview Taylor and
quoted a fee of 50 guineas to report on the lower line; by January 1903
the Board had had his report and in the following month it was
recommended that Taylor should be sacked. Aitchison was then called
to arbitrate between White's and the Company, and a compromise was
reached. The next month Taylor left the undertaking and Aitchison
was invited to take his place . . . a somewhat 'hot seat' as events were to
show. By April Aitchison was preparing drawings for sheds for the cars
and lavatories for the passengers: the pit of the engine house was to be
fenced and the upper winding wheel 'hutted'. Von Donop duly
inspected on 8th May and sent his report on 13th May; he did not fully
find matters to his liking and insisted on slipper brakes being fitted to
Upper Section cars, the position of the conductor's bell-push altered
and a speed indicator fitted in the engine house. He came again on 7th
July; being satisfied, services began on the next day, subject to the
4 m.p.h. speed limit.

The B.O.T. then put the Company into confusion by stating that
where the line left the roadway it was a 'Railway' not a 'Tramway' and
would be liable to Passenger Duty @ 5%.

On 10th October, 1903 the Board had to send a circular to shareholders appealing to them to increase their holdings and that £1,700 was
urgently required . . . 'there are a number of liabilities upon Capital
Account to be paid off'.

Problems were not all settled; the St. Helen's Cable Co. offered two
new cables at half price due to defects in the originals; White's enquired

if they could purchase the undertaking; and Taylor claimed for balance of money due to him. He was told that the claim against him for negligent handling of the construction of the line far outweighed any claim he had against the Company. There was then a nasty scene between the Board and Aitchison over his fee.

The upper portion, 3 furlongs 9.3 chains long, was more easily built than the lower, and free of roadway situations for the track. The lower half had opened in the previous Easter, so from early July the whole system, (albeit then and now being strictly two separate journeys divided by a change of car at the 'Plateau' or Halfway station), became operational. On the open hillside of the upper part, animals strayed on the track and Lord Mostyn backed up his rights and insisted on the line being fenced. However, other views prevailed and the line remains a hazard for sheep and cattle; the steepest portion of this section is 1 in 10.5, with an average of 1 in 15.5.

As completed the line was 1,706 yards long and its summit 637 feet above sea level; there were stated to be three passing places (one being that at Halfway station and therefore not a passing place in the accepted sense) otherwise the line was single. A ten-minute interval service using four cars was envisaged, each car being cable-hauled with a maximum speed of six m.p.h. (one car at each end of a separate cable on the Lower Section and two cars along one cable on the Upper Section). To some extent the weight of the descending car counter-balanced the ascending one, and was so arranged that cars passed each other at the intermediate loop on each section. The winding drums were worked by steam engine housed in a building, and the method of haulage effectively divided the line into two halves – the Lower Section was entitled The Great Orme Tramways, the Upper Section was The Great Orme Tramroad. Their construction differed.

The Lower Section starts on the site of the backyard of the former Victoria House, currently known as Victoria; from a junction of the Old Road and Plas Road it climbs the course of the Old Road to Ty Gwyn Road, following the latter to a site known as 'The Plateau' whence it reaches the Halfway station (489 ft above sea level). This lower length is notable for its steep gradients and curves, the steepest pitch being 1 in 3.6 (the B.O.T. report gives 1 in 4.3) but having an average climb of 1 in 6.6 overall. This section became the steepest cable tramway in the country. Minimum radius was 75 feet (the B.O.T. Report figure). On this lower portion the wire ropes run in conduit 14 in. deep and 6 in. wide (B.O.T. gives 18 in. × 5 in.) set between the rails; the conduit opened into inspection pits at each end of the section. Although resembling ordinary railway construction with stone pitching, concrete was used for the conduit and bed of the track. The upper part of the conduit had 'Z' steel rails, leaving a steel face 6 in. deep on either side with a slot 1¼ in. wide in the centre. As built, the conduit's side rails provided the bearing for the automatic emergency brake, whilst through the slot travelled the connection between the underframe of the bogie and wire rope; this was by means of a haulage lever and drawbar. In most other equipment of this period, cable-worked street cars only moved when the driver connected the car to the moving cable in a conduit, but here at the Orme the car moved permanently with the cable and its 'driver' was actually the winch-operator in the winding house.

The steel running rails were flat-bottomed, installed in 30 ft lengths weighing 50 lb. per yard, on longitudinal sleepers, secured by fang-bolts and dog spikes; the slot rails were in ½ in. steel with 6 in. web-plate, angle plates 3 in. × 3½ in. weighing 60 lb. per yard (though an 84 lb. had been approved earlier). Initially, steel tie rods 2½ in. × ⅜ in. were fixed between the rails at 6 ft intervals. All this was heavy construction for such comparatively light vehicles. The rails were rolled by Charles Cammel Ltd. of Workington, and pointwork was by Askham Bros & Wilson Ltd. of Sheffield. On the Lower Section a flangeway was formed by a 23 lb. per yard angle iron bolted to the longitudinal timbers set in concrete which held the running rails, on the inside of the running rail and forming a 1 in. groove. This arrangement was insisted upon by the Board of Trade as the Company had intended to use conventionally grooved tramway rails. (Today's rails are also 30 ft long, fishplated at joints.[5]) On this Lower Section the wire rope was supported inside the conduit by 12 in. diameter grooved steel sheaves and guided by vertical steel curve pulleys; the latter were 6 ft apart on curves. Inspection and lubrication of the grooved wheels was made through the lid of a box which contained each one.

Completely different was the Upper Section which was similar in finish to railway construction with wooden cross sleepers. The wire ropes were taken between the rails on both horizontal or vertical rollers and above ground level; there is no conduit. The rope was worked on the 'fore and aft' principle and all ropes were first supplied by the St. Helen's firm in 'Lang-lay' pattern from plough steel; the Lower ropes were 1¼ in. diameter with a breaking strain of 62 tons; the Upper of ⅞ in. diameter and a strain of 29½ tons. Each rope was half a mile long and with a car attached to each end of the rope the system of working a funicular railway was employed, the cars being used to balance one another and the winding plant providing the power and braking effect as either was needed. Contemporarily it was called the 'Tail Rope' system.

The simple stone-built winding and power house contained two sets of engines, winding drums and boilers. 'Boilers . . . are being con-structed at Newark' said the minutes, but Taylor doubted their suitability to do the work – a curious quotation if he himself was ultimately responsible for this part of the equipment; perhaps he had been overruled by both Fowler and Musker? Horizontal engines came from C. & A. Musker of Liverpool; there were two engines in each set and they were of 80 and 60 h.p. respectively, and had reversing gear and worked in opposite directions. The engines for the tramway section had cylinders 12 in. bore × 14 in. stroke; those for the tramroad 8 in. × 12 in. The winding drums were 5 ft 4 in. diameter and divided in the centre where a strap brake was fitted. Connections between engines and drums was by spur gearing with a gearing reduction of 4 to 1: all this machinery had been delivered to Llandudno railway station by November 1901 . . . far too soon it appeared! Taylor complained he had 'told White's many times' to keep it back.

From the beginning it was the Company's intention to work the Lower Section throughout the year (using the jockey cars in winter) and the Upper during the summer. They wished to promote light goods traffic, and hoped that the proximity of rail transport would encourage the nearby mines to re-open; consequently stock for both passenger and goods working was on order. The goods business must have been a disappointment for average receipts 1902–13 were only £14 12s. 0d.! The passenger stock comprised bogie cars, single-decked, and weighing about 6½ tons empty, having end platforms, and were 37 ft long over buffers, 7 ft 6 in. wide overall, 30 ft long inside the saloon which was of central gangway type with fixed transverse seats either side and arranged back to back except at the ends; the seats were of lath, for 48 persons (plus 12 standing). Access to the saloon was from the end platforms through a hinged door; the upper half of these doors and the upper end-quarters of the bodies were glazed; 'sun and rainproof curtains' were at first provided for the open sides but these proved most unsatisfactory and were removed. The oil lamps at opposite corners of the body served as both warning and interior lighting. At each end were wrought-iron buffers with 12 in. diameter heads fitted centrally; they were designed for link and pin coupling, and there were additional side safety chains. The cost of the stock was to be £2,000 payable in instalments of £400 per annum, the first to be paid twelve months after delivery of the cars. Bogie wheel-bases were 4 ft and wheels were 1 ft 9 in. diameter in cast steel on mild steel axles 3¾ in. diameter – the bogie side frames are still the originals with 'H.N. & Co. Ltd. G.O.T. 1901'[6] cast on the axlebox covers, and some retain an oval maker's plate.

As supplied, the four passenger cars (Nos. 4–7) had both wheel and slipper brakes. Nos. 4 and 5 used on the Lower Section had an automatic emergency brake fitted to each bogie. The wheel brakes took the form of cast-iron shoes to each wheel, worked from a handwheel on the end platform: the slipper or track brake had a contact face 12 in. × 4 in. and hung between each pair of wheels – it was worked from a second handwheel. The emergency or conduit brake was in the form of a double set of cam teeth normally sprung against the faces of the conduit and only drawn clear when the strain was taken off the haulage rope. If tensions slackened these teeth were forced against the conduit plates by strong springs . . . further, cams of eccentric outline in the linkage forced the brake more firmly against the conduit as the weight of the car (for instance) attempted to run away downgrade. Cars Nos. 6 and 7 used on the Upper Section had shoe and rail slipper (or sledge) brakes only; these have never been altered. The minutes suggest that had White's first intentions come to pass, the type of passenger car envisaged would have been quite different from those of the event. From the beginning the same cars have remained on their original sections – life guards are now fitted to the west side of the cars on the Lower Section only.

As to the jockey or goods cars, these have long remained something of a mystery: only three came to work on the line, carrying Nos. 1–3; each was mounted on a single four-wheeled truck and the conception of these cars is obscure, but the minutes hint that they were personal to Taylor. In November 1901 the Company's solicitors had written 'that Mr. Taylor had taken on himself the responsibility of ordering the makers to proceed with the jockey cars' and the umpire ruled that White & Son should have done so 'and must order them at once'. Hurst, Nelson complained that the position regarding White's was very unsatisfactory. A minute of 11th February, 1902 confirms Taylor had ordered 'four trucks totalling £138 . . . the Board . . . to ask him if they could manage with two only'; and 'it was decided to leave the colour of the cars to Mr. Taylor'. They were 16 ft 7 in. long over buffers, their bodies 9 ft long, 6 ft 10 in. wide and with end platforms 2 ft 6 in. long. Access to body was by inward opening doors in the body sides; total width of doors was 4 ft 6 in. In September 1902 it was decided to fit seats into two cars at a cost of £6 per car and to add two panes of glass to each side of these cars. The minutes (17th August, 1903) suggest that only two cars were actually on the line (those by then fitted with seats?) but at the same time refer to 'the two jockey cars still lying at the L.N.W.R. station' and that the latter might be used for carrying coal up the line. As only three jockey cars ever operated, presumably one was never taken into stock (or perhaps never reached the Great Orme Tramway at all) but the latter supposition is countered by (13th February, 1905) 'It was agreed to buy the two waggons' [sic] 'lying at the L.N.W.R. station from the Administrators of the late H.E. Taylor for £20'. Two of the cars were sometimes used for funerals on the Lower Section; there was a charge of 2/6d. for the body and mourners were carried at residents' rates. These jockey cars have seldom been illustrated, but there is pictorial evidence of one standing under load with coal at the winding station and one is rumoured to have been reduced to a simple open truck to carry fuel, and pushed up by a tram behind it. Their wheel brakes were similar to the bogie cars, but additionally 'hook' or 'catch' brakes were fitted; these consisted of two bars, each 2 ft 1 in. long, one end had a 'catch' on it, the other was attached to the haulage gear. An account said that if control of the car

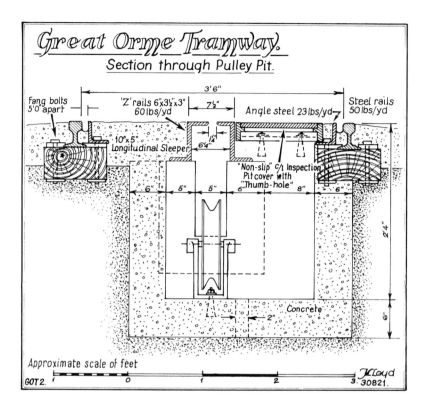

Great Orme Tramway.
Section through Pulley Pit.

was lost, the bar would be dropped onto the roadway of the Lower Section and by hooking up the sleepers, the car would be brought to a stand . . . just how this was done on a line where in places the track was covered over by concrete, is not clear; another account says the brake enabled 'the car to remain at rest unattached'. All were officially withdrawn in 1911.

On all cars communication between conductor and driver at the winding house is by telephone and electric bell, the wire being suspended from a light pole bracket which many have mistaken for a source of power as to an electric tram. A trolley boom from the car roof is part of the telephone circuit and enhances the appearance of a current collector from an overhead wire. When new, the telephone system used Hunnington-Sconte transmitters and receivers inside the cars. The overhead boom carries a small pick-up wheel. At first at least one bogie car had only a single boom and the others two booms; jockey cars had a single boom. The trolley wheel on the boom is in constant electrical contact with the overhead wire and the signal to start (or stop) is given to the engine house by bell code.

By 1903 £14,144 had been spent on construction, and the first Manager to be appointed was George White who was recommended by, and had served on, the Liverpool Overhead Railway. Now that the Company was fully in business it turned its attention to tourist facilities which were somewhat primitive. On 9th September, 1899 'THE NORTH WALES CHRONICLE' had said 'The Telegraph Inn and adjacent land' had been purchased 'in order to build a good hotel at the Summit'. It was George B. Morgan who, on becoming a Director on the strength of being the owner of the local Clarence Hotel, interested Worthington, the brewers, to support his scheme for the Inn. Morgan, who had been Catering Manager for the Great Northern Railway of Ireland, was obliged to do his first season of business from a marquee (1903) whilst Thomas McDonald of Dundalk began work in April 1903 on the intended hotel. Morgan also wished to lay out an 18-hole golf course on leased land nearby but he failed financially; the full scheme was cur-tailed, being completed at last in 1909 by a Club formed for that purpose. The hotel, on a raised plateau, remained a single storey affair and had the appearance of a castellated 'fortress', with one corner tower, and flanked by a covered verandah. However, it continued to do duty as a Telegraph or Semaphore station maintained by the Trustees of Liverpool Docks who used it to check movements of ships in the Mersey estuary. After becoming a R.A.F. Radar station during World War II it has since enjoyed a rather chequered career; it was sold to the U.D.C. in 1961 and is presently a Café.

The lower terminus was located in the yard of Victoria House, but early in 1904 such funds as were available were directed to building a deviation and proper station there, called Victoria. It stands on the site of Llandudno's first three storey house and was built by a mine agent. The present buildings occupy the site of its backyard, but the first station's running line used an offset-curved line into it with a second parallel siding to stable the jockey cars. The present layout has a single line only and its buildings are on the west side; there is an overall roof open on three sides and the building contains the manager's and booking offices. During winter one car stands under the roof. Ori-ginally the three other passenger vehicles were without shelter, so in 1905 and 1906 single car sheds were built, one at the summit and one either side of the winding house at Halfway: these buildings are 45 ft long with clearance 17 ft wide and 12 ft high inside. Applying pressure together, the Mostyn Estate and local opinion obliged the Company, who had postponed the work on account of cost, to improve the layout and site of the track at Black Gate where the line came up from the Old Road and joined Ty Gwyn Road on a gradient of 1 in 3.8. The revised arrangements were begun in spring and approved by Von Donop on 19th June, 1906.

The Board of Trade 'for securing to the public reasonable protection against danger . . . with respect to the use of mechanical power on the tramway and tramroad . . . authorised by the Great Orme Tramways act 1898', issued certain regulations and byelaws on 21st June, 1904. Summarised they were:

1. Every carriage shall have wheel brake blocks and a slipper brake; those running on the Lower Section to have an automatic emergency brake.
2. Every carriage to be conspicuously numbered inside and outside.
3. There shall be wheel guards to push away obstructions and a warning bell on each carriage.
4. Carriages must be built so as to give the driver the fullest possible view of the road.
5. Cables and pulleys must be so free of noise that they give no cause for complaint.
6. Stationary engines to be fitted with speed indicators and a governor which cannot be tampered-with; at a car speed of more than 6 m.p.h. steam must be automatically shut off.
7. 'No trailing carriage shall be used on the tramways, but a truck securely coupled to the carriage attached to the cable may occasionally be used for the conveyance of coals and goods'.
8. Carriages must carry (appropriate hours and fog conditions are specified) a white light to the front and a red to the rear.
9. There would be a speed limit of 4 m.p.h. on the Lower Section and 5 m.p.h. on the Upper.
10. No carriage would be allowed to leave the depot without grippers or slipper brake connections in working order.
11. Passengers were to be taken up and set down only at termini and also at
   (a) The Black Gate at the top of Old Road
   (b) 'At Killen's Shop about 150 yards from the engine house'.

A letter from the Company to the Board of Trade dated 26th April, 1904 anticipated the above and confirmed they had already been met.

Although Llandudno continued to grow and many new residences appeared before World War I, the Company made no attempt to restore the winter trams, much used by Orme residents in the beginning. Mostyn Estates Company had been formed to develop land, giving 999 year leases and reducing fares for residents on the Estate in addition to existing concessions for residents and golfers on the cars. Modest growth followed in the ensuing years and shareholders received an average of 6% until during World War I.

In 1906 Henry Sutcliffe succeeded George White as Manager; White was dismissed in 1904 and wrote a 'private and confidential' letter to the Board of Trade drawing attention to three items:

(a) the emergency brake was defective as the 'plough' had almost sheared through
(b) slipper brakes on Upper Section cars, insisted upon by the B.O.T. inspector, had not been added
(c) there had been an accident due to overwind, and not reported

The B.O.T. wrote to the Company (without revealing the source of their comments) to which the Company replied:

(a) the brake was satisfactory
(b) the slipper brakes had been removed by White without their consent
(c) no comment (but an official form was lodged later)

Plate CLVIII Victoria Tram Station at the foot of the Great Orme; the season has not yet begun: April 1979. *J.I.C. Boyd*

Plate CLIX The terminus from the north side . . . the season has just ended! October 1962. *D.L. Chatfield*

Plate CLX Looking up the steep and narrow Old Road where the 1932 accident occurred: April 1979.
J.I.C. Boyd

Plate CLXI Car No. 5 grinds up Old Road. The street sign forbids entry to motor cycles and cars during times of tramway operation, 'except for access': September 1981.　　　　*J.I.C. Boyd*

Plate CLXII The lower end of the passing loop at Black Gate. Right-hand running is practised: September 1981.   *J.I.C. Boyd*

Plate CLXIII Leaving the roadside section above Black Gate, a car approaches the Plateau and Halfway Station, with the hinterland of Llandudno stretching across to Deganwy, below: May 1964.
D.L. Chatfield

Plate CLXIV A 1920s view of Car No. 7 on the Lower Section at Halfway Station.   *L. & G.R.P.*

Plate CLXV The same site as above, but a new livery has transformed the appearance of Car No. 5: April 1979.   *J.I.C. Boyd*

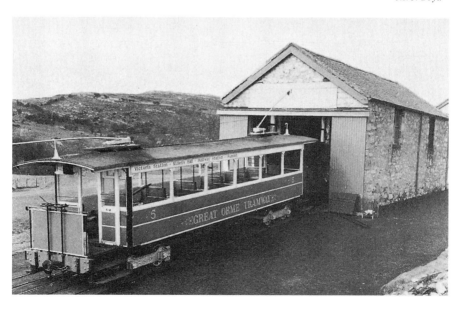

Plate CLXVI The lower shed of the Halfway Station (with obsolete signboard hanging therein), showing inspection pits, cables and rollers: April 1979.   *J.I.C. Boyd*

Plate CLXVII Car No. 4 waits at Halfway to descend to Victoria; note the lifeguards on this side only: March *1956.*   *D.L. Chatfield*

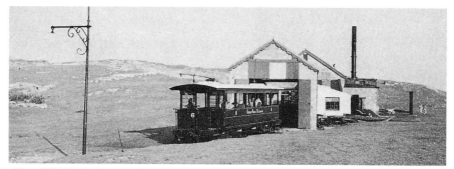

Plate CLXVIII On the same day as the foregoing, Car No. 6 waits on the upper side of Halfway. The new season is reflected by the new paint! *D.L. Chatfield*

Plate CLXIX By dint of cable lengths, cars are able to pass each other on the upper loop without stopping: September 1981. *J.I.C. Boyd*

Plate CLXX The Summit Station. The gale was so strong that photography was almost impossible - later a car was blown on its side here: September 1981. *J.I.C. Boyd*

Summit, Great Orme, Llandudno.

Plate CLXXI The Summit in the late 1920s; the scene has since changed but little.   *per J.I.C. Boyd*

Plate CLXXII Looking cast from the Summit, steam issues from the winding engine house chimney at Halfway; the Little Orme forms a back-cloth.   *D.L. Chatfield*

Plate CLXXIII 'The slot' at the lower end of Black Gate loop . . . it is filled with a wooden block when trams are not running.
J.I.C. Boyd

Plate CLXXIV Trackwork and cable slots at the upper end of Black Gate loop.
J.I.C. Boyd

Plates CLXXV, CLXXVI & CLXXVII The track and cable arrangements on the Upper Section are more railway-like than on the Lower.

J.I.C. Boyd

Plates CLXXVIII, CLXXIX & CLXXX Bogies, shoe-brakes and other safety features: April 1979.

J.I.C. Boyd

Plate CLXXXI Car interiors have changed little over three-quarters of a century but . . .   *J.I.C. Boyd*

Plate CLXXXII . . . not so fashions and our coinage!   *D.L. Chatfield*

Plate CLXXXIII Some civil engineering features survive on the Cedryn Quarry Tramway course. This fine stone embankment is one of them: March 1975.   *J.I.C. Boyd*

Plate CLXXXIV There were two loading platforms at the south end of the Blaenau Ffestiniog L.N.W.R. tunnel; on the left for Oakeley Quarry and bottom right for Greaves' Llechwedd Quarry. Wagon turntables for the slate wagons are seen on the latter's wharf.   *R.H. Bleasdale*

Plate CLXXXV The Cowlyd Tramway veers off round the bluff to the right; the incline down to Dolgarrog falls from a summit beside the two men; this was once a busy interchange yard: March 1975.

J.I.C. Boyd

Plate CLXXXVI Round the corner from the foregoing, 'the main line', tractor shed and turntable look abandoned, but occasionally a 'train' takes to the grass-covered rails.   *J.I.C. Boyd*

Plate CLXXXVII Looking west with Cowlyd Reservoir in the far distance (*right*) the tramway crosses the adit tramway of c 1853 to the Ardda Mine. (Map Ref: 761659)   *J.I.C. Boyd*

Plate CLXXXVIII Looking back towards Dolgarrog at Siglen, the pipeline resembles a giant black caterpillar: April 1945.   *J.I.C. Boyd*

Plate CLXXXIX Generally laid very much on the surface of the boggy terrain, in places the Cowlyd Tramway (here at Siglen) has been given a generous formation. (Map Ref. 743643)   *J.I.C. Boyd*

Plate CXC A day's outing for officials of the Conway & Colwyn Bay joint Water Supply Board, probably in mid-October 1917, with the German locomotive and a train of side-tipping wagons with bodies removed and benches and floors placed thereon. The reservoir stretches behind, as bleak then as it is today.   *Gwynedd Archives*

Plate CXCI During the building of the Eigiau Reservoir a standard gauge line was laid largely on the site of the old Cedryn Tramway; equipment was taken up and down the Dolgarrog escarpment in this manner. *Gwynedd Archives*

Plate CXCII In a spate of modernisation in 1927, the Little Orme's Head Quarry acquired three 80 h.p. Sentinel-built geared locomotives, themselves delivered by steam lorry. Here No. 2 is attached to loaded wagons to pose for an official picture in the firm's catalogue. *per J.I.C. Boyd*

It appears White had been sacked because he complained of under-staffing, especially in the engine house. He thought too, the signalling wires were inefficient. On 12th April, 1905 the Company further advised the B.O.T. that the late Manager and his assistant 'had made certain threats to some employees'.

The safety of the line was occasionally called into question; the above-mentioned incident was on 8th October, 1902 due to misjudge-ment by the operator of the upper winding cable; he pulled up instead of lowering the top car and the rope at the bottom slackened; the lower car 'started' with two awful jerks and the rope became entangled round the first pulley and the line came to a halt from 3 p.m. until noon on the following day. On 1st August, 1904 in an instance of overwinding the descending car collided with the buffer stop at the lower station. White feared loss of business. Judging the situation by occurrences of similar nature in 1903–5, Sutcliffe, his successor, removed the emergency brake and took the governor off the winding engine without notifying the Board of Trade! Some Directors averred that this had been done without their agreement, but it was not until 1932 that the consequ-ences of that action were to have horrific effect.

In 1905 and 1906 unspecified parties made offers to purchase the undertaking and in 1909 (and again in 1919) Llandudno U.D.C. negotiated to the same end, but no change of ownership took place. In 1909 the Company had offered the tramway to the Council, who were willing to pay only £7,000 for it. A special meeting of shareholders refused to allow a sale at this figure.

Before the 1914 season began, Sandycroft Ltd. supplied a new winding engine for the Lower Section – in 1920 electric haulage was considered but not adopted.

Season followed season, but from the beginning financial success was always elusive; in some years the plight was such that the line only operated for six weeks during the summer. Like all other holiday attractions, the Company's takings nose-dived during World War I and maintenance problems became a source of real worry – the cable was now worn to a point where it was deemed unfit for use but, with the Ministry of Munitions refusing a permit to purchase a new one, the Company operated in 1918 one of its shortest seasons on record, a mere 22 days. In due course wartime shortcomings were righted and with improved economic conditions Llandudno's business grew again. The Company was optimistic for the future when one of those events which was to change the whole situation took place. It was to be compared with the accident which befell the Snowdon Mountain line on the opening day in 1896 and which has dominated its history since that time. On 21st and 23rd August 1932 the Great Orme Tramway suffered in a way which placed it in the same category.

The first warning came on Sunday 21st August when No. 5 car on the Lower Section was satisfactorily halted by the brakes when its drawbar broke. Two days later, this happened to car No. 4 on the same section and the 'NORTH WALES CHRONICLE' (26th August) headlined 'All Llandudno was horrified on Tuesday to learn that one of the cable cars of the Great Orme Tramway had run away, crushing to death the driver (referred to as 'Brakesman' in most reports) Edward Harris, and creating some shocking injuries among the crowd of visitors who, a moment before, had been gaily singing as they returned from a happy morning on the summit of the Orme. A little girl, Margaret Worthington, whose foot was torn off, died at 3 p.m. in the hospital . . . Careering for a short distance at gathering speed, the tram left the metals and crashed into a twelve foot high wall. A tramway standard caught in its flight was torn up, a portion being flung into a neighbouring lane. As the top of the tram swept along the crest of the wall, it dislodged the coping stones which cascaded through the window spaces upon the passengers. The car was full of people, there probably being thirty-five persons in it'.

The time was about 12.30 p.m. and the drawbar broke on Tabor Hill just above Black Gate. The car's wheel and slipper brakes were ineffective and running away it left the track on a reverse curve and hit the wall on the east side of Old Road's entry; the impact hurled passengers violently forward, causing head injuries from the window opening uprights. The luckless brakesman on the front jumped off with 12 year old Margaret in his arms, but the car lurched over on the same side and crushed them against the wall – the girl had been up to the summit to take lunch to her father, an employee. Two passengers subsequently died in hospital and many were seriously injured.

Lt. Col. E.P. Anderson held an enquiry the following Monday, 29th August, in the Town Hall. Meanwhile the accident area was roped off and the tram secured by ropes to trees.

The enquiry was told by Sutcliffe that the drawbar of No. 5 had snapped and broken on the previous Sunday ("it was a unique occurrence") and that "about 10 days before the accident one of the 'Vibrac' steel drawbars, which had been in use for about a year, broke where it was in contact with the edges of the 'Z' bars at the top of the slot of the conduit". Fortunately no run-away resulted "because the rope remained attached to the car through the lower half of the drawgear and the 'cam-bar'". Anderson had already determined that the proper function of the cam-bars should have been to move longitudinally under the action of the spring, 'and force the jaws out against the webs of the 'Z' bars. These jaws, as had already been mentioned, have been removed for many years and now the only function of the apparatus is to provide a slight degree of cushioning between the cable and the tramcar'. Several drawbars shown to Anderson were worn where it passed through the slot in the conduit 'at a point about midway between its top pivot and the cam-bar'. Sutcliffe admitted the life of a drawbar was about a season, or six months; he had chosen 'Vibrac' steel for their construction as he felt they would be more resistant to wear; he had no experience of the metal. English Steel Corporation supplied the 'Vibrac V 45' to Messrs Craven Bros. Ltd. and he had had six bars made between 1930–32 by the latter firm. Though they cost more than the previous type Sutcliffe maintained that Cravens were perfectly aware of the end-purpose of the bars. The fractured bar had been in use for "seven or eight days, doing 60 journeys a day, and every bar shows the abrasion marks" referred to on the other bars. The enquiry was told by E.S.Co's metallurgist that 'V 45' was selected rather than any other on account of its resistance to wear, but no one in his firm had any notion of the use intended for the bars; he assumed that a reputable firm like Craven knew fully what they were ordering, but after seeing the conditions of working the line, he felt that the drawbar would bend considerably under stress, and might weaken more due to this than to tension. Craven Bros. spokesman said they had received an initial order in 1930 for two drawbars of 'Vibrac' steel 'as resistance to wear was important', 'no other information as to their use was given with the order . . .'; his opinion was that fracture was probably due to side pressure, of which they had had no previous suggestion; had they known better the conditions of use, they might have criticised the design. When the drawbar in question was submitted to the National Physical Laboratory, the test report read ". . . the material used . . . was generally unsuitable . . . in a component of hauling gear which would be subjected to a series of impacts during service . . . in the actual drawbar serious forging defects were also present . . .".

Anderson ruled that the use of such material was an error of judgement on the part of Sutcliffe. The cause of the rapid wear on the drawbars was due to sideplay in the running gear of the car, plus the excess width of the bars over the designed dimensions and to the design of the equipment; as it was, the clearance between drawgear and 'Z' bars was insufficient. Blame in part also rested on Craven Bros. who might have asked for more precise information against Sutcliffe's somewhat loosely worded initial order. Defects in the forging lay in the failure of E.S.Co's Openshaw Works – drawbars should have been supplied in machined state rather than the rough and then defects would have been more easily detected.

The accident showed that the existing slipper and wheel brakes were physically incapable of holding the car in such circumstances; if an automatic brake had been fitted according to the Statutory Regulations the consequences might not have been serious; there should have been some wedging or gripping action in addition to that of sliding friction, and this was what the automatic brake was fitted to provide. Sutcliffe was blamed for removing the brakes and Anderson felt that the drawbacks of the design which led to them being taken off might have been overcome by alterations of design or in adjustment. He added that the Company Chairman also knew the brakes were absent and though the cables had been well maintained, possible over-attention had been paid to these rather than other care of ancillary parts; he found the governors had been taken off the winding engines, again against the Regulations; responsibility for this too, rested on those he had previously indicted. The Engineer, (T. Ellis) who had been with the Company since work began, recalled that the governor was taken off the lower engine because there was insufficient power to pull a loaded car up the gradient at Black Gate (the scene of the accident). Finally Anderson forbade the re-opening of the tramway until the Statutory Regulations had been met and recommended that a design for an automatic brake should be reconsidered as should also be its materials, and that it should be less sensitive to mere variations in the tension of the cable. The drawbars should be accurately made; they should avoid contact with the 'Z' bars as much as possible, and the sideplay of cars must be reduced. Regular inspection should be introduced, using well-lighted pits, and passengers should not be allowed to ride on the front platform.

The Report was dated 18th November, 1932, and published on 2nd February, 1933.

No time was lost in setting things to rights. The Annual General Meeting on 13th February, 1933 was told that a new automatic brake designed by consulting engineers, Sloan & Lloyd Barnes of Castle Street, Liverpool, and supplied by Walker Bros., Pagefield Ironworks, Wigan, was in hand. Car No. 5 was fitted with this and tested in April 1933. But by now, claims totalling £14,000 had arisen from the accident and the insurance company had repudiated liability though they were prepared to make an *ex gratia* payment of £1,150 which was accepted. The Tramway Company intended to commence proceedings against Cravens for breakage of the drawbar (this does not seem to have been carried through), but was clearly insolvent and a committee of shareholders attempted to dissuade those making claims to delay their action until (1) the brake had proved itself, (2) the line was making money again, and (3) there were funds to meet the situation (there being no financial reserves for this purpose). However, Rabbi Harris Lewin of Cheetham, Manchester, whose wife, Sarah, was badly injured, had obtained judgement for £1,000 plus costs and after obtaining a writ, the sheriff took possession of the undertaking on 23rd May, 1933 and advertised the track and equipment for sale. In consequence the Board had no option but to apply on 7th June for a Winding-up Order which was granted on 24th July, there being assets of £6,839 3s. 0d. available to meet the reduced sum and other claims. A liquidator was appointed on 4th September, 1933.

It was agreed among the creditors that the closing of the Company was due to a series of circumstances – including an omission to comply with the terms of the policy of insurance – which had had a knock-on effect, and the likelihood of a repetition was slim. Further, the best hope they had for having their claims met under the circumstances was to satisfy the Board of Trade, have the line re-opened on a profitable basis and then sell it. They met on 25th August and agreed to continue the tests which had begun the previous April. The Ministry of Transport approved of the brake design which was a subject of Patent applied for on 9th June, 1933 between Walker Bros. (Wigan) Ltd. and H.E. Dance (an employee of Sloan & Ll. Barnes) of Birkenhead; it was fitted only to the upper bogies of a car and in total consisted of four sledges mounted on their own hubs to the wheel axles. When released by powerful springs the sledges dug into the roadway with a row of renewable teeth attached to their undersides: this would cause the vehicle to rise on the hubs so that all its weight was transferred to the sledges: to prevent complete derailment, guides to engage either running rails or conduit slot were specified in the Patent, these guides continuing to steer the car when and if the wheel flanges had ceased to do so. On test it was proved desirable to fit the new brake to both bogies; the sledges on the upper were inoperative until a governor attached to the car wheels reached a pre-determined speed when the retaining springs were released, and dropped the sledges firmly onto the roadway. The sledges on the lower bogie were released by the movement of the sledges on the upper by means of Bowden cables (or other methods).[7] The Orme's system uses plungers which if depressed by derailment trigger the brake through Bowden wires.

On 11th January, 1934 the liquidator gave approval to carry out the aforementioned brakework; as applied to car No. 5 the governing device was set at 6½ m.p.h. On test the emergency stop proved remarkably smooth, so car No. 5 was loaded with scrap iron and on 23rd March, 1934 its braking performance was publicly tested and filmed. Relying on car speed, the apparatus transformed the whole safety picture. Walker's then fitted car No. 4 similarly. Col. A.C. Tench from the Board of Trade inspected (Col. Anderson had died) on 11th May following and the tramway re-opened on 17th May, 1934; a condition was imposed that the emergency brakes be tested annually before the operating season commenced and for this purpose concrete weights, suitably marked with poundage and having carrying handles, are available.

The public evidently had no fears for another accident; the 1934 season proved to be a good one and the concern was offered for sale by the liquidator; it was purchased by a local syndicate based on a shareholders' committee under the chairmanship of Arthur Hewitt for the even-then modest sum of £5,600. Six shareholders formed the Great Orme Railway Ltd., a private limited company of £10,000 capital, which bought the line on 30th March, 1935. Out on the line itself however, whilst there was little evidence of this enforced change of ownership there was plenty to show that local enthusiasm for a tramway up the Orme was as strong in 1935 as it had been forty years earlier!

Although the new owners styled themselves a 'Railway' to distinguish the background change, the basic legislation of its original Act and subsequent Regulations remained unaltered – it was, and remains, a Tramway and Tramroad under its Act of 1898.

The excellent motives of the new owners soon put them into difficulties. Not being a Statutory Undertaking they were unable to levy fares then in force or needed in the future, and it was necessary to face the expense of firstly a Great Orme Tramways (Temporary Increase of Charges) Order and secondly the Great Orme Tramways Act of 1936 in order to charge the fares then in force; these were (1934 and 1935) 8d. single, 1/- return. The new owners continued in business for the next 14 years, punctuated by World War II and later the retirement of Sutcliffe who, despite the trauma through which he had passed, remained as Manager to be succeeded by C.C. Rhodes in October 1945. Summer operation continued on a reduced scale during World War II as the summit building was used as a R.A.F. Radar station. After the war the building was acquired by Randolph Turpin (the retired boxer) but after his failure it was taken over by Llandudno U.D.C. who thereafter leased it to the Forté catering organisation. One change introduced by the 1935 company was to usher in Sunday services, a feature which could hardly be opposed locally as the U.D.C. was already running summer charabancs up the Orme by another route to serve St. Tudno's church where Sunday open air services were held.

Llandudno U.D.C. has long had a history of acquisition of undertakings which might operate for its own benefit; some of these have been mentioned. They had had the greatest interest in the Orme tramway since before it opened and the Act of 1898 had given them powers to purchase the line in 1926 and every seventh year following, the price being equal to 28 years' purchase at 4½%: 1947 was a year of decision and on 18th October they gave notice of intention to exercise their powers – at this the Company considered the cost ought to be calculated on the capital outlaid on the concern since its opening (£19,464) making a total figure of £26,000. The case went before Mr. Justice Jenkins in the Chancery Division of the High Court on 13th October, 1948; he ruled that the figure should be limited to that spent by the 1935 company (£6,970) and so the undertaking passed to the local authority for a mere £8,407 on 1st January, 1949. The local company which had bridged the years since the 1932 disaster and seen the tramway through the war years, was wound up voluntarily; the final meeting was on 25th March, 1950, the ultimate distribution being 33/9d. for each £1 share, a fair reward. It was soon to be proved that the purchase was a bargain; with the expense of some track relaying the authority opened for business at Easter 1949 and by the season's end its takings had covered the cost of purchase and the relaying. Business was even better the next year even though throughout 1950 the Council was running buses wholly or part-way up the Orme.

Surplus funds were used for further track renewals, but concern at the cost of coke fuel which had risen dramatically gave rise to estimates for scrapping the steam generating plant and the installation of electrical gear. Actually the whole matter of fuel costs had been under review for some years and not only by the Company! In 1955 250 tons of coke @ £7 ton were burned each year: back in 1942 Llandudno U.D.C. had appointed a sub-committee to report on the question of providing a tram service during the winter or the alternative of running a bus service, but results were negative.

The Company had said 'operational difficulties and expenditure' would prevent them 'from entertaining the question' and the Deputy Regional Transport Commissioner said the route was quite unsuitable for operating public service vehicles, so the sub-committee had concluded it was to be a winter tram service or no winter service at all; the wartime conditions and the then crying need for a year-round service focussed their attention on Section 57 (1) of the Great Orme Act 1898 regarding takeover. Regretfully they had noted it would be 23rd May, 1947 before an opportunity for compulsory purchase came their way, but they had informal talks with the Company to see if they could buy before that date. The Company was interested but not in the suggested price. L.U.D.C. had previously prepared an estimate to show that the loss on working a 7 day winter service themselves would be equivalent to a rate increase of 2¾d. in the £1; overall, it was estimated a winter service would show a loss of £2,525 per annum. The Committee's Report (29th July, 1943) continues: 'Your Committee have also thought it well to make tentative enquiries as to electrification of the Railway . . .' and they had obtained figures from their electrical engineer. His report shows the Council had (some years before) initiated a similar enquiry into electrification but by now, the engineer conceded, those early proposals could be improved upon; the main problem was one of supply, and to avoid disfiguring the Orme with overhead cables. In all he felt the conversion from steam would cost £2,249, and running costs with current at 1½d. per unit would be £340 p.a. against an estimated sum of £664 for coke fuel.

On this aspect nothing is heard for a further twelve years; in June 1955 the L.U.D.C. approached The General Electric Company at Liverpool and correspondence between them includes references to numbers of 'hauls per day'; this showed that from early May, 25 hauls were made, increasing to 68 in late July down to 25–30 in late September; also that the regular pattern of traffic flow had upward/downward trends (i.e. uphill/downhill literally) in quite separate periods each morning, afternoon, and between 7 and 9 p.m. All other options including direct electric drive to the trams were considered – by now, (1955) the saving on conversion might be £1,615 p.a.

A decision was taken, the business given to The English Electric Co. Ltd. in 1956 and by Easter 1958 the electric winding apparatus was commissioned. From out of the boiler house – last used in October

1957 – came a Robey locomotive-type horizontal boiler, one Sandycroft 120 h.p., one original Musker 80 h.p. winding engine (the latter had taken up duty on the Upper Section when it was replaced on the Lower Section) and a small stand-by boiler.

The electrical gear now comprises two 415 volt three-phase 50-cycle A.C. slip-ring induction motors; the smaller (75 h.p.) works the Upper Section and the more powerful (125 h.p.) the Lower. Whilst the motors run at approximately 730 r.p.m. there is a reduction gear for the drums which give about 5 m.p.h. on the lower and 7 m.p.h. on the upper levels. The normal hand-operated action on the winding drum is retained, and this must be 'on' before the winding gear can be switched on. There is also automatic cut-out of the equipment . . . a successor to the steam governor; this comes into action at 15% over the set speed. Smooth starting and stopping is ensured by resistance control though in motion the cars operate at near-constant pace. To test the emergency brakes annually, it is necessary to cut out the reduction gear and so speed up the revolutions of the winding drums for the Lower Section; this is done with a temporary belt drive. This higher drum speed brings the emergency skate brakes into operation.

Times since then have been punctuated by the building of a passenger shelter at the summit in 1965, a bogie derailment on the upper loop during August 1966 when the two passing cars collided as a result (no injuries) and celebrations in both 1972 and 1977 to mark anniversaries. During a severe gale a car was blown on its side at the Summit in September 1982. Llandudno U.D.C. disappeared on 1st April, 1974 and the administrator is now Aberconwy District Council. During the 1977 festivities the existing plaque on Victoria station was unveiled summarising the line's history. In season the employee strength is fourteen including four drivers, four conductors and two engineers.

Fares are only mentioned herein as of passing interest as since the late 1960s financial inflation has made the comparison of fares somewhat ridiculous; up to then, only modest increases were made, as seldom as possible.

Passenger tickets were of paper type issued by Bell Punch machines until 1964 when the booking office (only) was provided with a strip-ticket machine: cancellation is by hand-nippers. The line is usually open Easter–October and cars run to the demands of traffic rather than a timetable.

Further modifications to the brakes on cars 4 and 5 have taken place: their sledge brakes, operated manually from the platform ends, have been taken off as, if they were applied at the same time as the Walker sledges were operating, the effectiveness of the latter would be reduced by some weight being removed. These two cars carry watertanks to emit water under control of a foot pedal; curves are watered to reduce friction. On the Upper Section the two cars retain their rail-type sledge brakes, and have received no further modification.

The original livery was a deep yellow, with white roofs and black ironwork; the yellow was then changed to royal blue, but this became dulled with constant re-varnishing. In 1962–3 all cars became lighter blue and were given black lining-out; roofs, numerals and lettering remain white as they always were. In 1967 bodies became royal blue again, with cream above waist and in very recent times the running gear has become light grey. Car interiors are brown, ceilings white. The present body livery is Trafalgar Blue with light grey roofs, window frames in ivory picked out with Cambridge Blue on the beading – this was adopted for the 75th anniversary. Beneath the cant rail there reads in black characters '*Victoria Station* ★ *Killens Hill* ★ *Halfway Station* ★ *Summit*'.

When the 1935 Company was formed the car-side lettering was changed from GREAT ORME TRAMWAYS to GREAT ORME RAILWAY, which it remained until 1977 when the original style re-appeared. The jockey cars were painted similarly but with detail differences to the positions of the car numbers.

The Route Described: Operation

Hundreds of young people today have never been inside a conventional train; the convenience of a car and the cost of rail travel combine to deter them. On a unique system like the Great Orme Tramway these criteria do not apply; by offering an unusual mode of ascending an attractive vantage point at a holiday resort, expense becomes a secondary consideration. In a Britain which has eschewed its railways, the Edwardian atmosphere of the Orme tram remains as strong as ever – even though today there is the rival method of travel by chair lift.

The operation is divided into two distinct portions; it follows there is a passing loop within each section and as it is not feasible to cross the cables, each car uses the same side of a loop throughout. There are no platforms or bridges. The Lower Section resembles a street tramway, the track running along or at the side of the highway; such are the hazards of a tram meeting road traffic that Old Road is closed to traffic during the hours of tramway operation. This Lower Section is 872 yards long and rises 400 feet; on leaving the covered Victoria station the line climbs up the centre of stone-walled Old Road, crosses Ty Gwyn Road and enters the raised section described earlier – here is Black Gate request stop. Above this the track divides by means of a typical spring-operated single-bladed tramway-type turnout to form the passing loop; due to the geometrics of cable length and the drum diameters when winding/unwinding, the loop is somewhat below the precise halfway point of the section. At these same points the running rails are broken to allow the cable drawbars to pass through them; at the point where the conduit slots bifurcate, a long 'V' is formed in the roadway and this somewhat treacherous aperture is infilled by a shaped wooden insert when trams are not running. On the top side of the loop the tracks are interlaced with a common groove between them for the remainder of the section; this is done to enable the cables (they are side by side hereafter) to run in their individual conduits to the winding house – it is not practical to house them (running in opposing directions) in one conduit. After Tyn-y-Coed Halt the Lower Section terminates at the Plateau (known initially as First Station and now, Halfway) and passengers are forewarned at this somewhat open hillside site to 'Change Here for the Summit Car' by a large hoarding (489 ft above sea level). The Lower Section car halts just outside a stone car shed for this purpose and at the end of the day's working there follows the somewhat clumsy practice of dragging a length of cable from the conduit here to allow the engineer to winch this car into the shed . . . meanwhile its mate is firmly bedded against the buffer stop at Victoria. The shed contains two separate inspection pits, interlaced track without guard rails and a cable passes over rollers through each pit.

Two cables are sufficient to work the Lower Section but three are needed for the Upper, due to the position of the winding drums below the worked line. The first cable passes from drum to the first car, the second from first car round the idle return wheel at the summit and on to the second car, and the third from the second car back to the other Upper Section drum in the winding house. The Upper Section is, therefore, alike to a string of beads with beads threaded at intervals. Any change in speed of cable affects each car equally.

Passengers must pass on foot around the winding house to reach the Upper Section car. This windswept site – as it can be – is somewhat in contrast with the urban surroundings from which they began the ascent and many travellers are bemused by the Two-for-the-Price-of-One journey. In earlier days there was a rail connection round the west side of the winding house between the two sections and one siding on each side for the jockey cars serving the boiler house. Former trackwork may still be traced. This upper line is more like a railway as this open hillside, free of buildings, makes it a complete contrast to the section below – the line runs over unfenced grassland to the summit – with small civil engineering works to complete the 'railway' resemblance, and passing through an area of bygone quarries and copper mines.

The Upper Section is worked by cars Nos. 6 and 7: is 827 yards long but rises only 148 feet. The rails are spiked and occasionally clipped to the wooden sleepers, being cut down standard gauge timbers laid at yard intervals and ballasted. The section begins with a length of level line and rises on a low embankment as far as the passing loop, *en route* there is a level crossing with the road which gives access to St. Tudno's Church (Llandudno itself derives its name from this Saint) and apart from here – where each cable runs in a channel – all the Upper Section cabling, pulleys, etc. are open and above ground. At this crossing a notice for road users reads:

BEWARE OF TRAMS CROSSING
WAIT UNTIL ROPES DROP

warning vehicles not only of oncoming rail traffic but also not to cross
the line before the cables slacken and fall back into their slots! (There is
additionally a conventional ungated level-crossing warning – of 'Highway Code' variety – depicting a steam locomotive!). On reaching the
loop each car keeps to its customary side as on the lower part, the
drawbars being fixed off-centre beneath the car to ensure their respective cables being kept apart; in this way it is feasible simply to have
single tracks below and above this loop while the two cables lie inside
the running rails. The passing loop is laid out in railway fashion using
White's point-gear and as each car leaves the loop it sets its own point
for right-hand running and overhead blades for its own return. There
are conventional weighted hand-levers for each point but as their
regular action is automatic the levers are only used in emergency; to
prevent vandalism each lever is contained within a wire cage and
additionally, the point indicators are numbered to agree with the
number of the car. At the point where the cable passes through the
running lines at the two turnouts, the rail is broken by a slot. Since the
last war the overhead wire at this passing place has been made into a
loop though previously it was only a single wire (the descending car's
conductor removed his trolley to allow the ascending one the use of the
wire). There now follows a reverse curve and the deepest cutting on the
system, together with the steepest portion on this section, 1 in 10.3;
then the gradient flattens out, the summit (637 ft above sea level) is
reached with its 'hotel' building to the east of, and 29 ft above, the
terminal. Ahead stands a stone shed where the upper car is stabled and
the cable wheel is hidden away. It is a fine place to be; sea, mountainous
views along Snowdonia down to the sea, Anglesey away to the west . . .
altogether a narrow gauge journey not to be missed, though quite
different from any other in Wales.

Shortly after the last war the author of 'GREAT ORME TRAMWAY'
(R.C. Anderson) set down his recollections as a season's 'driver' on the
line; he would await the start at Victoria and by calling the conductor of
the top car at Halfway by means of a hand-generator to provide the
current would ascertain by telephone if he too, was ready to go. If the
reply was favourable, he would press a bell push twice in the roof of the
cab; at this, the Lower Section engineer-driver would set the cables in
motion; if there was no need for a halt at the request stops, two short
rings would be given, but if a stop at Black Gate was required, it was
ensured by ringing one long and one short, and the converse for a stop
at Tyn-y-Coed Road. In emergency a single bell was rung. Restarting
was always signalled by two bells; the downcoming car gives no bell
signals except in emergency. Should a car make any kind of stop, the
other car must necessarily halt also . . . a circumstance which often
puzzles passengers when no one is alighting or boarding! Normally,
Lower Section drivers do not require to use their handbrakes at all.

Anderson described the Upper Section working where starting

arrangements were exactly the same. There is a separate engineer-driver for this section (who sits back-to-back with his companion) and on it the conductors may use handbrakes to ensure smooth starting and stopping; due to the varying gradients involved and its position on the section, the amount of pressure applied will vary for each car. The object is to keep the cable taut as, should it slacken too much it will fall beneath the cable pulleys.

Altogether, there is much more to the Great Orme Tramway than meets the eye and that which does is full of peculiar interest.

	1902	1903	1904	1905	1906	1907	1908	1909	1910
Gross Passenger Receipts	£ 1,356	1,781	2,039	2,103	2,247	2,175	1,918	2,239	2,338
Net Receipts	249	31	434	652	776	556	349	721	795
Passengers Carried	109,710	111,302	76,519	73,091	102,590	79,879	71,839	82,799	85,854
Car Miles	5,987	8,213	10,100	8,127	9,310	10,721	9,545	10,321	10,197
Av. Pass. per Car Mile	18.32	13.55	7.57	8.99	11.01	7.45	7.5	8.02	8.41

	1911	1912	1913	1914	1928	1929	1930	1931	1932*
Gross Passenger Receipts	2,130	2,351	2,866	2,393†	5,668‡	5,620‡	4,938‡	4,391‡	3,401
Net Receipts	675	831	1,341		1,389‡	392‡	938‡	331‡	–92
Passengers Carried	80,717	84,352	100,097						
Car Miles	9,673	9,551	11,022						
Av. Pass. per Car Mile	8.36	8.83	9.08						

Average Passenger per Car Mile 1902–13 = 9.75 passengers in a 48-seat vehicle!

*To 23rd August only.

†From Annual Report. No official returns published hereafter.

‡From Winding-up Petition.

REFERENCES

1. His obituary (August 1904) links him with River Dee Conservancy Board, Hawarden Water Works Co. and Chester Race Course.
2. This tale has its imperfections as cable trams in San Francisco did not begin service until August 1862, and said to have been conceived by Andrew Hallidie, a cable maker who deplored the distress of tram horses.
3. Further details:– THE MATLOCK STEEP GRADIENT TRAMWAY (reprint) [The Arkwright Society] 1972. The Board of Trade files advise the inspection of an experimental line at Swansea with a gradient of 1 in 5 which had been passed by Colonel Yorke.
4. R. White & Sons sent a description of the tramway to the B.O.T. on 22 February, 1901 "when used in conjunction with the American system of jockey cars which are permanently attached to the ends of the hauling ropes".
5. The scrap rail dump at Halfway contained specimens of many old and light sections, slide chairs of primitive 1860 period, 40 lb. rail and sections of the original 50 lb. rails not now used.
6. Dates: 1909, 1912, 1923 and 1932 also appear.
7. Patent Specification 423,855 finally accepted 11 February, 1935, gives full mechanical details and drawings.

PART 8
OTHER RAIL SYSTEMS

(The dates in brackets following each title refer to the period when a rail system existed)

PENMAENMAWR & WELSH GRANITE CO. LTD. (c.1832–1967)

(Formed by an amalgamation of three following concerns on 31st January, 1911, this title covers the greatest period during which this quarrying combine owned and operated railways.)

This very large granite-quarrying business was taken over by Kingston Minerals Ltd. in 1965. Its then-redundant railway system was utterly different from others herein, being largely formed of inclines from mountainside down to sea shore with relatively short runs of near-level trackage, and possibly for this reason (and having no 'main line' as did the other large slate quarries in the neighbourhood), it did not attract so much interest despite its long-dated background. As with contiguous quarries working granite, the stone was extracted up on the hillside on the hinterland, processed to the form required (setts, stone for tarmacadam, railway ballast etc.) and despatched either by sea or rail at the shore line. As time progressed, earlier workings were closed down, worked out or buried by rubbish from above; the picture was of constant change and improvement in transport – this improvement ultimately swept away the railway system in favour of other methods. Traditionally in this type of quarry the rail gauge was 3 ft. Existing accounts of the undertaking are not numerous but have done full justice to the overall history of the industry there.[1]

Geographically these quarries enjoy an exciting and windswept north-facing aspect along the shore of Conway Bay; they have eaten large tonnages of rock from the sides and summit of Penmaen-Mawr Mountain 'a vast, naked, gloomy rock, presenting towards the sea a rugged and almost perpendicular front, . . . height 1,545 ft'. Now gnawed away completely by quarrying, on the top stood Braich-y-Dinas an ancient British fort, deemed impregnable and capable of housing 20,000 men. From this point in the west the P.&W.G.Co. workings extended to Graiglwyd Mountain, approximately 1½ miles to the east. Commercial exploitation by English entrepreneurs over 150 years has produced a mongrel vernacular of place names within the workings.

There have been three main sources of stone hereabouts; firstly the west side of Penmaen (mainly the collection of scree from the hill slopes), secondly on Penmaen (Mountain) itself to the east of there, and lastly in the extreme east of the Estate, on Graiglwyd Mountain. Though not co-existent, each sphere of working had its own pier and, after the opening of the Chester & Holyhead Railway along the coast on 1st May 1848, the alternative of rail to ship despatch was available. The

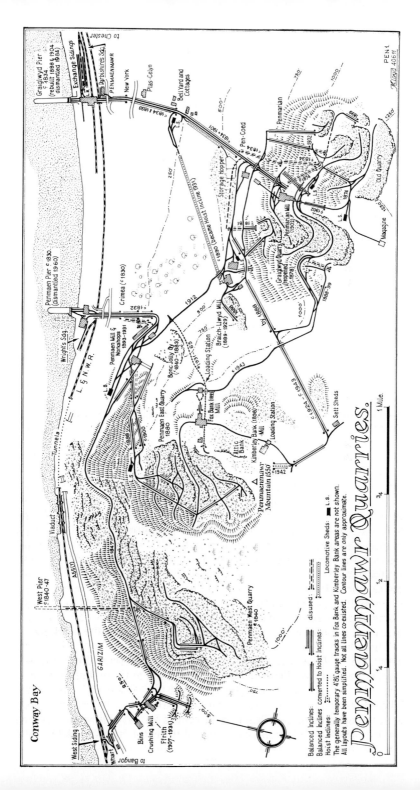

Penmaenmawr Quarries.

Conway Bay

Graiglwyd Pier c.1834 (rebuilt 1888 & 1904 dismantled 1934)

Exchange Sidings

to Chester

Dyhshire's Sdg.

PENMAENMAWR

New York

Plas Celyn

Bell Yard and Cottages

c.1834 & 1889

Pen-Coed

1834-1901

Penmanian

Penmanian Quarry 1902

Penmanian Mill (1902)

Old Quarry

Magazine

1874

Storage Hopper

c.1890 (became Hoist Incline (1931)

Graiglwyd Quarry (reopened 1978)

1888-99

by 1889

Loading Station

c.1943

Sett Sheds

c.1924 - c.1943

1942

Kimberley Mill

Loading Station

Attic Bank

Fox Bank (1889) Mill

Kimberley Bank (1898)

Braich-Llwyd Mill (1889-1929)

Bonc Jolly Dŷy (1840-1889)

750'

Penmaen East Quarry 1880

c.1900

1889

L.S.

Penmaenmawr Mountain 1550

Penmaen West Quarry c.1840

Crimea (c.1830)

1832

Penmaen Pier c.1830 (dismantled 1960)

Penmaen Mill & Workshops 1893-1931

Wright's Sdg.

L. & N.W.R.

Tunnels

Viaduct

A55(1)

GARIZIM

West Pier c.1840-47

West Siding

Wharf

to Bangor

Bins

Crushing Mill Ffrith (1907-1931)

250'

PEN.t A.Lloyd '06.tt

Balanced Inclines:

Balanced Inclines converted to Hoist Inclines:

Hoist Inclines:

disused:

Locomotive Sheds: L.S.

The generally temporary 4'8½ gauge tracks in Fox Bank and Kimberley Bank areas are not shown. All layouts have been simplified. Not all lines co-existed. Contour lines are only approximate.

0   ½   ¾   1 Mile.

quarry transport problem was to carry stone from a maximum height of 1,550 ft to the seaboard in a horizontal distance of about ¾ mile and to keep the resultant inclines within reason, some were angled at 1 in 1½ across the mountain face: the remainder fell almost at right-angles. The three working areas were connected by two main contour lines; the first of 1847 linking West and East Penmaen Quarries, and the more recent 1912 line connecting the foregoing with Graiglwyd following the formation of the P.&W.G.Co. in 1911, and dubbed the 'Canadian Pacific Railway' by the workers! It was a form of marriage bond! Unfortunately it was not a blissful union; the land between the ends of the 'C.P.R.' was owned by the Bryn Mor Estate who proved to be a stubborn opponent of the rail link. They were appeased by a generous royalty 'per ton' to which the new Company responded by running their trains at night . . . until somebody sneaked. Gravity, cable, man, horse, steam, diesel and petrol-powered forms of traction have played a part over the years but in contrast with the slate quarries to the west, there were no long hauls of wagons along a private railway.

BRUNDRIT & CO. LTD. (Penmaen West and East Quarries) [Company: Brundrit & Co. 1873 until 28th September, 1897]

This firm had operated the two sites on leases from Baron Hill and The Crown at the west end of the P.&W.G.Co. complex. It was formed by two Lancastrians, Philip Whiteway and Denis Brundrit[2] in 1830 for the purpose of gathering cobbles from the shore at low water and loading them into ships beached thereon; the cobbles were consigned to pave Lancashire streets. The ships returned with coal or Runcorn sandstone used as building material, as ballast. About 1830, off Pen-Maenan, the first Penmaen Pier or jetty was built to replace this primitive loading method with all its dangers of an open coast; the dangers persist but even these frail-looking narrow piers were better than beaching. The 1833 lease from The Crown gave access to quarrying on the mountain itself and a chain-operated balanced incline brought wagons down to the pier. In time there were to be three inclines (locally dubbed 'banks') and Bonc Jolly Quarry was developed at the summit of them (approx. 600 ft). Some early inclines had narrow vertically-mounted drums at the summit.

To the west the same partners leased part of the Mountain from Lord Newborough and purchased the mineral rights to obtain scree there, so about 1840 a West Pier was built under Thomas Wright's management (approximately ¾ mile west of Penmaen Pier) with attendant incline, the latter being extended upwards to reach the nucleus of the West Quarry by the same date. Workings and inclines then proliferated. Trouble loomed when the projected Chester & Holyhead Railway claimed a course along the limited shoreline and proposed a conflicting right at the point where the West Pier and incline stood. Compromise was reached and Brundrits relinquished the use of the incline and pier in payment for the substitution of a link railway between these West Quarries and the older Penmaen Pier, down to which all Brundrit's products now flowed. Exchange sidings were provided with the L.N.W.R. here also, and some standard-gauge ballast business developed: this connection was by "Wright's Siding" (¾ m. west of Penmaenmawr station).[3]

A locomotive, MONA, was acquired in the 1870s to haul from Penmaen Quarry to Bonc Jolly, but it was unsatisfactory and sold; the first de Winton locomotive of 1878 was next, and served for about 70 years!

Above Bonc Jolly Quarry and to the west of it, the East Quarry opened out from 1880 and a new larger pier was built in 1888; in the early new century the main inclines were improved and straightened and in about 1913 yet another larger jetty was built, to the east of that existing. By the early years of the twentieth century the rock drills were threatening the very summit of the mountain and a small band of ecologists protested in vain.

On the most westerly slopes at Ffrith new workings were opened up in 1907 to recover scree from the slopes facing Llanfairfechan. Inclines led down over the coast road to exchange sidings with the L.N.W.R. but there was never a jetty hereabouts. For shipment stone had to be worked eastwards along the 1847 line and down to Penmaen Pier; Ffrith Mill was built for processing. In due course this source of stone was exhausted, and the whole area closed down in 1931.

Brundrit & Co. Ltd. was liquidated on 10th March, 1911.

DARBISHIRES LTD. (Old and Graiglwyd Quarries)
[Company: Darbishire & Co. until 18th June 1890]

This firm took over the initial business started by Thomas Brassey (the railway contractor) and his partner John Tompkinson who in 1834 had taken a lease from The Crown of part of Graiglwyd Mountain, an area directly behind Penmaenmawr itself. The initial trade involved taking down stone off the screes by sledge to the shore for shipment. In due course a series of five inclines replaced this primitive system – but not at this early time – and a pier was built at Penmaenmawr. The workings were actually in two parts, the older (Old Quarry) to the east of the summit whilst those to the west of it would form the Graiglwyd Quarry later. In 1840 the workings were taken over by Liverpudlians Richard Kneeshaw, J.T. Raynes and William Lupton who developed the site, enlarged it but did nothing to improve substantially the rail system. Due to a fall in demand, the end of the lease and failure to come to terms with the lessors together with a desire on the part of the lessees to operate interests elsewhere along the coast they removed, taking all equipment, incline drums and tramways with them.[4]

With Charles H. Darbishire as Manager,[5] a partnership of William A. Darbishire, Dr. S.D. Darbishire and himself (owners of the nearby Ty-Mawr Estate), purchased a part of the land of the undertaking on 1st January, 1878, but this did not include the pier or the Old Quarry where the Crown lease did not fall in until 1887, at which date the site once carrying three inclines down to the pier was replaced by four new ones. Meanwhile interchange sidings were provided with the L.N.W.R. and the emphasis was on rail-borne despatch. If shipments were needed they were railed to Cei'r-Ynys Wharf on the east bank of the Conway beside the Tubular Bridge, and boats loaded there; shipments for N. Ireland were taken to Connah's Quay for loading. The new lease of 1887 provided an opportunity for a fresh Graiglwyd Pier, and as at Penmaen, the incline foot was run right on to the jetty; it opened in June 1888. Simultaneously working at the Old Quarry recommenced, and new tramways and inclines proliferated. The new focal point became Braich-Llwyd Mill, opened in 1889 and connected with all Darbishire's workings by inclines and contour tracks. Then began a long history of supply of railway ballast for which this Mill was the nucleus; until World War II one of the most familiar of privately-owned wagons was from the fleet which was to carry the Penmaenmawr & Welsh Granite Co.'s standard gauge wagons far afield into the railway system and allow their name to become a household term.

Below and to the east of Graiglwyd workings the Penmarian Mill was erected in 1902, and soon afterwards all the inclines below it to the pier had been given quadruple trackage i.e. double inclines. Yet again the pier was renewed in 1904 to incorporate an ingenious system whereby loaded wagons could discharge either into storage hoppers or directly into ships; a hinged movable section was formed at the foot of the lowest incline to allow for variations in the tide and the height of ships' sides alongside at the pier.

The Company was liquidated on 4th April, 1911, Henry Watkin Darbishire being liquidator.

PENMAENMAWR & WELSH GRANITE CO. LTD.

The foregoing concerns, together with the Welsh Granite Co., amalgamated in 1911, and in 1912 Braich-Llwyd and Penmaen Mills were linked by contour railway as mentioned previously. Each of the old centres of production remained somewhat independent nonetheless, and Penmaen Pier became secondary in importance when Graiglwyd's was replaced by yet another one to the east of that existing. From 1924 the 3 ft gauge system was taken upwards from Braich-Llwyd until it approached Pen-Dinas. For Attic bank, (the very summit of Penmaenmawr Mountain) and the penultimate level (Kimberley; 1,360 ft), a standard gauge railway was begun in 1931. By converting certain balanced inclines to single-tracked hoist-operated inclines (using electric winches for haulage), standard gauge rolling stock and quarry equipment was brought up in part or whole on special 3 ft gauge trolleys. By this means two Avonside Engine Co. diesel locomotives of 1932 and an ex-Lancashire & Yorkshire Railway four-coupled 'pug' saddle tank (L.M.S.R. No. 11245 ex L.&Y.R. No. 43, from Hull Docks, for use as a stand-by) were each taken up intact (plus five further diesel units in due course), whilst a crusher and face-shovel were taken up in parts and erected on the level (1932–33). Attic was worked away completely by winter 1932; Kimberley ended about eleven years later. (This period marked also a time when the Old and Graiglwyd Quarries were largely abandoned in favour of Attic and Kimberley potential.)

A feature without compare hereabouts was the ingenious use of hump and gravity shunting at the crusher/tippler near the 'Thomas Davies' landing. Here the Quarry Engineer (Pierce) contrived a system whereby whole incoming trains were fly-shunted up a hump and held there; then one at a time wagons were let down on the other side into the tippler. Once emptied, they left it by gravity at some speed, passing over sprung trailing points and were stopped by a severe upward incline. This reversed their direction and they returned, changing tracks onto a loop at the said point and continuing by gravity, so to form into line as a train of empties on the adjoining line to that on which they had arrived.

External circumstances and internal changes in quarrying methods had brought about retrenchment and reduction of the railway system from July 1932 when an entirely new system was introduced whereby the face-workings on Attic and Kimberley were mechanised and most of the older working-faces and their attendant inclines were abandoned. Closure of Ffrith (due to other causes) has received mention; Penmaen Mill closed in 1932 and the pier below saw its last vessel in 1955. Inclines above Graiglwyd were replaced by conveyor in 1937, and by 1961 all tracks had gone from Penmaen and the pier was taken down. The area served by the standard gauge first on Kimberley and moved to Fox Bank (1,255 ft) in 1940–1 was ultimately worked out, but from 1949 road vehicles had replaced it. Above Graiglwyd Pier the inclines were gradually replaced from March 1957 by a conveyor until the last rail section (Penmarian Mill and Pencoed – opened 1901–2) was converted in 1962. By 1965 there were only remnants of railway and rolling stock to be seen, and the vestige of non-cable working remaining, all was closed down in June 1967 when the last rail tractor ceased work.

Motive Power – general note

The pattern of locomotion passed through very similar phases to other quarrying sites in the region; first of all man or horses, and then the vertically-boilered steam engine built by de Winton & Co., Caernarvon, the first of which came in 1878 being one of three of this type worked by Brundrit & Co. Ltd. Darbishire introduced steam engines in 1891; seven were de Winton type acquired by them between then and 1895. Hunslet then made entry as they had done elsewhere, and Darbishire had four of their familiar saddle tanks in 1899–1905. Brundrit took delivery of a similar but unusual inside-cylindered version (presumably because of limited clearance?) in 1902 and an Orenstein & Koppel A.G. engine in 1907 – the only one of overseas make in these quarries. It was the last steam purchase, and after many years diesel tractors were introduced from 1929 until 1941. All the foregoing were to 3 ft gauge.

The de Wintons 'gave service' long after withdrawal and parts could be seen cunningly embodied into other machinery whilst the cannibal-ised unused remains lay around for years. They were similar to the 2 ft gauge machines described in other parts of this book, save that they had inside frames and disc wheels outside them and were of course, larger units. The Hunslet engines too were based on their customary four-coupled engines, save that here also the design was enlarged and being of wider gauge, the frames were inside, with the one exception before-mentioned. It was the increased cost of coal and of taking it to the upper levels that marked the introduction of diesel rail tractors there.

Of the rail tractors/locomotives, ALICE, supplied by Sir W.G. Arm-strong Whitworth & Co. Ltd. in 1935 was noteworthy as being a diesel-electric machine.

An 'outsider' which seems to have escaped precise notice was a battery-electric tractor with four-coupled chassis suggesting it had come from a steam locomotive, and having a central 'steeple' cab. This was working between Bell Yard and the foot of Braich-Llwyd Incline in the mid-1930s.

Engines from de Winton & Co.

(B = ex Brundrit & Co. Ltd.   D = ex Darbishires Ltd.)

PENMAEN	B	0–4–0VBT	1878	disused by 1943; still stored East Quarry Jan. 1967	(1)
LILIAN	D	0–4–0VBT	1891	disused by 1933; scrapped	(2)
LOUISA	D	0–4–0VBT	1892	disused by 1936; scrapped by 1951	(3)
ADA	D	0–4–0VBT	1892	disused by 1931; scrapped	(4)
PUFFIN	B	0–4–0VBT	1893	disused by 1934; scrapped but remains extant 1967	(5)
WATKIN	D	0–4–0VBT	1893	disused by 1944; sold Feb. 1966	(6)
HAROLD	D	0–4–0VBT	1894	disused by 1938; dismantled c.1942; chassis became wagon; scrapped 1967	(7)
LLANFAIR	B	0–4–0VBT	1895	abandoned by April 1940; sold Feb. 1966	(8)

All locos unsprung – frames curved round near foundation ring.

Brundrit engines were named after local places: Darbishire after members of the family e.g. H. Watkin Darbishire, (or) Louisa (Mrs. Hewan) a sister of H.W. Darbishire.

Dimensions supplied by the owners:

	Cylinders	Driving Wheel diameter	Wheelbase	Pressure lb./sq. in.	Weight in Working Order
(1)	5¾* × 10 in.	1 ft 8 in.	4 ft	120	4½ tons
(2)	5¾* × 10 in.	1 ft 8 in.	4 ft	120	4½ tons
(3)	5¾* × 10 in.	1 ft 8 in.	4 ft	120	4½ tons
(4)	5¾* × 10 in.	1 ft 8 in.	4 ft	120	4½ tons
(5)[a]	5¾* × 10 in.	1 ft 8 in.	4 ft	120	4½ tons
(6)[b]	5¾* × 10 in.	1 ft 8 in.	4 ft	120	4½ tons
(7)[c]	6¾ × 11½ in.	1 ft 8 in.	4 ft 5 in.	120	5¾ tons
(8)[d]	6¾ × 11½ in.	1 ft 8 in.	4 ft 5 in.	120	5¾ tons

(One of these engines reputed to have had jackshaft drive – ADA?)
Some wheels when new were 1 ft 10 in.

- a. On shed, East Quay; derelict 1967
- b. On Graiglwyd exchange sidings 1946
- c. On Graiglwyd exchange sidings 1932.
- d. Old Quarry, abandoned 1936. Boiler outside diam. 3 ft, length overall 11 ft 6 in., width overall 4 ft 3 in.

*5¾ in. increased to 6 in. later.

Engines from The Hunslet Engine Co. Ltd. (all ceased work 1943)

(B = Brundrit   D = Darbishires)

HUGHIE†	D	0–4–0ST	Works No. 706 of 1899; scrapped 1951	(9)
TIGER	B	0–4–0ST	Works No. 764 of 1902; scrapped 1951; frame used as jig	(10)
STEPHEN	D	0–4–0ST	Works No. 771 of 1902; scrapped pre 1950 but chassis extant then	(11)
SINGAPORE†	D	0–4–0ST	Works No. 798 of 1903; scrapped 1951	(12)
DONALD† (later HUGHIE)	D	0–4–0ST	Works No. 866 of 1905; dismantled by 1951; scrapped	(13)
DUTCHMAN	B	0–4–0WT	Works No. 2464 of 1907; scrapped 1932	(14)

†extant but part dismantled by April 1950.
(Considerable exchanges of saddle tanks).
Locos fitted "SKEFKO" roller-bearings on big ends (TIGER excepted). Salter safety valves in cabs. Cross-head pumps left hand side.

	Cylinders	Driving Wheel diameter	Wheelbase	Pressure lb./sq. in.	Water
(9)	7¼ × 10 in.	1 ft 9 in.	3 ft 3 in.	120	c.120 gall.
(10)	7 × 10 in.	1 ft 10 in.	4 ft		
(11)	7¼ × 10 in.	1 ft 9 in.	3 ft 3 in.	120	c.120 gall.
(12)	7¼ × 10 in.	1 ft 9 in.	3 ft 3 in.	120	c.120 gall.
(13)	7¼ × 10 in.	1 ft 9 in.	3 ft 3 in.	120	c.120 gall.

(14) new from Orenstein & Koppel A.G. Berlin.

Painting (1930s):

de Winton: Black, ³⁄₁₆ in. blue lining;
Hunslet: Green, ½ in. yellow lining.

Rail Tractors and Locomotives*

No.	Name	Type			Works No.	Date	Date disused	Note
–	(COED)	4 wh.	PM	Motor-Rail	5024	1929	1967	(1)
–	—	4 wh.	DM	Motor-Rail	5611	1931	gone by 1953	(2)
–	(LLWYD)	4 wh.	DM	Motor-Rail	5905	1933	1962	(3)
–	(MARIAN)	4 wh.	DM	Motor-Rail	5941	1936	1967	(4)
–	HAROLD	4 wh.	DM	Motor-Rail	5950	1938	1967	(5)
14	LLWYD	4 wh.	DM	Motor-Rail	5951	1938	1962	(6)
–	NANT	4 wh.	DM†	Motor-Rail	5513	1930	1967	(7)
–	(STEPHEN)	4 wh.	DM	Motor-Rail	5949	1937		(8)
–	ALICE	0–4–0	DE	Armstrong Whitworth	D53	1935	1967	(9)
–	VIXEN	0–4–0	DM	Hunslet	3129	1944	1967	(10)
–	TAFF	4 wh.	DM	Hunslet	1770	1935	1967	(11)
–	(CRIMEA)	4 wh.	DM	Ruston & Hornsby	202987	1941	1966	(12)
–	(WELLS)	4 wh.	DM	Ruston & Hornsby	202989	1941	Scrapped 1967	(13)

PM = Petrol mechanical;   DM = Diesel mechanical;   DE = Diesel electric.

Notes
1. Built as Petrol Mechanical – converted to Diesel Mechanical. New
2. New
3. New
4. New
5. New
6. ex-STEPHEN. New
7. ex-Trevor Quarries: returned ex-2 ft gauge PM converted to 3 ft gauge 1933 and to Diesel 20/28 April 1934
8. ex-DINAS: to Trevor Quarries 1953–4 (from whence it came)
9. New – see THE NARROW GAUGE No. 50, p.40
10. New
11. Purchased secondhand 1947/8   All ex B.C.S. (Engineers & Contractors) Ltd.
12. Purchased secondhand 1947/8 ⎫ Taffs Well (ex-Balfour Beatty & Co. Ltd.
13. Purchased secondhand 1947/8 ⎬ Orkney)

*See INDUSTRIAL RAILWAY RECORD No. 68, p.293 – general article.
†See note 7.
(Acknowledgement to Neville Fields for assistance with loco notes compiled in 1949–50.)

Wagons (All of 'contractors type' basis i.e. adapted bodies on plain oak chassis with wheels outside the frame)

The main business was conducted by four differing types of open wagon:–

(1) *Mill Side-tipper*	An open box containing approximately 2 tons used for carrying crushed granite or rubbish – discharge and tipping mechanism released by lever at one end; body laterally pivotted on chassis to this end.
(2) *Three-sided 'Breaker'* [sic]	An open box having one open side to carry approximately 2½ tons of setts. Loading etc. was done through the open side. Mostly rebuilds of (1) using complete chassis.
(3) *Side-door Hopper*	Specifically for loading ships at the piers, with side discharge. Steel-sheet floor. Capacity approximately 3 tons.
(4) *Open Wagon*	A large 4 ton (nominally 3 ton) box wagon for carrying stone within the quarry, and especially between crushers. Emptied by rotary tippler (often in pairs together).

Type	Body Length overall	Body Width overall	Height overall	Wheelbase
1	6 ft 6 in.	5 ft	3 ft 9 in.	3 ft
2	6 ft 6 in.	5 ft	5 ft	3 ft
3	7 ft 3 in.	5 ft 2 in.	5 ft 3 in.	3 ft 3 in.
4	6 ft 6 in.	5 ft	5 ft	3 ft

The first two and the last type ran similar wooden chassis as to size, frame, wheels and pedestal bearings. The third type was similar but of larger chassis and ran on sealed roller bearings and was immediately recognisable by their pressed steel wheels. (Originally 7-curved spoke wheels and plain bearings as for other stock.) On the other types wheels were seven-curved spoke, 13–13¾ in. diameter.

Wagons built by the Company in timber with locally made ironwork, save that Britannia Foundry, Portmadoc (and others) supplied it from time to time. Painting was in light grey or red oxide with black ironwork. Lettering and numbering was in white, usually by stencil. Some bodies had white ends.

Workshop for building and repair of stock employed eight men; deterioration rate was comparatively high among the 3 and 4 ton types.

Also used, embodying many of the standard parts from the foregoing or using rebuilt wagons for the purpose:

Tank wagons for diesel oil; flat wagons for constructional work; tool wagons; mobile chutes; man-riding incline cars; gunpowder vans.

Couplings by upturned hinged hooks and loose link; 'buffers' formed by extension of the main frame members (which were in all cases behind the wheels).

In times past an *estimated total of approximately* 400 wagons was in operation.

Trackwork

Mainly conventional in flat bottomed rail spiked to wooden sleepers approximately 5 ft × 6 in. × 5 in. and sometimes secured on the outside of sharp curves by wooden blocks to prevent the rails from spreading. All early trackwork in 30 lb. (occasionally 16 lb.) rail with sleepers at 3 ft intervals; later replacements in varying weights of heavier rail, in most recent times 45 lb./yd.

Maximum mileage of track about 70; number of inclines (not co-existent) 42.

Although it was naturally the aim of the Company to minimise the number of accidents which might occur on these exceptionally steep inclines, 'THE QUARRY MANAGER'S JOURNAL' has several records: in 1932 two runaway laden wagons crashed into two wagons in which men were riding up the incline, a young man being killed, one man who escaped was catapulted over a 6 ft wall. The loaded wagons had been jerked off the head of the incline when seven men were coming up in one of two empty wagons, the leading one of which derailed and hit a bridge buttress. The practice of riding in the wagons or standing on the buffers was not prohibited. Two years later a man riding on the buffer of an ascending wagon slipped and fell into the path of descending wagons with fatal results.

The Shed Master at Bangor was sent for to inspect the standard-gauge engines on the mountain top:

> We rode up the mountain . . . in a cable-hauled truck . . . at the top we had to change and then travelled for a little over a mile on the footplate of a diesel locomotive that was banking a train of about 20 quarry wagons. This part of the journey was along a railway roughly laid along a ledge cut in the hillside about 1,000 ft above the sea and the rocking and pitching as the engine pushed its load around blind corners with apparently nothing either ahead or below and only the rockface on the inner side was rather a grim experience . . .

He returned via a different route:

> . . . found ourselves on a flat piece of ground about 12 ft wide which went straight out to sea below with no intervening ground. Across this flat piece of terra firma ran a 3 ft gauge track whose rails, bent at a very acute angle, disappeared from sight over the edge . . . on (it) stood a fourwheeled trolley with two rows of seats placed almost on their backs and attached to the end of a cable . . . we were invited to take our seats . . . and I did so rather fearfully after having had a good look at the coupling pin and the cable!

Clearly, the scenario and methods of a quarry system as opposed to those of the L.M.S.R. were sharply contrasted in the mind of J.M. Dunn on that occasion.

John Hicklin's 'THE HANDBOOK OF LLANDUDNO' published in the late nineteenth century states that even then there was a 'nice summer house part way up the mountain for the accommodation of visitors where picnic parties are continually found' and that parties could ascend in the returning wagons 'but being very perpendicular requires a strong nerve.'

PENMAENMAWR SHIPS
BRUNDRIT & CO. LTD.

Brundrit & Whiteway, Runcorn }
John Brundrit, Runcorn }
Penmaenmawr Shipping Co. Ltd., Liverpool

Name	Period of above-named ownership	Builder	Type	Gross Tons
JOHN	1840–1883*	Brundrit & Whiteway, Runcorn	Schooner	62
PHILIP	1842–1865*	Brundrit & Whiteway, Runcorn	Schooner	72
SARAH	1846–1865*	Brundrit & Whiteway, Runcorn	Schooner	77
THE PORT	1847–1865	Brundrit & Whiteway, Runcorn	Schooner	69
DUKE	1848–1884	Brundrit & Whiteway, Runcorn	Schooner	74
ELLESMERE	1850–1901	Brundrit & Whiteway, Runcorn	Schooner	72
SIR ROBERT	1851–1878	Brundrit & Whiteway, Runcorn	Schooner	60
LLANFAIR	1852–1873	Brundrit & Whiteway, Runcorn	Sloop	52
ANNE CHESHYRE	1853–1873	Brundrit & Whiteway, Runcorn	Sailing Ship	413
BRACKLEY	1854–1883	Brundrit & Whiteway, Runcorn	Schooner	80
ALMA	1855–1881	Brundrit & Whiteway, Runcorn	Schooner	78
DENNIS BRUNDRIT	1856–1874	Brundrit & Whiteway, Runcorn	Sailing Ship	462
SQUALL	1857–1869	Brundrit & Whiteway, Runcorn	Sloop	7
GWYDIR	1858–1873	Brundrit & Whiteway, Runcorn	Smack	55
BERTIE	1859–1909	Brundrit & Whiteway, Runcorn	?Schooner	61
PRIORY	1861–1865	Brundrit & Whiteway, Runcorn	Schooner	88
ECLIPSE	1863–1882	Brundrit & Whiteway, Runcorn	Schooner	78
SWIFT	1865–1906	Brundrit & Whiteway, Runcorn	Flat	66
PARKER	1866–1873	Brundrit & Whiteway, Runcorn	Smack	58
SWALLOW	1868–1909	Brundrit & Whiteway, Runcorn	Smack	67
JULIA	1874–1901	Brundrit & Whiteway, Runcorn	Schooner	66
INO	1876–1877	Frodsham in 1846	Schooner	75
MARTEN	1878–1888	John Brundrit	Sloop	67
REGINALD	1881–1888	Brundrit & Co. Runcorn	Steamer	116
A.M. BRUNDRIT	1882–1885	Brundrit & Co. Runcorn	Schooner	113
PERCY	1887–1906	John Brundrit	Flat†	89
CECIL	1890–1909	R. Smith & Co. Lytham	Steamer	235
TAFFY	1894–1899	D.J. Dunlop & Co. Port Glasgow	Steamer	173
SUNBEAM	1898–1909	Brundrit & Co. Runcorn	Schooner	148
PUFFIN	1900–1909	Ailsa Shipbuilding Co. Troon	Steamer	404

*Gone by
†Converted to steam 1891

TREFRIW AREA TRAMWAYS (c.1840–1958)

There is a region of attractive upland country on the west of the Conway, south-west of Trefriw and so south to the Llugwy Valley, much of which today is worked by the Forestry Commission. It is a

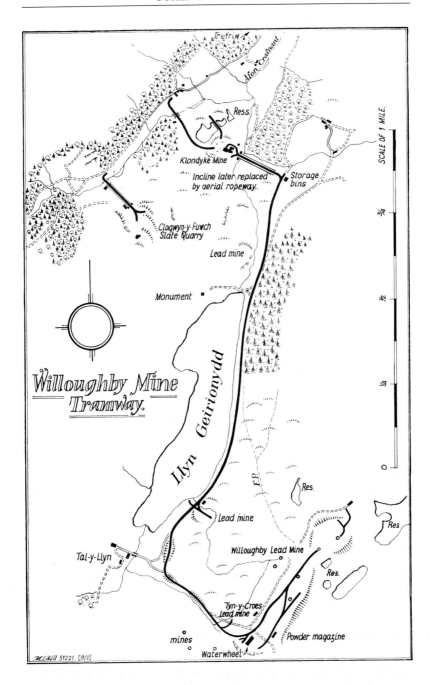

Trefriw

Afon Crafnant

Ress.

Klondyke Mine

Incline later replaced
by aerial ropeway.

Storage
bins

Cloqwyn-y-Fuwch
Slate Quarry

Lead mine

Monument

SCALE OF 1 MILE.

¾

½

½

0

Willoughby Mine
Tramway.

Llyn Geirionydd

FP

Res.

Res

Lead mine

Willoughby Lead Mine

Res.

Tal-y-Llyn

Tyn-y-Croes
Lead mine

mines

Powder magazine

Waterwheel

tract of broken high ground above 600 ft and many small lakes (some created by the mining companies) in the pockets between. There is a history of working for metal ores from Roman times; more recently slate was gained. The wharf at Trefriw was the shipping point. The number of sites is too numerous to list here but most of the small workings had internal tramways, few of which can be traced as most have been swept away in recent years as afforestation has taken over.

Of perhaps about two dozen sites where rails were once laid, only two systems were of such age and magnitude as to deserve individual mention, and one is only notable in that it was worked until the early 1960s, though it must be said that, like an iceberg, most of the rail system was out of sight (a conclusion supported by informed present-day exploration). Of the others, David Bick has written ". . . lead mines near Llanrwst . . . none of which were doing any good, at least for the shareholders."

At Willoughby Mine (1888) [Ref: 767603] between 1877 and 1911 tonnages were such as to substitute carts by a tramway to carry lead and zinc ores; 1,400 tons of the former and 1,880 tons of the latter were taken to the smelter in that period, the name of the undertaking changing with successive owners viz: Welsh Foxdale (1901), Welsh Crown Spelter (1906), New Pandora (1914), with no record of continuous working.[7] An early petrol-driven rail tractor by Kerr Stuart & Co. Ltd (No. 861 of 1904) is reputed to have worked from 1904 which may also date from a rebuilding of the tramway . . . it is shown extant on the 1887 Survey. In 1907 there was a typical closure when all was dismantled only to re-open with wartime demands in 1914. The gauge was 1 ft 10 in. and length just under 1½ miles. Of similar output but without significant tramway systems were Pool Mine (Bettws-y-Coed) and more recently, Tre-Castell, southwest of Conway – the most productive of the period.

During successive ownerships water power derived by wheels driven from reservoir sources was abandoned in favour of electrical power, and tramways were drastically curtailed in extent. Water remained in demand only for the washing of ore.

At Willoughby tramroads were laid in light bridge or flat bottomed rail, the smallest being only 5 lb./yd. A steep grade of approximately 1 in 20 at each end of the line was a distinctive feature, as was a considerable stone-walled embankment about 6 ft wide and 10 ft high, filled with 'arisings', emphasising a 'permanent' image to the work.

Small wooden tub wagons were in use (3 ft 8 in. long: 2 ft 2 in. wide: 3 ft height from rail running on 12 in. diameter wheels at 1 ft 3 in. wheelbase). The waterwheel here was stated to be only second to that at Laxey (Isle of Man) in size; during World War I it was blown up for scrap.

The second most extensive rail system was largely underground at Parc Mine [Ref: 788602] which like the others has a long history but most importantly in the century from the 1850s. In 1887 it was the D'Eresby Mountain Mine, becoming Llanrwst Park Lead Mine then simply Parc Mine in which form it finally closed. Like neighbouring workings it has opened and closed repeatedly and recently was subjected to the most modern techniques by its owners, Johannesburg Consolidated Investments (inc. 1951). The first flimsy tramways (possibly early 19th century) were of 1 ft 2 in. gauge and horse-worked using wooden tub-wagons: underground gradients were considerable e.g. approximately 1 in 40. It was only approximately 400 yards long. In the most recent phase (1951) a new tramway of 24 in. gauge using 40 lb. flat bottomed track and modern mining wagons evolved largely out of World War II for mineral exploitation when overseas supplies were cut off, together with modern motive power (including battery-electric rail tractors underground), was in evidence. Underground workings were extended south west, to approximately 1½ miles when work ceased in 1958.

After a period of closure the mill worked briefly in 1960, but subsequently all equipment was scrapped soon after. The latterday appearance of the site with its vast spoil tips and use of concrete was utterly different from any other described, and with a daily tonnage of c.300 tons was one of the largest British metal mines.

Extremely large steel-bodied 3-ton tippler cars were used, plus over 100 1-ton side-tippers with three Ruston & Hornsby 20DLU rail tractors as motive power. The latter could haul eight 3 ton or fifteen 1 ton wagons when loaded and there was a considerable yard layout with fan of sidings, tippler and loco shed and workshop at the mine entrance.[8]

Underground, considerable sophistication was evident but the whole system never realised the potential which it was designed to meet, as the ore proved too poor in quality.

It is of interest that Samual Worthington, so prominent in his early work at Port Penrhyn, constructed the Trefriw – Llyn Crafnant road to give employment at a time of great distress.

ARDDA MINE TRAMWAY (1853–1864)

In extraordinary contrast to the pleasant soft mountainscape of west Trefriw only two miles to the south, the district west of Dolgarrog is a wild upland desolation (not without attraction in that respect) most fitted today for rearing of sheep and the collection of water! The region lies south-west to north-east, bounded on the west by a high ridge having some spectacular shapes, an arm of which projects almost into Dolgarrog village itself which lies at the foot of the west escarpment of the Conway Valley. This ridge acts as a watershed and catchwater between – to the north – the Afon Porth-Llwyd Valley, and – to the south – the Afon Ddu Valley. At the head of each re-entrant formed by

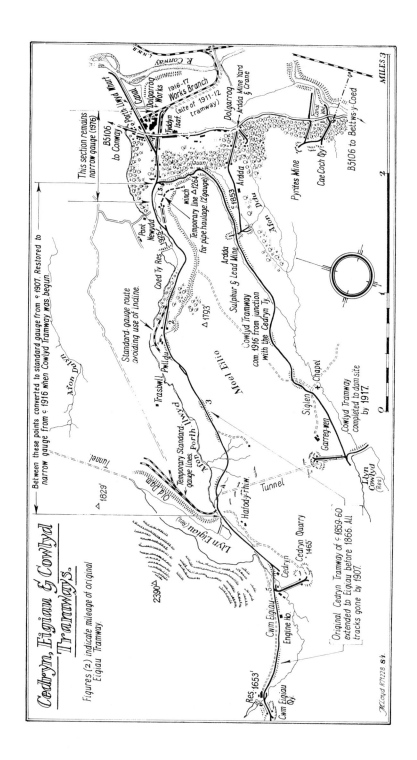

Cedryn, Eigiau & Cowlyd Tramways.

Figures (2) indicate original mileage of original Eigiau Tramway.

Between these points converted to standard gauge from c.1907. Restored to narrow gauge from c.1916 when Cowlyd Tramway was begun.

This section remains narrow gauge (1976)

R. Conway

L.N.W.R.

Canal

Dolgarrog Works

1916-17 Works Branch

Porth Llwyd Wharf

B5106 to Conway

Tyddyn Isaf

(site of 1911-12 tramway)

Dolgarrog

Arda Mine Yard & Crane

B5106 to Betws-y-Coed

Jauun

L.S.

winch line △1264

Temporary line △1264 for pipe haulage (2gauge)

Arda

Arda Ddu

Afon

Pyrites Mine

Cae Coch Qy.

Canal Head

Pont Newydd 1935'

Coed Ty Res.

Arda Sulphur & Lead Mine

Cowlyd Tramway com.1916 from junction with the Cedryn Ty

Afon Dylan

Standard-gauge route avoiding use of incline.

△1793

Moel Eilio

Trasswll Phillau

2

Afon y Porth

3

Temporary Standard-gauge lines

Hafod-y-Fnim

A

Tunnel

Siglen

Chapel

Garreg-wen

Cowlyd Tramway completed to dam site by 1917.

Llyn Cowlyd (Res)

Old Dam

Tunnel

△1829'

Afon Ddu

Llyn Eigiau (Res)

Cedryn

Cedryn Quarry '1465'

2390△

Cedryn

Engine Ho.

Cwm Eigiau

5

Original Cedryn Tramway of c.1859-60 extended to Eigiau before 1866. All tracks gone by 1907.

Res. 1653'

Cwm Eigiau Qy.

MILES: 3

2

1

0

H.Lloyd R71228 81

these two rivers is today a reservoir, each responsible in its time for two
of the most remote tramways in North Wales.

Sulphur, slate, slab and the gathering of water for urban and
industrial supplies have been the reason for the construction of several
narrow gauge tramways (and one standard gauge contractor's railway)
hereabouts.

Ardda Tramway was the earliest line in the area and brought iron
sulphide (pyrites) down from a mine at 1,100 ft [Ref: 760659] to a
walled yard where the stock was held for security [Ref: 774663]. It was
then taken mostly by cart to Conway for shipment to Lancashire, via
Merseyside and Deeside ports where by two processes then in use,
sulphuric acid was made for the textile industry. A lease for 21 years
from Lord Newborough to 'The Ardda Sulphur Mine Co.' of April
1854 permitted the construction of a tramway – the mine itself was
leased from the Gwydyr Estate and some of the tramway lay thereon;
this lease recites 'a continued line of iron railway either with a single or
double line . . . to carry sulphur . . . engines either fixed or locomotive.' [Sulphur itself would not have been extracted from such local
workings and the term 'Sulphus Mine' used in this district is a mis-
nomer. Iron Sulphide was extracted from which Sulphuric Acid was
made in a host of small works in south Lancashire.] A warehouse was
erected on the opposite side of the Conway road. Lord Newborough
had the right to use the line himself after three years of the lease, and
purchase at the end of it. The Company gave notice of cessation to use
in March 1864.[9]

Part or all of the line was in use by March 1853 and had closed by
1864. The course may be followed from where it passes out of the mine
under the Cowlyd Tramway bridge with smithy and office adjacent,
then easterly to a point in the woodland where it runs along a shelf to
the head of an incline [Ref: 769663] which drops the line in an E.S.E.
direction to the mine yard beside the Royal Oak Inn (now the Newborough Arms Hotel). The whole line was a little under a mile in length
and probably of 2 ft gauge. Surviving rails in the vicinity suggest some
use of fish-bellied track, perhaps second-hand from the Nantlle Railway whose materials were identical? The tramway on the Gwydyr
portion may have been ready by 1852, as it is described in March 1853
as 'has lately been made'.

Previous transport had been by sledge.

The 'CARNARVON & DENBIGH HERALD' 12th March, 1864 advertised
an auction at Trefriw for tramway materials 'About 1,500 yards of flat
iron rails, 1,000 yards of wire rope . . . 6 new iron wagons, 6 old iron
wagons . . . also a very powerful break [sic] and drum . . . a large
quantity of sleepers . . .' and there is little doubt this marked the end.

CAE-COCH (or RHIBO) PYRITES MINE, TREFRIW
(c.1860–1919)

According to contemporary records of shipments from Trefriw down the Conway, this was probably the most successful of the many mines which were scattered over the Gwydyr Estate; it was approximately 4 miles northwest of Llanrwst and about the 600 ft contour high up on the western escarpment of the Conway Valley [Ref: 775654]. Iron pyrites and sulphur were worked and in the earliest times the pyrites were brought down the hillside on sledges to the turnpike: the largest working was a cave-like entrance in the steep hillside above Trefriw chalybeate wells. Sledges also carried the output to the river bank to reach river boats and transfer their loads; at first the output was taken to Thompson & Hill's Vitriol premises in Vauxhall Road, Liverpool.

There is much conflicting information about the various periods in which the main mine and various smaller adits were worked, and the dates on which tramways and the use of its own wharf came into use are not known for certain.[10]

Following a sample assay of Cae-Coch pyrites by John Hawkesley Thompson in 1818, his relatives Messrs. Thompson & Hill of Liverpool took a lease of the mine for 14 years from 1st June, 1821. Between 1826–40 they remained the tenants; it was quite the most productive of the Gwydyr mines with an average of 394 tons of ore in 1827–35. Only four men worked there up to 1834, then the number doubled. After 1832, with the death of John Hawkesley Thompson, the firm continued as William Hill & Sons, Liverpool, chemical manufacturers who now loaded at Cae-Coch wharf (rather than at Trefriw wharf further south, which involved road cartage). By 1872 – and probably existing well before then – a tramway is mentioned in the lease. Hill operated until 1876 and then closed due to competition from Spain and Scandinavia. Then William Veitch, trading from Crieff from 1880 until 1886 and then at Trefriw until 1889. By 1886, employee strength was 103, the highest attained. Veitch's lease authorised 'laying a tramroad to the turnpike' but there must have been an incline to replace sledges long before this time. Between 1889–98 tenants were the North Wales Sulphur Mining Co. Ltd. (or locally "Muspratt's") of Trefriw (who had been obliged to move from Liverpool to Newton-le-Willows and later were forced to move again to Flint in view of the evil fumes from the Works) with employment about 60, but reduced to 3 in 1895 when work ceased again due to competition from abroad. During this time Veitch was agent.

No work took place until World War I created a demand for sulphur which could not be met by shortage of shipping; Morris & Roberts of Bangor worked the site 1915–16 but only employed 2 men; in 1917–18 the work was taken over by the Ministry of Munitions who employed over 200 men for a brief period. The history of the mine is wholly intermittent, with Cae-Coch Pyrites Ltd. formed in 1888 never doing any effective trade! During World War I, The Mineral Resources Development Committee was deputed to find large quantities '. . . for the manufacture of sulphuric acid'. The mine was hastily re-equipped at a cost of £50,000 to produce 600 tons a week, and equally hastily closed in July 1919. During 1941–42 the Ministry of Supply carried out development work but production was not resumed. In 1945 the tenants were British Non-Ferrous Mining Co. Ltd. of Holywell. Between 1860–75 the mine produced 90,000 tons of ore, most being shipped to the Merseyside ports, including Liverpool and Runcorn. During World War I 16,000 tons were extracted in two years.

To confuse further the rail-transport situation, from 1929 the main incline (abandoned then for the past ten years) was rebuilt for the use of a granite quarry about the same contour, and as there are relics of all the foregoing periods, the materials in use being the main evidence of date, the site is of especial interest. Early maps show an abandoned incline leading down from the mine along the northern boundary of Trefriw Wells; there may have been a tramway on this or it may have been a sledgeway; maps show it as abruptly curtailed some distance above and west of the Trefriw–Conway road here. If used by sledges, perhaps these could be dragged over the adjacent field to the road; if a tramway incline there may have been failure to complete to the foot (leasing problems) . . . there are several possibilities. Unclear too, is the evidence of a primitive canal off the Conway, leading to the east edge of the road opposite to where this incline would cease; there is now no trace of such. [References: incline head 775653; canal head 778653].

No doubts exist however, about the second(?) and more southerly incline, with a gallery extending northwards to the original mine, and another some way down to the south to a second adit. The incline head is at Ref: 775652 with the remains of at least two winding gears, probably a legacy of various ownerships, the most modern being the Government period. The original drumhouse survives as does a modern steel framework with a horizontal wheel. On the descent a small crane to the north edge stands beside the skeleton of a workshop with 12 ft lathe bed inside! At a forestry road further down there is a derelict granite loading point for the (later) stone-quarrying period to which the incline was put to use, the effect being to divide the old incline into two at this point. The former sulphur incline comes down beside these works but throws off a branch above them (as above mentioned) southward to the second adit; the stone works have not entirely erased the terminal works of this branch. Continuing down over the forestry road the incline (some of whose trackwork still survives though the sleepers have gone) course drops down beside another granite quarry at its roadside foot and some of the incline stonework has been quarried away here. Once at the road level, the sulphur tramway was obliged to make a sharp 'S' bend, cross the road on the level and continue eastwards along a stonesided embankment, over a weighbridge and out to a banjo-shaped wharf built in enormous blocks of stone [Ref: 781652] forming a 'T'-shaped terminal with discharging sidings. Doubtless in later times the excursion steamers on the river used this wharf for those passengers anxious to take the waters at the nearby Trefriw Well!

There is some old material lying about suggesting a tramway was installed in the Thompson & Hill period; there are 'T'-bulb rails (as used also at nearby Ardda) in chairs, light bridge rails of about 10 lb./yd. and some unique-section flat bottomed rail with a section resembling a crushed collar stud! During the 1917–18 period the Ministry installed a wire ropeway to take the output overhead direct from the mine to a siding by the L.N.W.R. Conway Valley branch.

CEDRYN QUARRY TRAMWAY (c.1861–c.1888)

A small slate and slab quarry on Lord Newborough's land [Ref: 719636] is noted in Samuel Holland's diary as being worked by him about 1827 whilst waiting for legal proceedings to be clarified regarding his interests at Blaenau Ffestiniog. Access to this very remote site was by an extremely rough track – possibly unsuited to carts – and Holland had but a short flirtation with it. Following this it was worked by at least four lessees, including W.A. Darbishire of the Pen-Dyffryn Quarry, Nantlle. In 1863 the "Caedryn" [sic] Slate Quarry Co. Ltd. took it over but assigned it to the British Slate Co. Ltd. [formed in 1860 to work three Welsh quarries: Cwm Eigiau, Cedryn and Vron (Nantlle) in 1865, but probably assigned earlier, in fact.] British Slate liquidated in 1874 and the following year the Caedryn [sic] & Cwm Eigiau Slate Co. Ltd. formed, only to be dissolved 11 years later. Cedryn Quarry closed for all time before 1890 but there must have been earlier periods of disuse when British Slate announced they would concentrate on Vron only in 1871. Although there were tramways in the Quarry by 1854 output at first used the primitive road from the head of the valley to the foot of the Dolgarrog escarpment (i.e. Holland's time) and though some accounts have credited a tramway with this early period, it was 1861–3 when such was built, from the Quarry [Ref: 720635] to a wharf on the Conway [Ref: 775681] about 5 miles long involving a number of inclines from quarry floor level to riverside wharf. 'THE NORTH WALES CHRONICLE' has; "Tenders invited to construct a tramroad 5 miles long from Cwm Eigia [sic] slate quarry to River Conway, 6 miles from Llanrwst, for H.E. Sullivan . . . includes an incline 600 yd in Dolgarrog Woods and a bridge under the turnpike. (George Felton, Mostyn Estates Office, Llandudno, 15.8.1861.)"

The gauge was a nominal 2 ft and the track identical with that of the Croesor Tramway, built also at this time; i.e. wrought iron rails 18 ft long, 'T' section with strengthening 'bulb' flange on one bottom edge, carried in chairs with small wooden keys on wood sleepers.[11] The route of the line from the quarry incline down to the main line passed over the infant Eigiau on a wooden trestle, past a small reservoir to feed the waterwheel at the main mill and turning east, crossed the river again [Ref: 718639] by a timber bridge on piles at Bont-y-Cedryn. The small dwelling "Cedrun" was nearby, and traces of a siding to it. The primitive road struck up the hillside above, direct to the quarry and a small barrack. For a time until the extension to the Eigiau Quarry this was the head of the line. It is a bleak, treeless upland tract. Now on the south side of the river the course passes Bont-y-Hafod-Rhiw and the rejuvenated site of the Eigiau Reservoir with its broken walling of the 1925 collapse still evident, and rounding a col at Hafod-y-Rhiw makes lonely progress along the 1,200 ft contour, over the water tunnel linking Eigiau and Cowlyd [Ref: 726651] so over a stone embankment with the site of the standard gauge 'avoiding line' now a road alongside. There is a second such embankment [Ref: 732651] but little to break the monotonous scene as the route passes along the hillside, save for an occasional earthwork.

Here and there are traces of passing loops; the roadway and tramway merged for a distance but the former drops below whilst the tramway crosses two stone embankments and at Ref: 749664 is forced to drop by incline to road level beside the present Coed-Ty concentration reservoir. There has been some woodland here and the surroundings are much softer; present day catchwater leats make casual walking for the investigator almost impossible without the availability of a portable bridge! About Pwll-Du [Ref: 764672] comes the junction with the later Cowlyd line, and in connection with 1925 activities there are remains of sidings, a stockyard for pipes and materials for waterworks. Curving round the contour (c.850 ft) now the track survives as an access from the Works below; there is a more modern winding house, a primitive loading platform and the head of two inclines which at 1 in 1½ and 1 in 3½ fall steeply down through the Cae Ty-Mawr and Dolgarrog woodland [Ref: 767673]: the foot of the second passed under the turnpike road at Tyddyn-Isaf by an 18 ft 'tunnel', 7 ft wide and 5 ft 9 in. high and is in the Works' complex: most signs beyond are now obliterated, but the tramway continued across flat marshy meadowland to the river's edge at Porth-Llwyd wharf, the valley of that river having been followed from Llyn Eigiau. There was a small yard here and the main wharf lay alongside a short northward twist of the track. It was a traditional point for water craft to moor and existed long before the time of the tramway.[12]

(In C.C.R.O. ref: X/M/Maps 680/9 are details of a proposed bridge 'tramroad crossing the Conway and Llanrwst Turnpike Road . . . altered afterwards': the highway is 16 ft 6 in. wide and the rail gauge 2 ft 6 in.)

An interesting issue in its story is the employment of Charles E. Spooner to survey the proposed line in the early 1850s and near Bankfield House, (the foot of the lower of the two Dolgarrog inclines) and a tunnel under the road, there was a depot (Cei-Coed) alongside, perhaps suggesting that some products went thence by cart? There was certainly a crane here, used by Penmachno Quarry as the nearest place for unloading carted slab! An account of Spooner's visit, given verbally by W.O. Roberts a former licencee, speaks of his being loaned a horse by the Royal Oak Inn in order to reach the Quarry, and taking dinner there afterwards. Ten years later (April 1860) C.W. Ramsden made an unfinished survey also, and in August 1861 George Felton of Mostyn Estate Offices, Llandudno made a third![13]

After transport costs rendered such quarries at the ends of remote valleys uneconomical, the course of the lifted tramway became a rough road.

Apart from the finding of a double-flanged wheel in the Quarry, nothing is known of its equipment. Leases only refer to 'iron rail' or 'tram rail'. Cedryn was an open working but Eigiau Quarry (about to be described) was a mine.

EIGIAU (or EIGIA) QUARRY TRAMWAY (c.1863–c.1888)

This Mine (later worked more nearly as an open quarry) [Ref: 702635] was about a mile further west than Cedryn, and on about the same contour (c.1600 ft) – a survey from Conway to Eigiau (not exactly followed) was made by C.W. Ramsden in April 1860 – and the Cedryn Tramway was extended the intervening distance about 1863; the 'CARNARVON & DENBIGH HERALD' on 14th March, 1863 contains W.A. Darbishire's advertisement for a contractor 'to build a tramway from Cedryn Quarry to the River Conway' which may suggest the Eigiau line was as yet incomplete but on evidence is more likely to refer to an extension westwards of that tramway.

Sir Richard Bulkeley leased the 'slates under a sheepwalk at Cwm Eigia in the parish of Caerhun with rights to make . . . tramways . . .' for 21 years in 1827 to James Rigby of Hawarden (and others) and tenants covenanting to employ 100 men by the third year and subsequently. In 1853 working passed to the Cwm Eigiau Quarry Slate & Slab Co. Ltd. which was liquidated in 1859; they were 'shortly to lay a tram road across a mountain, being a descent from the quarry'.[14] There must have been an interregnum, as another lease of 6th September, 1861 was taken by Henry Eden Sullivan of Cwm Eigia [sic] Lodge (trading as Cwm Eigia Slate Co.); this lease underlines the 'sandwiched' position of the quarry between Lord Penrhyn's land to the west and Lord Newborough's to the east. This carried the right to 'use the present road' but on the landlord's copy is pencilled '. . . over which the said (Sullivan) has constructed or is constructing a tramway for the use of said quarry or mines'. Next, The British Slate Co. Ltd. took a lease 1st July 1865 and the plan shows a complete tramroad.[15]

It has already been seen that British Slate was a poor performer and closed down in 1874, abandoning Eigia before then but paying rent up to that time. To complicate matters a portion of the quarry was worked by Caerhun Slate Co. Ltd. from late 1865 – this company too was dissolved in 1883. On 1st January, 1875 'THE CAMBRIAN NEWS' advertised for sale a 'Slate Quarry with tramway to the river Conway . . .'.

Examination of all issues suggests production ceased in about June 1868, the tramway enjoying only brief usage.

A Sale Catalogue (N.L.W. Caerns. 125) of 1889 says 'A tramway has been made to connect the quarry with another tramway by which the produce can be taken down and shipped on the Conway, a tidal river distance about 6 miles'. This description conflicts with some earlier ones which suggest the tramway extended the full distance as part of the Eigia lease, but it is likely that the Eigia's portion of line only extended to the boundary between Bulkeley and Newborough lands.

Warrington Smythe ('REPORT TO THE OFFICE OF WOODS & FORESTS' 1867) writes of 'the wastes of Caerhun and Llanbedr' where he found these two quarries working on 'an important scale by the same Company'. Eigia employed 60 men in production of slate and slab, and Smythe refers to a 1½ mile tramway connecting the two. 'Cedryn employs fewer men but has a fine incline constructed to carry its produce down to the machinery placed on the main valley'.

HAFOD-LAS or THE BETTWS-y-COED QUARRY
(c.1862–c.1927)

This medium sized open quarry [Ref: 780560] was in business by 1862 and worked on the gallery system mainly for slate but also produced slab; it was taken down to Bettws railway station along the main Holyhead road, one mile to the east. The quarry lay to the south and above that road at a height of 750 ft. A second pit to the east of the mill appears to be a 'second generation' working.

It had a short main tramroad of less than half a mile in fullest extent and most of this was a double-tracked balanced incline leading from the mills at the summit to a roadside wharf at the foot, this being a little distance off the main road itself. A feature of the incline is the considerable cutting *en route*, an unusual necessity generally capable of avoidance in other situations; the incline is also bounded by some substantial slab walling near the summit. Here, barrack buildings extend to the west and two mills with a water wheel between to the east, the latter bearing the date 'A.D. 1863'. There are two further individual inclines behind the mill – an ecclesiastical-looking structure – and the eastern is not topped by a drumhouse as conventionally in Wales, but has a horizontal cable wheel let into a slab lined pit beneath ground level. In the galleries round the excavation are several small tunnels for the tramway, which was of 1 ft 11 in. gauge. Various patterns of 10 lb./yd. bridge rail, 5–8 lb./yd. flat-bottomed and elsewhere, characteristic 'T'-bulb cast rails in chairs were used. All these were carried on primitive wooden sleepers and everywhere the materials used were extremely light.

The pit to the east of the mill was approached by a tunnel, more recently opened out into a cutting, and to the east side is another incline down whose side came a 24 in. diameter cast-iron water pipe bringing a supply from Llyn Elsi to drive water wheels (and later, turbines). The landowner is the Gwydyr Estate.

Leaseholders have included:

William E. Cooke & Others 1862– ?1864.

James Swinton Spooner & Others trading as Bettws-y-Coed Slab & Slate Quarry Co. Ltd. 1865–1882.[16] Company put up for auction 8/1882; working stopped 12/1883.

Rev. John Gower & J. Evan Jones & Others trading as The Bettws-y-Coed Slab Slate & Cistern Co. Ltd. 1886–1892.

Bettws-y-Coed Slate Quarry Co. Ltd. 1895–1906 (in receivership). Traded again in hope of a sale but dissolved 1915 – quarry closed 1913.

J.J. Riley of Deganwy (*see also Rhos Quarry, Capel Curig*) by 1922 (closed 1927). (Riley's interests sold 1940).

Output in 1900 was 3,000 tons per annum; until that time annual average number of employees was 15 persons.

There was no Registered Company with title 'Hafod-Las Slate . . .' nor reference in D.C. Davies 'SLATE & SLATE MINING IN NORTH WALES' 1880 Edition, suggesting it was closed at this time.[17]

In the Auction Notice of 16th August, 1882 the machinery (all the property of James Swinton Spooner) includes 'two 32 ft waterwheels'. Products included coping stones, railway platforms, curbs etc. The machinery was again advertised in late summer 1883.[18]

Outstanding in the matter of this quarry is its connection with two well-known railway-connected surnames, Gooch and Spooner, however different their stature may have been. In 'SIR DANIEL GOOCH – MEMOIRS & DIARY' (R.B. Wilson), Gooch writes (1865) "I had much reason to be dissatisfied the latter part of this year with the manner in which Harry was treated by Whitworth in Manchester. I therefore took him away and purchased for him an interest in some slate quarries at Bettws-y-Coed in North Wales, then chiefly belonging to a Mr. Cooper . . .". (A footnote by the Editor suggests this was Cooper (unclear) but could be James C. Cooper of the Pen-Llyn Slate Quarry, Dolwyddelan. Henry (Harry) Daniel Gooch was the eldest son and a director of the Whitworth Manchester Works 1863–65.

Other prominent names in the 1872 list of shareholders are William Fothergill Cooke (of Cooke & Wheatstone telegraph fame, knighted in 1869) who was associated in the original lease of 1862 and probably introduced Gooch to the venture. Cooke was already a shareholder in the Maenofferen Slate Quarry, Blaenau Ffestiniog, as was C.B. Skinner who had also become by 1872 a shareholder in Hafod-Las. Other Civil Engineers with interest included H. Daniel Gooch, G.W.M. Hellyer and Hedworth Lee (Resident Engineer on the Chester & Holyhead section.) Original capital was an impressive £50,000.

At the start (1862) James Swinton Spooner, plus Cooke and Hellyer, were among signatories to the lease and the machinery in 1872 was subject to a lien for £900 due to James Spooner.[19] H.D. Gooch informed the Registrar of Companies that the Company had been sold (it was stopped by default on 30th September, 1884) the quarry having closed down on 7th December, 1883.

Letters (some by Cooke in atrocious handwriting) of 1865–66 suggest the undertaking was short of money until the Goochs were interested. Gooch wrote (16th June, 1866) '. . . the inclines are not finished, the drums not having arrived' and there are references to the road from the incline foot to the turnpike (about 220 yards) '. . . or relaying railway double . . .'.[20] The shortage of cash may be reflected in the exceptionally light nature of the tramway materials.

The only vehicle unearthed is a three-sided iron-bodied rubbish wagon (less chassis) 5 ft long × 2 ft 11 in. wide and only 1 ft 3 in. deep – as with most of the other effects at this site, quite different from those found hereabouts!

MOEL SIABOD TRAMWAYS (c.1863–c.1901)

A pair of scarcely-known slate and slab quarries opened near Capel Curig in the second part of the 19th century and their products fell to the 500 ft contour by means of a 1 ft 11 in. gauge tramway containing four inclines: occupancy was frequently by Liverpool or Manchester builders. At the most westerly end of the line was Moel Siabod Slate & Slab Quarry, a pit of uncertain depth as it has been flooded for years, 1,600 ft above sea level, and about 1¾ miles from the road wharf at the foot of the tramway's last incline; this was close beside Pont-Cyfyng, just east of Rhos Farm [Ref: 734570]. From here the output was taken by their own horses and carts to Trefriw (and placed in boats on the Conway, for transfer when necessary into sea-going vessels at Conway itself). Later, when the standard gauge reached Bettws (1868), cartage was restricted to there, whilst great hopes for the competitiveness of the works were entertained in the projected North Wales Narrow Gauge Railway's General Undertaking of 1872 which would have passed very close to the bottom wharf, and taken products into Bettws. By 1902 Rhos Quarry had obtained a steam tractor and wagons for the road journey.[21]

At 1,400 yards from the foot of the tramway (and a little over half way along its full length) was the later Rhos or Capel Curig Quarry, into which a branch tramway was constructed by means of a rather curious junction part way up the third incline. This quarry was at 1,000 ft and the working was a pit 200 ft deep. It remained at work intermittently until the early 1950s, and used the tramway to the last. The Moel Siabod enterprise had built and was owner of the tramway; it had closed at an earlier (unknown) date and considerable parts of the whole tramway remained in situ in September 1945 (author's first visit) and smaller lengths in April 1976.

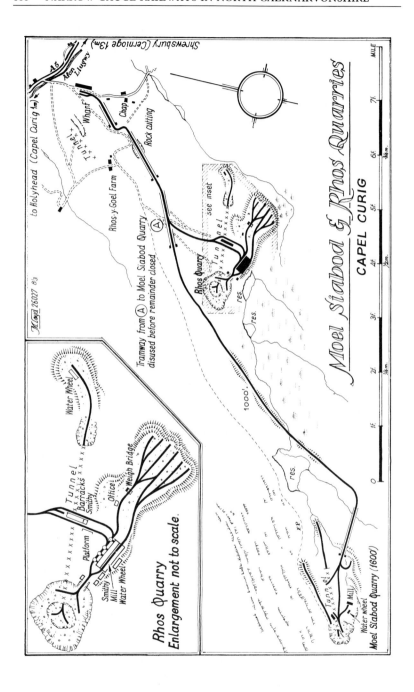

Moel Siabod & Rhos Quarries

CAPEL CURIG

There are impressive tunnels into the pits of both quarries and that at Rhos is not flooded. Extensive use of water wheels is also evident. The quarries lie on the Gwydyr Estate though some of the Rhos tramway was subject to a lease from Moel Siabod. The lessees were responsible for tramway upkeep, that portion west of the Rhos Quarry junction must have been abandoned earlier than the remainder.

Moel Siabod Quarry [Ref: 717555]

Opened before 1867
Worked by Robert Williams of Capel Curig [22]
Moel Siabod Slate & Slab Works   ?1873
Owen J. Owen   Working in 1901 but only 45 tons produced
(Nothing further known but probably not operated after 1901 – closed in 1902)

Rhos Quarry [Ref: 728563]

Quarry on lease from 1861 and probably this was starting date – lessees where known were:

Samuel Clift (trading as Clift & Blackmore, Builders' Merchants, Ardwick, Manchester.)	1861–
Rhos Slate & Slab Quarry Co. Ltd.	1869–
Capel Curig Slate & Slab Quarry Co. Ltd.	1872–1882
The Capel Curig Slate Co. Ltd.	1883–1890
P. & H. Lewis & Others (trading as Timber, Slate and Builders' Merchants, Conway.)	1893–1901
Frederick Kitchen of Trefriw	1903–1904
(Various local operators	1906–1915)
J.J. Riley of Deganwy [23] trading as Rhos Slate Quarry (Capel Curig) Co. Ltd.	

Between 1882–86 output had averaged 1,000 tons per year and this figure is again recorded in 1938 and approximately in 1939: in 1940, 70 tons; 1950, (when there was an exceptional demand after the blitz) 2,310 tons; and in 1951, 96 tons. No work after 1951; Riley in liquidation 1955.

Tramway

Began at a small roadside wharf and immediately rose by double-tracked incline; a second single-track (intermediate/passing loop) incline began close by the summit of the first, and in conventional manner there was a brief contour track linking the two. In 1945 there was evidence that longitudinal sleepering existed here, supported by a

Sale Catalogue[24] of 1882 which states 'road in repair which has recently been relaid with longitudinal sleepers and is in good order' (suggesting it may have been built up to 15 years previously). The Catalogue continues 'the proposed railway from Corwen to Capel Curig will pass close to the Incline . . .' (i.e. N.W.N.G.Rlys. Undertaking No. 1). Certainly in recent times conventional cross-sleepering was evident, and the rails varied from an extremely light bridge rail of 8 lb. to a 16 lb./yd. version of the same.

The second incline passed through a cutting to reach the third (a double-track type) part way along which the branch to Rhos Quarry went off to the left with evidence of a newer winding drum above the junction. At the original third summit the course wound and climbed its way over open mountainscape, rising at about 1 in 15 from 1,000 ft there and by means of a final incline into Moel Siabod Quarry, to 1,600 ft at the site. The 'main line' is said to have been worked by horsepower and a notice nearby in recent times "DOGS WILL BE SHOT" is not conclusive evidence that it was worked by Huskies!

The tunnels also carried tramways on a lower level; they were recommended in a Report of December 1889[25] by J.J. Evans (lately Manager at Penrhyn) and subsequently built. Water wheels were used for pumping the galleries and pits.

The rails were carried on 3 ft 6 in. – 3 ft 9 in. lateral sleepers at approximately 3 ft 6 in. intervals.

Wagons

An inventory of 1889 reveals two varieties of wagon: the conventional open-ended steel-bodied double-flanged wheel open rubbish wagon so widespread in the industry, and some less conventional iron-framed body slate wagons running on double-flanged wheels used on the 'main line'. The latter embodied some very heavy timber framing with side members extended to form buffers, but their framed bodies were built up with verticals of flat iron strip and used round bar iron as a frame-work (a construction unique to this venture). The rods passed through eyes burned in the ends of the flat bars, and wheel and pedestals apart, no doubt all was constructed in the smithy locally. 'Blondins' were used to lift the rubbish wagons from the pits.

The wheels were lighter than usually found, having four rather delicate curved spokes. Their diameter was also greater than 1 ft 6 in. and all had brake handles (suggesting gravity working in one direction, in single wagons?). A surviving part-body was 4 ft long × 3 ft wide.[26] A wheelset found in 1945 confirmed the gauge but confusingly had single-flanged wheels.

Motive Power

Conversation locally suggested a de Winton & Co. locomotive had operated in Rhos Quarry for a period in the 1890s; this is unconfirmed.

There was also a diesel rail tractor by Deutz (sold to W.O. Williams of Harlech as scrap in the 1950s) and another by Ruston & Hornsby (171902 of 1934) bought new. [27] It was bought from a Conway dealer by Votty & Bowydd Slate Quarries Ltd. in the late 1950s.

DOLWYDDELAN AREA TRAMWAYS (c.1865–1917)

Of this district the 'CARNARVON & DENBIGH HERALD' wrote on 15th March, 1873 that the quarries were as yet young and not properly developed. A group of about half a dozen small slate quarries, whose output was at first carted to Trefriw and later to Bettws-y-Coed, clustered around the village of Dolwyddelan and on both sides of the Lledr Valley, some of which dated back to early in the 19th century. The largest pair, Tyn-y-Bryn [Ref: 743520] and Pen-Llyn [Ref: 745522] was immediately to the southeast of the standard gauge station and an interchange siding and wharf was served by inclines falling from these quarries. East again, was the isolated Chwarel-y-Fedw [Ref: 747527] which, having no mill on the quarry site, had an incline which took the stone down under the L.N.W.R.;[28] then the tramway crossed the Lledr by a slab-and-pier bridge and ran up alongside the valley road. Here, by a reverse shunt, wagons could be taken over one of two road level crossings into the Bwlch or Prince Llewellyn Quarry [Ref: 744528] which also owned a small tramway network; its mill was used by the stone coming across from Chwarel-y-Fedw. There were one or two other small quarries in the district (e.g. Rhiw-Goch [Ref: 759543] an underground working worked from 1865), but their short tramways were insignificant and competition forced closure in the late 1870s. The

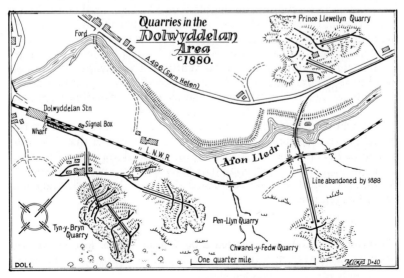

principal landowners were Baroness Willoughby D'Eresby (Gwydyr Estate), and George Henry Ellis.

Dolwyddelan station (L.N.W.R.) was important enough to have been enlarged in later years, but the interchange siding was not affected. This section of the Conway Valley branch (projected originally as a narrow gauge line as between Blaenau Ffestiniog and Bettws-y-Coed) was opened in 1879 and post-dated the start of these workings. As with most similar situations all these works had long periods of disuse; Chwarel-y-Fedw had closed by 1888 and did not re-open. Known details are:

Tyn-y-Bryn

Opened 1863	?1863–1866
Lledr Vale Slate & Slab Co. Ltd.	1866–1869
Tyn-y-Bryn Quarries Ltd.	1919–1926

Pen-Llyn

Opened c.1870 "Small number of men employed" ('CARNARVON & DENBIGH HERALD' 1873)
Closed c.1920 (ref: Lindsay p.327)

Prince Llewellyn

Opened by 1865: in 1873 an open pit employing about 40 men

James C. Cooper (see also Hafod-Las Quarry)	pre 1865
Bwlch Slate Co.	pre 1870–pre 1887
Prince Llewellyn Slate Quarry Co. Ltd.	1896–1903
E. Richards & Co. Ltd. (name reverted to Prince Llewellyn Slate Quarry Co. Ltd. 1/1906)	1903–1910
?	Sold 1917

Approximately 420 ton/annum output.

Chwarel-y-Fedw or Hendre

Opened pre 1870	
Beddw Slate Co.	pre 1870
"Not working" ('CARNARVON & DENBIGH HERALD' 1873)	
Hendre Slate Co. Ltd.	by 1882 – closed by 1890

Track

All tramways appear to have been of nominal 2 ft gauge and built in bridge rails pinned to wooden sleepers.

BETHESDA AREA TRAMWAYS (by 1870–1911)

There is a generous array of company titles (some incorporating the word 'Bangor' or 'Port Bangor') covering this area, all relating to quarries in the Bethesda district on the east bank of the river Ogwen. The four most important formed a shallow arc on the map, stretching north to south along the flanks of Moel Faban and Gyrn Wigau whose lower slopes fall right beside the main street of Bethesda itself.

The most northerly near Llanlechid was Bryn-Hafod-y-Wern Quarry [Ref: 632692]; to the southwest of it, Tan-y-Bwlch Quarry [Ref: 627683]; then to the south again was Moel Faban Quarry [Ref: 626678] and south of this the last, right on the edge of Bethesda itself, Pant-Dreiniog Quarry [Ref: 624672]. There was also a small working, Coetmor [Ref: 618673] which was filled with rubbish from Pant-Dreiniog Quarry alongside from 1873. It was first let in 1830 and advertised in 1859 having eight wagons.

There were internal tramroads in these four, but only that at Pant-Dreiniog was of any extent. These slate quarries had begun life in the 1820s; the detailed vicissitudes of their history have no place here save to mention that Bryn-Hafod-y-Wern planned to be served by a branch of the Chester & Holyhead Railway[29] and its owners were concerned in management of companies formed to have physical links with the L.N.W.R. in Bangor when these plans failed.

All quarries were forced to cart to Bangor for shipment; and worse, Lord Penrhyn became involved in some, to their eventual detriment!

Tan-y-Bwlch pit required two stationary steam engines, one to hoist wagons up a shaft which fell to a tunnel level driven in from the pit; another engine was needed "to hoist wagons to the level of the old tunnel" and though the tramway system may have been of considerable interest it was considered "a disaster that two (engines) should be needed for an unfortunate location; all is on a gigantic scale" (1873).

The North Wales Quarries Society Ltd. was a child of the Penrhyn Strike of 1900–03; it was a co-operative formed to work Pant-Dreiniog, Tan-y-Bwlch and Moel Faban (Bryn-Hafod-y-Wern had closed for good in 1884) but economic circumstances closed them all in 1911. The first-mentioned was thoroughly modernised and provided with a new tramway system and two steam locomotives, and issued an illustrated brochure; some workings were freehold and others under lease from The Crown. Manpower was available as this was a time of labour troubles at the nearby Penrhyn Quarry; it was the intent to work Moel Faban and Tan-y-Bwlch (which were adjacent) in conjunction with each other. Of Pant-Dreiniog is said "The Society has constructed new tram roads for locomotives . . . additional drum buildings and connections attached to the old engine . . . built a locomotive shed . . .". 'THE CO-OPERATIVE NEWS' 19th November, 1904 wrote in glowing terms of the new tramroads which linked Moel Faban and Tan-y-Bwlch. It was, unfortunately, an ill-starred venture, short of capital throughout its life, even though backed by the co-operative movement and trade unions.

The 2 ft gauge tramways were rebuilt in flat bottomed 20 lb./yd. rails; rubbish was carried in conventional open-ended steel bodied wagons for tipping. It is believed slate wagons were not used as the quarried stone was stacked in rubbish wagons and taken to the mill; when products left the mill they did so in carts.

Locomotives

> RICHARD BELL   0–4–0ST Outside Cylinders 6 in. × 9 in. Driving Wheels 1 ft 6⅞ in. W.G. Bagnall & Sons, Stafford. No. 1726 of 10/1903
>
> J.C. GRAY   0–4–0ST Outside Cylinders 6½ in. × 10 in. Driving Wheels 1 ft 7 in. W.G. Bagnall & Sons, Stafford. No. 1863 of 1907

both of which were sold when the undertaking went into liquidation. BELL was named after the ex railway guard–later M.P. for Derby– and General Secretary of the Amalgamated Society of Railway Servants (1897–1910) who in that capacity, was involved in the notorious Taff Vale Railway Case of 1900.

At Bryn-Hafod-y-Wern the driving force was Edwyn John Jeffrey Dixon (its proprietor in the early 1850s) who has already come to notice in Volume 2 on the Penrhyn Railway. Dixon brought out a patent (14165 of 12th June, 1852) for an Improved Slate Wagon (it was more like a rubbish wagon in appearance) while the 'MINING JOURNAL' 1850 p.610 has other references to his inventiveness. The drawing accompanying the patent is not of relevance here but shows double-flanged wheels running on round bars set at 24 in. centres, and invites the suggestion that this quarry may have been using discarded Penrhyn Railroad materials.[30]

CONWAY MOUNTAIN AREA TRAMWAYS (c.1875–c.1962)

Penmaenbach Stone Quarry

Besides the Penmaenmawr complex (which was quite the largest working on granite) there were smaller local quarries working the same material, the most significant of which was Conway Stone Quarries which operated under a lease from Conway Borough. J.Y. Fisher and Henry Henshaw were the first to work the site (1874), trading as Penmaenbach Stone Quarries Co. and after auctioning their lease and quarry equipment was bought by Isaac Anwyl in 1878.

The Borough Minutes suggest that both main road and L.N.W.R. line were crossed on the level by a tramway, and a pier then in existence had been extended by 225 ft. There was a succession of short term operators including the cleaning materials firm Kleeneze Ltd; there

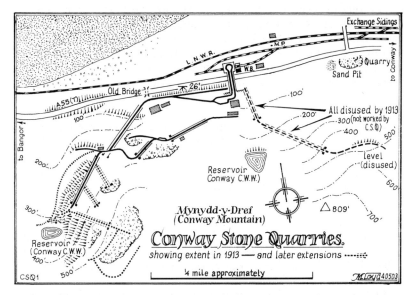

Conway Stone Quarries.
showing extent in 1913 — and later extensions ·····⇉

¼ mile approximately

followed Carder's Stone Lino Ltd. (1907); Conway Stone Quarries Ltd. (1908) who changed the name to the North Wales Granite Co. Ltd. (1913). (The North Wales Granite Co. had worked the site from 1916.)

Fisher and Henshaw's 30-year lease from Conway Borough granted a right of level crossing over the L.N.W.R. – rail variety; they had started the pier by November 1874. Anwyl stopped work on the pier on acquiring the lease and submitted plans showing an existing jetty 500 ft long (with the aforementioned 225 ft included) a 3 ft gauge proposed tramway along it and height of pier 20 ft from sea bed to rails. At this time there were no interchange sidings with the L.N.W.R. In 1878 Col. Yolland of the Board of Trade reported there was one self-acting plane in the quarry which fell to a gated crossing of the L.N.W.R. On the seaward side the quarry had erected a crushing plant. Each quarry wagon with 1½ tons of stone was placed on a four-wheeled trolley which stood on a tramway laid at right angles to the incline and ran along the occupation road up to the field gates on either side of the railway (Penmaenbach signal box). Each loaded truck was hauled or pushed along (whilst resting on the trolley) and across the railway, thence back along the far side of the L.N.W.R. to the crusher! Yolland was told that the previous day 28 trips of two trucks in each meant that 56 wagons had crossed the L.N.W.R. main line separately, and the same number returned as empties. During that time twelve passenger and eighteen L.N.W.R. goods trains used the crossing. The pier had apparently been built in defiance of the B.O.T., but if taken down the "boats would be beached and use of the rail level crossing continue"! There was also doubt if The Crown or Conway Corporation was the owner of the foreshore.[31]

The remainder of the system up above on the mountain comprised largely an incline series on 3 ft gauge which in due course was linked to exchange sidings with the L.N.W.R. whilst the main road was crossed by a bridge. At first only hand and horse power was used in the quarry, but the North Wales Granite Co. Ltd. owned a standard gauge locomotive (ex-Bradford Corporation) for the exchange sidings.

The undertaking settled down into a somewhat uninteresting and respectably-worked site having several levels and balanced inclines. The tramway system reached the upper levels by World War I, being over 350 ft above sea level and a problem of reconstructing a diagram of the tramway layout has been the effect of periods/sites effacing earlier work. Once the extraordinary pick-a-back rail crossing of the L.N.W.R. had been discarded in favour of an overbridge, its one idiosyncrasy was lost!

Though the premises produced the traditional granite chippings output, Carder's speciality was flint linings for tube mills, pulverising cylinders, grinding pans; also chert pavers and runners (these products appear listed on their letter-head).

Conway Stone Quarries Ltd. was a branch of Brookes Ltd. of Halifax.[32] They had changed the name Conway Stone Quarries Ltd. to North Wales Granite Co. Ltd. by 1913 and it was intended that an aerial ropeway should be used for loading ships from a hopper bin in the quarry served by the tramway. Work on this was begun but never completed. The quarry was extended westward and before World War I a steam locomotive came to the quarry; by then the east end of the workings had been abandoned. In the depression after the War the locomotive was laid off in favour of horses again. Business continued until the late 1940s, supplying crushed stone and dust to make concrete paving materials in premises beside the main line; the exchange sidings remained purely on the south side and much main line ballast was loaded there. Some of the tramway system survived to the early 1960s, out of use.

Track and Wagons

Early portions were in 16 lb./yd. bridge rails, replaced later by 24 lb. and 30 lb./yd. flat-bottomed spiked to wooden sleepers.

Wagons were similar to those at Penmaenmawr and all carried on four wheels; one type was a simple 3-sided box open wagon and the other a side tipper, having the door opening on one side only. The open wagons may have been rebuilds of the tippers, again similar to developments in the neighbouring workings. Couplings, frames and running gear were similar to those next door also and the inventory of 1927 reads:

No. of	Capacity	Body Length	Body Width	Body Height	Type
55	2 ton	5 ft 6 in.	4 ft 6 in.	2 ft 3 in.	Side tipping
20	1 ton	4 ft 8 in.	3 ft 10 in.	2 ft 2 in.	Side tipping
4	1 ton	4 ft 8 in.	3 ft 10 in.	2 ft	End tipper

Also two wagons each carrying two water barrels. It will be noted that body sizes were somewhat smaller than Penmaenmawr. From the list it is deduced that conversion into open wagons had not begun in 1927.

Motive Power

This was POPSY, 0–4–2T by Dick, Kerr & Co. Ltd. of Kilmarnock, which came from The Shap Granite Co. (another of Brookes' interests) and after heavy overhaul and a new boiler, was leased to Conway between 31st May, 1915 and 31st March, 1920 (and maybe longer but had gone by 1926). It was built to an unknown gauge and conversion to 3 ft was undertaken at Manning Wardle & Co. Ltd., Leeds, who also fitted the new boiler and copper firebox, amended coupling gear, painted it green and black and were sent the new nameplates MORFA, and owner's plates. The engine left Leeds on a crocodile wagon in May 1915 for use on the only near level section of the quarry system on the second level. As rebuilt the engine remained 0–4–2 with 7⅛ in. × 12 in. outside cylinders, with 2 ft 1 in. driving wheels (suggesting her original gauge was 2 ft), rigid wheelbase was 4 ft and total 8 ft 6 in.

A curious feature of the undertaking was that it was on Corporation land and sited between two of Conway's reservoirs. At one stage the Corporation was in doubt about reletting, as the Government Inspector maintained that the old reservoir was not in the right place and that the correct place was that and the same one where Fisher & Henshaw wished to quarry! ('CARNARVON & DENBIGH HERALD' 15th June, 1878). The holder of the lease thereby acquired the sole right to supplying Liverpool with stone 'raised from the land the property of the Corporation of Conway'. Initially all business was done in setts.

Finally, all the evidence points to the tramway system being of 3 ft gauge until World War II when the 2 ft gauge was adopted.

LITTLE ORME'S HEAD QUARRY, Porth Dyniewyd (1889–1931)

This (ultimately) large excavation was a limestone working at Trwyn-y-Fuwchon [Ref: 819826] at the northeast end of the headland facing Penrhyn Bay. It was one of the biggest and most economical sites, it being possible to load stone mainly by gravity into ships at all states of the tide. Latterly, ships of 800 tons capacity could be loaded within the hour.

This place was a typical North Wales quarry undertaking, with its two main periods of history; firstly as The Little Orme's Head Limestone Co. founded by Joseph Storey of Lancashire, and his son Robert, formed in July 1889 (they also worked the Station Quarry, Miller's Dale) which purchased Edward Fidler's 30 year lease of the foreshore

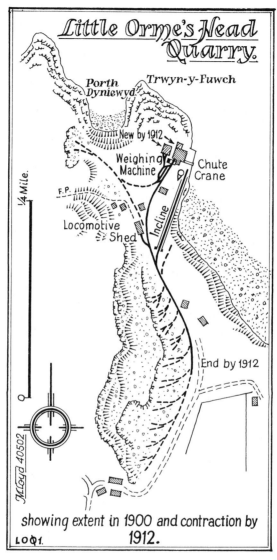

Little Orme's Head Quarry. showing extent in 1900 and contraction by 1912.

here from Lord Mostyn. In 1896, 50 men were employed in, and 29 outside, the quarry. This concern shipped limestone to the Clyde and Argyll coast ports for use in blast furnaces and chemical works. A 3 ft gauge (sometimes given as 3 ft 6 in.) railway conveyed the stone in wagons drawn by steam engines from the quarry face to the crusher where large lumps of stone were reduced and the results screened; from here the coarser pieces fell in sheet iron troughs to storage bins above a wharf. Three ships – loading one at a time – could load a total of 1,300 tons in four hours. Le Neve Foster commended the site as the most highly productive in his Report (1896). The Company was liquidated in June 1913 and was wound up in 1914.

It had re-opened in 1920 under The Ship Canal Portland Cement Manufacturers Co. Ltd. of 1912 (who were renamed Allied Cement Manufacturers Ltd. in August 1929, becoming Associated Portland Cement Manufacturers Ltd. in December 1931). In the early 1920s output was approximately 67,000 tons annually with 87 operatives within and 45 outside the quarry. In 1927 the whole site was re-vamped and modernised; the previous year the conventional steam stud was replaced by three 'Sentinel' chain-driven locomotives which were delivered simultaneously on three steam lorries. At the same time the original 3 ton-capacity wooden wagons were replaced by 'Easton' side tipping steam open wagons with inside bearings, supplied by Cambrian Wagon Co. Ltd. of Cardiff. These had a capacity of 7 tons and were loaded at the quarry face by one of three steam shovels. Trains of wagons were taken to the new crusher and each wagon lifted and emptied; thereafter the railway system had no further purpose as the stone fell by gravity as required.

There were three levels of railway, the uppermost in the workings reached by rope-worked incline. The middle or main level had on it the shiploading hoppers, main mill and loco shed and the bottom level was gained by a steep falling incline worked by locomotive.

Locomotives

Name	Type	Builder	Builders No.	Notes
MONA	0–4–0VBT	Hughes' Valley Foundry, Bangor		1
LITTLE ORME	0–4–0ST	Manning Wardle & Co. Ltd.	478 of 1873	2
ELLESMERE	0–4–2ST	Kerr, Stuart & Co. Ltd.	1255 of 1912	3
GARTH	0–4–2ST	Kerr, Stuart & Co. Ltd.	1257 of 1914	4
PENRHYN	0–4–2ST	Kerr, Stuart & Co. Ltd.	3092 of 1918	5
No. 1	4 wh.VB	'Sentinel' geared	6256 of 1926	6
No. 2	4 wh.VB	'Sentinel' geared	6255 of 1926	7
No. 3	4 wh.VB	'Sentinel' geared	6257 of 1926	8

The Quarry had closed by 1931 and No. 1 went to the A.P.C.M. plant at Harbury, Warwickshire.

1) May have acquired name whilst on Anglesey, perhaps then passing to Brundrit & Co. Ltd., Penmaen Granite Quarries, who found it too small and part-exchanged it in 1878 or 1895 for new loco with de Winton & Co.

2) Built for Leeds Corporation Water Works at Swinsty Reservoir as WASHBURN but sold to Little Orme; reboilered 1899 by Hough & Sons, Newton Boiler Works, Wigan. Cylinders 6 in. × 12 in.; Driving Wheels 2 ft 6 in.; Wheelbase 4 ft 7 in. No cab.

3–5) Standard outside cylindered saddle tank, 'Brazil' type, outside frames. Cylinders 9 in. × 15 in.; Driving Wheels 2 ft 6 in.; Total Wheelbase 9 ft 6 in.; Weight 12½ tons.

5)   Still at Little Orme April 1940 but scrapped soon after.
     (Reference to 2–5 in 'LOCOMOTIVE MAGAZINE' 1917 (ii) p.185).
6–8) 80hp. 4-wheeled type with specially enclosed cabs of type also supplied to Field &
     McKay, Clee Hill Quarry near Ludlow. Cylinders 6¾ in. × 9 in. Driving Wheels
     1 ft 8 in. Wheelbase 3 ft 6 in.

In conjunction with the Little Orme Quarry, the Ship Canal people
also worked the Garth Farm Shale Quarry, Mochdre [Ref: 819788]
between 1911–22, where a 2 ft gauge system connected the quarry face
with an overhead aerial ropeway which led to a siding at the former
Mochdre & Pabo station site on the Colwyn Bay – Llandudno Junction
section of the North Wales main line. There were two steam locos, both
built by Kerr, Stuart & Co. Ltd.

Name	Type		Builders No.	Notes
BABY	0–4–0T	outside cylinders	639 of 1898	9
BABY SENIOR	0–4–2ST	outside cylinders	1265 of 1914	10

 9) Came from firm's Stanlow site before July 1924. Scrapped c.1943 having stood on
     length of line, disused, on site – similar to DIANA of Pen-yr-Orsedd Slate Quarry,
     Nantlle. Outside frame; canopy cab.
10) Probably delivered new to Garth – first loco to work there. Replaced by BABY, and
     to Holborough Cement Works, Kent, c.1923.

NORTH WALES POWER & TRACTION CO. LTD. (1904–1906: part 1934)

(Roman Bridge and Cwm Dyli 'No. 1 Route'.)

From its formation in 1903 and an Act of 1904 to supply electricity,
the North Wales Power & Traction Co. Ltd.[33] was engaged in building
a hydro-electric power system to supply a considerable portion of
Caernarvonshire and Merionethshire in an area of about 10 miles radius
from its Power Station in Cwm Dyli [Ref: 654540] opened August
1906, which was driven by water turbine. Sections 5 & 6 of the
enterprise involved (as did other sections) 'new roads, tramroads,
inclines with winch haulage and mule teams etc. . . . haulage machinery, pipes, poles, cement etc. . . . and the employment of 800 men'.[34]
In this wild upland terrain it was a mammoth task to construct the pole
route for this section, there being no nearby roads, which for instance,
had enabled Cwm Dyli Power Station to have its machinery taken to
Llanberis by L.N.W.R. and then transported over the Llanberis Pass
by 'three traction engines and numerous horse haulages'. The Section
in question 'makes a bee-line over the mountains (from Cwm Dyli) in
an easterly direction to a point near Roman Bridge where it turns to the
south terminating at the Oakeley Quarries, a distance of 7 miles'. It was
a three-phase line, carried mainly on stout wooden poles, providing a
high-tension 10,000 volt supply to the first Blaenau Ffestiniog slate

quarry to accept the new power age. Of the 7 miles, 5 were constructed by means of a temporary tramroad of that length, using horses and mules on its level sections and steam winches 'where the line is steep'.[35, 36] The earthworks of these incline summits where vertical boilers supplied steam to twin-cylindered winches, plus their attendant coal bunkers, may still be traced today, as may parts of the route especially where the ground was built up in stonework to form light embankments. For some time after the route was complete the tramroad was left in situ to assist the early maintenance; heavy rain and boggy terrain gave a tramroad complete advantage over other access. In accounts of the scheme repeated reference was given to the North Wales Narrow Gauge Railways 'a line which with its extensions will eventually be supplied with electrical power for operating purposes', (and adds 'an electric railway to benefit quarry owner and tourist is progressing towards completion') but this never came to fruition.[37, 38]

Contractor for the scheme was that same company which was also pushing south towards Portmadoc the projects which would extend the North Wales Narrow Gauge Railways from Rhydd-Ddu to Beddgelert and beyond, namely Bruce, Peebles & Co. Ltd. of Edinburgh. The engineers were Harper Bros & Co. and Sir Douglas Fox & Partners. The pole work 'necessitated the laying down of temporary tramroads of which some 10 miles were used for hauling the line material over frequently boggy ground'.

The most fascinating of these tramroads climbed from Cwm Dyli to the col [Ref: 676542] between Ceunant Mawr and Clogwyn-Bwlch-y-Maen; there was an incline from the Power Station to the Pen-y-Gwryd – Beddgelert road (660 ft) followed by a second which winched poles on trolleys to the col at about 1,400 ft; the line (being easterly to this point) turned north-easterly and then dropped easterly again from the col (by pole no. 76) by incline to the north shore of Llynau Diwaunedd; the route round the lake – if completed – and there may be a little doubt[39] – swung south at the east end of the water and then dropped steeply and in portions by winched inclines [Ref: 689525], in a south-easterly direction to a point alongside the old Dolwyddelan – Ffestiniog road just east of Garnedd (550 ft) where there was a construction base [Ref: 706519]. The whole line was about 4½ miles long, and traversed some of the most inhospitable ground in the county.[40] There still survive some considerable stone or earth embankments and portions of stone-piered bridges, but along the upper lengths the site has subsided in the bog e.g. around pole no. 58. The gauge was a nominal 2 ft and the rails a light bridge section.

The Garnedd end may be most conveniently traced in the form of a long incline still revealing certain stone walling, cuttings and earthworks up to a point where it swings westerly round a bluff of Cribau and round above the Afon Diwaunedd valley [Ref: 691525].

The wagons were little more than stout wooden trolleys, crudely but strongly made either as flats or cradle wagons. The former were four-wheeled but the latter, to carry one pole each, or sections of water pipe, were long wooden frames with shaped formers to keep the leading end of the pole clear of the haulage cable on the inclines; their fore end was carried on a bogie but a single set of wheels was sufficient at the rear!

WHARF TRAMWAY, DOLGARROG (1911–1912)

Built by the Aluminium Corporation from Dolgarrog Works to the west bank of the Conway to enable materials to be brought by water. After off-loading, the loaded wagons were hauled into the Works by cable, powered by an electrically driven winch in the Works. Most traffic however, was hand-operated.

The system must have proved inadequate as the short tramway was replaced when, to meet wartime demands and the rebuilding of Cowlyd Reservoir by the Corporation, a standard gauge branch railway was built 1916–17 with a trailing junction on the Tal-y-Cafn to Llanrwst section of the Conway Valley line, a halt established south of the junction and conveyance of materials and work people inaugurated. This branch obliterated the Wharf Tramway.

COWLYD RESERVOIR TRAMWAY (1916–c.1975)

The Conway & Colwyn Bay Joint Water Supply Board was formed on 10th June, 1891. It had purchased from Gwalia Ltd. (formed by Gethin Jones and Roberts) the natural lake, Llyn Cowlyd, in the valley to the south of Llyn Eigiau, together with part of the watershed and adjacent gathering grounds. With a total area of 1,100 acres (including the lake which had become a reservoir in 1908 – a lake whose bottom was so deep it had then not been found) confidence was shattered by the extraordinary drought of summer 1915. [Years before when Gwalia Ltd. had been formed to acquire water rights in Snowdonia they were unable to carry out development and sold part of their water rights to the North Wales Power & Traction Co. Ltd. who prosecuted some hydro-electric schemes as a result – it was intended that the Snowdon Mountain Tramway and Portmadoc, Beddgelert & South Snowdon Railway would use electric traction. North Wales Power & Traction Co. Ltd. however, sold Conway Valley water rights to Aluminium Corporation Ltd. for since 1908 some of the gathering ground surrounding the Cowlyd reservoir had been acquired by the Aluminium Corporation Ltd. to supplement their own reservoir (formerly Llyn Eigiau) supplies.] (In 1918 A.C.L. purchased controlling interest in N.W.P. & T.Co. Ltd. which continued trading under that title.) With only 20 days' supply left in Cowlyd the Board was forced to review its position and further gathering ground and a larger reservoir proved an immediate necessity. An Agreement with the A.C.L. on 27th May,

1916 allowed the latter to build a new dam 40 ft higher than the old and downstream from that existing and to Board designs, the works to be the property of the Board but maintenance to be the responsibility of A.C.L.[41] There were many other arrangements regarding water supply which do not concern us here, but the maintenance issue led to the building of a tramway with junction made from that series of inclines which led from A.C.L. Works to the top lip of the Dolgarrog escarpment. These steps allowed the obtaining of a statutory authority by Act of 17th August, 1916.

Apart from carrying the materials, machinery etc. required, the dam itself was made entirely from rock quarried on the mountainside above the new dam wall, to which a tramway incline was led. Granite was also quarried 200 ft above the works and brought down by counterbalanced incline to be made into concrete; from the mixers 1 cu. yd skip wagons were hauled out to the dam site by cables powered by electric winch, electricity being available from the N.W.P.&T. Co. Ltd. line passing along the Cowlyd Valley from Cwm Dyli. Further temporary lines carried earth for dam filling in 4 cu. yd wagons hauled by steam locomotives or, where steeply inclined, cable powered by steam winches – a well-tried method of N.W.P.&T.Co. Ltd.! As to the tramway proper, it was stated 'Cowlyd Lake is very difficult of access, the only road leading up to it being from Trefriw . . . and a very poor one and very precipitous . . . a 2 ft gauge railway had to be constructed for a distance of about 3 miles from the top of the existing incline belonging to the A.C.L. which leads from the Works to a point near the concentration reservoir. The plant is delivered at the Dolgarrog station by the L.N.W.R. . . .' The L.N.W.R. wagons were run over the new standard gauge branch into the Works, the contents put into narrow gauge wagons and hauled up the incline, then using a steam (later electric) winch. The Engineers were Sir Douglas Fox & Partners and the contractors Sir Robert McAlpine & Sons. Tramway construction began in 1916 and by February 1917 had reached Ardda Farm where there was a stoppage re purchase of the property. The mine was passed in March and Siglen reached by May.

The dam work was not completed until December 1921, with an official opening on 20th September 1922 when the weather was more suitable! Then, it was remarked that (as mentioned frequently in this Series) Dolgarrog had now become the control centre of the N.W.P. & T. Co. Ltd., A.C.L., P.B. & S.S.R., N.W.N.G.R. (shortly to become the Welsh Highland Railway), Festiniog Rly. Co., Snowdon Mountain Tramroad & Hotels Co. Ltd., with continued emphasis that in due course electricity would become the common denominator of them all. For the official opening visitors were conveyed up the Works' inclines, 'a nerve wracking experience'; at the top they 'were transferred into specially constructed trucks'.[42, 43] A water-tunnel connection between Eigiau and Cowlyd was begun in March 1919 but was completed some time after the dam: it is recalled that tramway employees spent half their working week hauling up the inclines and the remainder in taking this material to Cowlyd!

During a storm on 31st December, 1934 there was a partial failure of the Cowlyd Reservoir's dam when the downstream side was washed out; this fact was not made public and the tramway enjoyed a further spate of usefulness during the improvements which followed.[44] During the 1930s onwards various contractors were employed to maintain the works (including pipelines), but during the mid-1960s a road was led up to a point near the reservoir so that Land Rovers and other specialised road vehicles might reach the reservoir. Some destruction of the tramway resulted from this, but a closure in 1968 which was intended to be temporary, proved to be complete – closure arose from derailment of a train carrying workmen and C.E.G.B. was obliged to classify such transport as unsafe: a 'road' was continued up to the tramway terminus by means of a rough track and Land Rovers could now complete the journey.

The Route (First inspection made 1942, and following notes based thereon)

To traverse the route of the line can be, according to season and weather, an upland walk requiring some determination of purpose and a highly unpleasant undertaking! It is not recommended for its scenic potential nor significant tramway engineering. From the A.C.L. Works the 2 ft gauge line passes in a loop under the west-of-valley main road (now B5106) by a concrete underbridge to enter a single-tracked incline in woodland and pass over the old main road just ahead. Huge twin pipelines from the Power Station below are met and climbing very steeply there comes a loop above which the incline is three-rail: next, the pipeline passes overhead, and as the incline comes over the lip of the escarpment, it also leaves the woodland to end at the junction with the former Eigiau line at 825 ft a.s.l. (Preceding this come the various sheds, winding house, sidings loop with trap points – left in derailing position and worked by ground lever – at incline head etc.)

The Cowlyd line proper reverses direction towards the south, passes through a rock cutting behind the winding house and takes up a sinuous wooded course along the contour of valley rim, following alongside a leat on the right for about half the total distance to Cowlyd Reservoir. First comes, on the right, a short siding to a corrugated iron engine shed, with small turntable outside to relieve the rail tractor used on this line from uni-directional running and enable it and the wagon stock some flexibility in train make-up and loading. It is beyond that the deep concrete lined catchwater leat is crossed for the first time, and shortly the pipeline passes overhead too, on its way down the cliff-side. Now follows a length of exceptionally sharp curves, some check railing, with very crude trackwork laid primitively over the surface with many undulations. Ultimately comes a rocky ledge and with a considerable climb the line lifts itself from the woodland and begins a long curve to take it westwards out of the Conway Valley (with exceptional views of the valley below lying to the south and beyond) into the shallow upland valley of the Afon Ddu. It is a bleak prospect, few trees, moorland, rock, scrub and marsh [Ref: 767664]. Ultimately the course crosses the water-filled site of the tramway leading into the cavelike entrance of the Ardda Sulphur Mine (easily recognisable by the remains of dumps and pits all around), by means of a bridge with a single timber span carried by stone piers. The mine adit is on the right and those with an eye for detail will have noted the earthwork of the Ardda Tramway coming up alongside from the left (east) for some distance past. Now comes a lonely stretch, part-fenced, and there are numerous gates to prevent straying of sheep: then the leat ultimately passes under the line and leaves it; turning northeast the track crosses a bog, very wet, partially flooded and poorly maintained in places to reach the pipeline again and cross the Roman Road. Now comes a winding shelf [Ref: 743643] 1,150 ft up, with earthworks to support the course to Siglen and the nearby Pont Brwynog chapel; then over another track and under 6 ft diameter pipes for the last time. In front stretches a dreary length of boulder-strewn tundra-like wilderness.

Looking ahead, the northern shoulder of Creigiau Gleision, buttressed up to 2,213 ft dominates the sheet of water held by the grey dam wall which is Llyn Cowlyd; to its right the flanks of Pen Llithrig-y-Wrach (2,622 ft) fall sheer to the reservoir side on the north. The memory of the Icelandic appearance of the tramway seen below from the latter's summit on a winter's day will ever separate it from those Welsh railways which lurk in lush valleys. At Ref. 736635 the northern corner of the same wall is reached and the track is crossed again. There are visible reminders of construction tramways leading both to the left and along it and ahead, the building of the linking water-tunnel to Llyn Eigiau and the wall itself. The line ends in two simple sidings, a couple of stone sheds with signs of a loop nearby; almost immediately beyond these rises to the right, the earthworks of an incline to the quarry which supplied the building stone; beyond it the water-tunnel 'junction' also featured a storage loop, all perhaps an anticlimax to the conventional narrow gauge terminus but adequate for the visit of an occasional maintenance train!

Even forty-odd years ago there was evidence that little time and money was spent on the tramway itself; insufficient consolidation had led to subsidence in bogs and parts of the line had slewed as the unstable hillside slid away in the heavy wet. Witness of trouble was in the long length of check rail even on straight lengths! From the incline-head onwards all rail was flat bottomed (in 18 or 21 ft lengths), much of 'Jubilee' 25 lb./yd. and never less than 20 lb.; some pressed steel sleepers of similar source remained, but most were cut-down standard gauge specimens where considerable renewals had taken place. Two and four-bolt fishplates were in evidence. Where washouts had occurred the track was left to hang and the occasional tractor and wagon simply brought it back to earth; no 'ballast' as such was ever used, not even broken rock. There was an unbroken climb to the west, save at Ref. 754652 where the line dipped to cross the leat.

Odd pieces of 'T'-bulb rail as used on the Cedryn line of 1861 were much evident in the past, evidence perhaps that sufficient had survived to provide useful material in 1916–17!

Motive Power

On the Cowlyd line motive power had a certain shadowy quality not only as regards doubts expressed that so few steam locomotives were employed as are recorded, but also that the tramway was only operated for a few days each week as materials accumulated at the incline-head, Dolgarrog. Bearing in mind the problems of access from the valley, sightings of a train would be rare.

McAlpine used two steam engines to build the line, (the first became EIGIAU but not initially) the earlier purchased from Charles Lawton Warren by the Aluminium Corporation, and the other being the property of McAlpine; it was nameless. The two were used indiscriminately, however. The Warren engine came through his road and rail haulage business at Seacombe in the Wirral, established in 1890 – the firm was still in business as road rolling contractors in the 1950s. He owned two locomotives by Orenstein & Koppel of Dortmund by 1913, being No. 5637 of August 1912 and No. 5668 of April 1913 which were in use on the construction of the garden village adjoining Lever Bros. Ltd. Port Sunlight factory, not far from Warren who, moving to a new house 'Overstrand' in Seabank Road, dubbed his engines OVERSTRAND and SUNLIGHT; they carried Nos. 4 and 5 on that project.[45] Work on the garden village ceased in 1914, and subsequently the Aluminium Corporation bought the latter engine which was at Dolgarrog by 1916 and was given its name between 1919 and 1921. It was a four-coupled well tank of a standard design from this firm, nominally of 30 h.p. and to run on 600 mm. gauge. The Cowlyd job being finished, and only maintenance usage being foreseen for the tramway, EIGIAU was laid aside after the Corporation acquired its first rail tractor in 1922. It was offered for sale at £95 and bought by Penrhyn Quarry, arriving at Port Penrhyn by rail on 18th July, 1928.

The second steam engine was a four-coupled saddle tank by W.G. Bagnall Ltd. of Stafford, Works No. 2080 of 1918, so indicating that Warren's engine had had to (apparently) work alone until the tramway was completed in May 1917. The Bagnall had been new to the Ministry of Munitions, later going to Thornton & Co. of Swansea (after the Cowlyd contract McAlpine sent it to Dinas Junction for the building of the Welsh Highland Railway).[46]

Name	Outside Cylinders	Driving Wheels	Wheelbase	Boiler Pressure	Weight in Working Order	Tractive Effort
EIGIAU	6 in. × 10 in.	1 ft 10 in.	3 ft 6 in.	175 lb.	6½ tons	2530 lb.
—	6 in. × 9 in.	1 ft 7 in.	3 ft 6 in.	150 lb.	5½ tons	2174 lb.

Correspondence between Dolgarrog and S.E. Tyrwhitt (Manager of the Festiniog Railway) in October 1922 confirms that the Corporation had EIGIAU on offer and being linked – by then – to the F.R., they had suggested they might purchase it. The letters suggest that Joseph Buggins & Co. of Birmingham was acting as the Corporation's agent for they supplied the F.R. with dimensions of similar engines on their hands (not identified). Strangely, Dolgarrog offered '2 small locomotives for sale'.

Buggins informed Robert Williams at Boston Lodge that the tank capacity of EIGIAU 'was 100 gallons (against 370 on the F.R.) and that a lower buffer height by 7¼ in. would be a hindrance'. Williams wrote '. . . I am convinced . . . would be of no use to us.'[47]

The intermittent use of EIGIAU was clearly inconvenient; in 1922 Edward Boydell Ltd. of Old Trafford, Manchester, supplied a 'Muir-Hill' rail tractor, being a 'Fordson' engine and gearbox assembly (20 h.p.) mounted on a four-wheeled frame. After starting up on petrol, it could run on paraffin when warm; the drive from gearbox to front axle was by chain. It had three forward speeds and a reverse which only gave 2½ m.p.h., so a turntable was installed at each end of the line. When Col. Stephens was mounting his anti-steam policy on the Festiniog the tractor was sent there for evaluation in 1924; naturally the heavy slate wagons overcame it easily! (These tractors cost £250 – they had a four-cylinder engine with 2 ft 11 in. wheelbase, 1 ft 8 in. diameter wheels and weighed 4 tons in working order.) Dolgarrog sold it in the late 1930s.[48,49]

Two other tractors were actually stationed on the tramway; the first was a new 'Simplex' – resembling a four-wheeled petrol-engined machine by F.C. Hibberd & Co. Ltd. of London, No. 1988 of 1936, strictly of 'Planet' type, with 20 h.p. engine and weighing about 2½ tons. This was one of four used by the J.L. Eve Construction Co. Ltd. of London from June 1936 in connection with pipeline work, and purchased by the N.W.P. & T.Co. Ltd. at the end of contract to replace the 'Muir-Hill'. It served until 1962, was bought by Oldham Bros. of Liverpool in 1967 and taken there for scrapping. When Eve finished the contract in 1938 his other three tractors were removed.[50]

The second was also new, delivered to a 1961 order of the Central Electricity Generating Board from Motor Rail Ltd. of Bedford, to replace the Hibberd. It was No. 22154 of 1962 weighing 2½ tons with a 28–30 h.p. 2LB diesel engine which led a charmed and seldom-used existence until removed to the C.E.G.B. Llanberis contract in September 1975 in connection with cable-laying; it accompanied some ex Dolgarrog wagons there.[51]

Other tractors have been used on the tramway but these had been obtained for temporary use there by contractors in both 1965 and 1967 and were removed after completion.

Wagons

Most early traffic was carried on flats and open wagons, with side-tipping skips for contracting work: the last named were of steel, the others of wood.

The 5-plank wooden wagons were carried on oak frames, with extended solebars to form buffers (and which must have conflicted with EIGIAU's central buffer-couplers) having bodies with a removable side approximately 4 ft 10 in. × 3 ft 4 in. wide and 2 ft 6 in. high. Opposite the removable side the corners were stiffened by sheet-iron corner plates, and the end by 'T' irons. Axles ran in plain bearings behind the wheels supplied by Millers of Edinburgh and having 1 ft 2 in. diameter and five curved spokes – and an unusual pattern. Hook and chain couplings were fitted. There were several pairs of bolster wagons to carry long loads (pipes etc.), one pair at least having outside wooden frames and bearings. The steel-framed tip wagons were given wooden seats and footboards on special trains for visitors, and the tip bodies taken off for the occasion. The C.E.G.B. also purchased six steel channel-framed open wagons with central buffing plates, outside roller bearings and disc wheels 1 ft diameter; bodies of these are 6 ft × 3 ft 1 in. wide × 2 ft high; they have drop sides and were painted green on delivery. They accompanied the C.E.G.B. tractor to Llanberis in 1975. Supplier was W.G. Allen Ltd. of Tipton.[52]

Two other small schemes involving temporary narrow gauge systems in the area included the building of a tunnel linking Llyn Eigiau with Llyn Cowlyd and following the collapse of Eigiau and Coed-Ty dams in November 1925, a small system in connection with the reconstruction of the latter. (Care has to be used in distinguishing inclines in the vicinity – some were used simply to haul pipework up the hillside but have the appearance of railway purpose!)

PENGWERN & GWYDYR QUARRIES LTD.

There had been some granite quarrying at the foot of the Cae Coch Sulphur Mine (q.v.) tramway incline for many years, and similar quarries also nearby relied on the river services in early years. The coming of the standard gauge railway left the river – in due course – without steamer traffic and some stone was carted to Llanrwst station. After the abandonment of the sulphur workings by the Ministry, granite was sent by its overhead wire ropeway to what had become the L.M.S. Railway siding, (recalls Ivor E. Davies of Penmaenmawr).

In 1929 Pengwern & Gwydyr Quarries Ltd. was formed by agreement between T.W. Ward Ltd. of Sheffield (the other working sites can be ignored here) which hereabouts acquired the "Coed Gwydyr Granite Quarries, Cae Coch Mine and the Cae Coch Mine Wharf". Modern tramway equipment was introduced and at the incline-head a quarry [Ref: 775650] was opened out to the south of the drumhouse. Rails of 25 lb./yd were laid throughout and the winding equipment overhauled. Wooden-bodied end-tipping and side-tipping skip wagons were provided in large numbers; many of the latter survive with trees growing through them! There were sheet-iron bodied trucks for carrying rubbish; surviving buildings suggest horse haulage on the levels. Much of this uppermost working and tramway survives as it was abandoned, claimed by trees and scrub but retaining its 2 ft gauge tramway in the face of reclamation by the undergrowth.

Although the tramway system of both the sulphur and granite periods is limited, the site encapsulates the Welsh narrow gauge mineral tramway era, leading as it does to water transport and embodying an interlude when a ropeway was used. Though not employing a steam locomotive, the site has much to commend for its industrial archaeology!

REFERENCES

1. A HISTORY OF THE PENMAENMAWR QUARRIES (*Ivor E. Davies*) Trans. Caerns. Hist. Soc. Vol. 35 (1974) p.27.
    NARROW GAUGE WAGONS - PENMAENMAWR QUARRIES (*C.G. Down*) Ind. Rly. Record No. 64 (1976).
    A QUARRY RAILWAY AT PENMAENMAWR (*Philip Hindley*) Ind. Rly. Record No. 68 (1976).
    THE PENMAENMAWR QUARRY INCLINES (*Philip Hindley*) Ind. Rly. Record No. 86 (1980).
2. Born in Stretford, Lancs. 1796, but then living at Runcorn, Cheshire. In 1823 they had formed a partnership in Runcorn as stone merchants and ship-builders. (See SCHOONER PORT: (*H.F. Starkey*) (1981) for detail.)
3. Wright's Siding: William Wright was Brundrit's father-in-law. Thomas Wright was manager here for over 50 years.
4. CARNARVON & DENBIGH HERALD, 12 January, 1878.
5. His brother William was Manager and principal shareholder of the Pen-yr-Orsedd Slate Quarry, Nantlle.
6. THE OLD COPPER MINES OF SNOWDONIA (*D. Bick.*) pp.41–2.
7. Pandora Lead Mining Co. (formed 1871) acquired by Western Developments Co. Ltd. (formed 1919) to take over Pandora & Hafna Mines.
8. I am indebted to John L.H. Bate for modern details of this site.
9. C.R.O. Glynllifon Collection 514 etc. and U.C.N.W. Tyn-y-Gongel Collection 585.
10. Sources consulted: H.M. Insp. of Mines Reports: Trans. of Caerns. Hist. Soc. Vol. 33 p.244: U.C.N.W. Bangor Mss. 7057: TOPOGRAPHICAL DICTIONARY OF WALES (*Samuel Lewis*) 1833 Edition: Corres. with Ivor Davies, Penmaenmawr: SKINNER'S MINING MANUAL: LIVERPOOL DAILY POST (various) November 1965.
11. Croesor Tramway – see NARROW GAUGE RAILWAYS IN SOUTH CAERNARVONSHIRE (*J.I.C. Boyd*) p.92 on.
12. Glynllifon Collection C.R.O. 510–518. NORTH WALES CHRONICLE, 2 December, 1865: (Prospectus of Caerhun Slate Co.) writes of "a tramway . . . constructed to a port at a cost of more than £10,000"(!)
13. X/M/MAPS 680/9 C.C.R.O. has additional drawings.
14. MINING JOURNAL 1853 p.786 etc.

15. U.C.N.W. Baron Hill Mss. 4403: 4431–34: 4911–29: 6449–64.
16. Lincolnshire R.O. ANCASTER MSS. No. 88.
17. A more complete list of lessees has proved elusive.
18. MINING JOURNAL 1882 p.978, and 1883 pp.1,098 and 1,382.
19. In the intervening years James had become Engineer to the Talyllyn Railway Co.
20. U.C.N.W. Bangor 24527.
21. P.R.O. BT31/10113/75758.
22. MINING JOURNAL 1873 p.295.
23. Formed the Caernarvonshire Crown Slate Co. Ltd. in 1932.
24. N.L.W. Caernarvonshire No. 235 of 1882.
25. N.L.W. 7771E.
26. Description taken in part from photos in C.R.O. XS/1608/1.
27. A petrol/paraffin machine probably acquired in December 1935 according to the Accounts. (Source: *Gwynfor P. Jones*.)
28. L.N.W.R. plans show standard gauge overbridge 15 ft span × 14 ft 6 in. high, 5 m. 2 ch. from Bettws.
29. For details see CARNARVON & DENBIGH HERALD (June 1873) and A HISTORY OF THE NORTH WALES SLATE INDUSTRY (*Jean Lindsay*)
30. THE NARROW GAUGE No. 71 p.13 on contains an article and reproduction of the drawing.
31. P.R.O. MT/263H 4287/1878.
32. See BROOKES' INDUSTRIAL RAILWAYS (*S.A. Leleux*) Oakwood Press (1972) for detail of other Brookes' interests.
33. ENGINEERING 15 June 1923 p.751.
34. THE ELECTRICAL REVIEW 1905 p.911 on.
35. ON THE WELSH NARROW GAUGE (*J.I.C. Boyd*) p.94 Ceunant Mawr winch.
36. THE ELECTRICAL ENGINEER Dec. 1905 p.763 has illustrations showing tramways, inclines and winching gear.
37. Additional notes; THE NARROW GAUGE No. 94 p.14.
38. NARROW GAUGE RAILWAYS IN SOUTH CAERNARVONSHIRE (*J.I.C. Boyd*) chaps. 6 and 7.
39. When the poles were re-armed in 1934 a few sections of the line were still usable. Poles requiring complete renewal were then – if convenient for site – floated across Llynau Diwaunedd, a method which may have been used initially in lieu of the tramroad, allowing the system to be worked from each end if need be. (I am indebted to R. Jones, Gwynfa, Trefriw, who worked on the 1934 renewals for many details of this enterprise.)
40. C.R.O. X/S/2 N.W.P. & T. Co. Ltd. Transmission lines added to 6 in. O.S. Maps (1901 Edition).
41. COWLYD WATERWORKS (*Charles F. Farrington*): Trans. Liverpool Engineering Society 2 March 1921.
42. THE ELECTRICAL REVIEW 22 September 1922 p.443 on.
43. ENGINEERING 20 July 1923 p.71.
44. Proc. Instn. of Civil Engineers. Vol. 27 p.366–8 (1964).
45. THE RAILWAYS OF PORT SUNLIGHT & BROMBOROUGH PORT (Oakwood Press) has some detailed but conflicting data.
46. NARROW GAUGE RAILWAYS IN SOUTH CAERNARVONSHIRE (*J.I.C.Boyd*) p.334.
47. Joseph Buggins & Co., Wholesale Ironmongers in Birmingham 1870–76, becoming merchants for contractor's plant, tools, railway and colliery stores 1877–1932: thereafter in the building trade until 1942. Joseph Buggins & Sons (apparently associated) contractor Wexford & Rosslare Railway c.1905 and Birmingham Tame & Rea Drainage Board c.1906.
48. THE FESTINIOG RAILWAY Vol. 2 (*J.I.C. Boyd*) p.330.
49. THE NARROW GAUGE No. 72 p.29.
50. THE NARROW GAUGE No. 86 p.17.
51. THE NARROW GAUGE No. 86 p.18–9.
52. THE NARROW GAUGE No. 86 p.18, and No. 91 p.29.

PART 9
THE ALUMINIUM CORPORATION LTD.

This concern was formed on 10th April, 1907 to produce aluminium at a smelter in Dolgarrog by electrical means derived from power supplied by a hydro-electric power station there (the generating station was transferred by A.C.L. to N.W.P. & T.Co. Ltd. in 1929). It has already been seen that pipelines from Eigiau and Cowlyd reservoirs would ultimately serve for that purpose, though at that year they had not been commenced. It was ideal country in which construction could involve narrow gauge railways; the scheme was initially designed and superintended by Harper Bros & Co. the executive engineers (who were currently associated with the building of the Portmadoc, Beddgelert & South Snowdon Railway project) and Kincaid, Waller, Manville & Dawson, the reservoirs to be created by the building of dams on the slopes of Garnedd Llewelyn and Pen Llithrig-y-Wrach respectively, the rivers being the Porth-Llwyd and the Ddu. Later in 1907 Bott & Stennett Ltd. of Westminster – fresh from Hever Castle where they had been working for engineers Sir Douglas Fox & Partners in the modernisation of Mr. Astor's estate – became contractors for the work on the Eigiau site and laid five miles of standard gauge railway off and on much of the former Cedryn Tramway site as between the top of the escarpment behind the Dolgarrog Works [Ref: 763672] and along the east shore of Llyn Eigiau, then a natural lake.

According to George Waters (one of their employees, still living in 1970) and confirmed by photographs, the locomotives and rolling stock were taken up the escarpment by re-laid narrow gauge inclines, but it will be noted that the new route was not exactly on the same site as that of the long-abandoned Cedryn Tramway. Additionally, other narrow lines on inclines with an average gradient of 1 in 1.3 were provided temporarily at the site for hauling up the pipes. The recollection is that the main narrow gauge incline leading down to Bankfield House was given a third set of rails which extended to the incline top and thence a short distance to 'The Marble Arch'; thenceforward only standard gauge track in flat-bottomed rails drove westwards from the sidings laid at this point. The Coed-Ty incline of the former Cedryn Tramway was avoided by means of some steep grades on the new railway, but this section apart, the Tramway site was utilised except at places where new bridges had to be built, the 2 ft gauge works (which still survive) being unsuited. 'After installing a steam winch at the head of the (Bankfield House) incline, the locomotive UXBRIDGE (0–6–0ST Hunslet No. 761 of 1902) was hauled up assisted by another loco (believed to be the LUCERO) pulling a wire rope in the opposite direction eastwards through the Works' yard . . . further traction was provided by a steam wagon pulling in a northerly direction along the main Llanrwst–Conway road.'[1] The steep gradient involved to by-pass the old Coed-Ty incline was ultimately reduced by the purchase of fresh land for £100 in

March 1910 to divert the line. It took a year to position the materials in order to commence the dam.

Bott & Stennett worked for two years (1907–8) but ceased in October 1908 pending payment for work done for the Corporation which went into voluntary liquidation in the following December but was reconstructed under the same name. (This financial embarrassment had other effects on Harper Bros who had at the same period ceased work on the P.B. & S.S.R. construction, and it is significant that by early 1909 the various bodies in the district involved in development of hydro-electric current supplies to quarries, railway, manufacturing etc., found themselves in difficulties.) Besides both the Corporation and Bruce, Peebles & Co. Ltd. (contractors to the P.B. & S.S.R.) going into voluntary liquidation (the former's problem was due mainly to the sharp fall in the price of aluminium) Bott & Stennett had not been paid for the last pouring of concrete into the dam; this part of the work was never certified with the result that it took much of the responsibility for failure of the dam on 2nd November, 1925. At the inquest it was averred that the concrete 'used in the construction was very poor'. It is recalled that some of the railway was removed before the Corporation was reformed in December 1909. Bott & Stennett resumed work in 1910 and completed it in 1911 and during this second phase the Corporation paid £600 to them for the narrow gauge track on the inclines plus winding gear which continued in use for their own maintenance purposes. During this second phase, Sir Douglas Fox & Partners alone were Consulting Engineers.

There were two recorded standard gauge engines on this contract but local opinion has it there were seven ('THE ELECTRICAL REVIEW' 6th November, 1908 states five were taken up the incline). They returned to river level by the same means as they rose above it. Due to the extremely sharp curves, the engines' tyres were sprayed with water from a device to reduce friction; UXBRIDGE was "a poor steamer and primed dreadfully on the steeper pitches."

Bott & Stennett had a sale at Dolgarrog 18th August, 1911 which included:

UXBRIDGE 'the top level engine'; this was not sold, going to B. & S., Cosford Loop contract, Coventry, but returned to Dolgarrog by the end of 1917.

LUCERO	0–6–0T	Manning Wardle	1098 of 1888
INCE	0–4–0ST Hunslet		425 of 1887 sold to Redpath Brown & Co.
GORDON	0–60ST	Manning Wardle	of 1894

The sale was repeated on 27–28th March, 1912 but other locos from B. & S. were then included in it, making for confusion. The fate of LUCERO and GORDON is not known.[2]

To bring in aluminium from Germany by water, the Corporation in 1911 built a 2 ft gauge tramway from the Works to a wharf on the

Conway (as already considered), but this was inefficient and a canal was dug into the Works the following year instead. The tramway was worked by wire ropes drawn by an electric winch. During World War I a standard gauge line was laid over this Wharf Tramway but rather than service the river it bridged the Conway and linked with an exchange siding on the L.N.W.R.'s Conway Valley line. In 1918 A.C.L. purchased a controlling interest in the North Wales Power & Traction Co. Ltd. and on 1st July, 1929 all 'waterborne interests' and the Power Station were sold to the North Wales Power Co. Ltd. (as it had become).

REFERENCES

1. For much of this detail I am indebted to Gethin Jones, then Works' engineer and A.L. Jones of Maenan, a historian of the Corporation. The road engine was Burrell compound No. 1667 – see TRACTION ENGINES AT WORK (Oakwood Press).
2. Information per Bernard Roberts.

PART 10
CONWAY VALLEY – RAILWAY PROPOSALS

The whole North Wales railway scene would have been very different if plans of the late 1870s had become reality (which was a possibility with some but only a pipe dream with others!) The two major factions were nominally independent companies backed by the L.N.W.R. and the N.W.N.G.Rlys; watching suspiciously in the background were the big landowners, conspicuously Baroness Willoughby d'Eresby of the Gwydyr Estate, Llanrwst. When the excitement ceased, and while some narrow gauge schemes became standard gauge in reality and others never left the drawing board, two decades would pass before the Conway Valley was prey to the fervour of the Light Railway Era and another round of narrow gauge proposals.

The Chester & Holyhead opened on 1st May, 1848. As a railway to serve any part of North Wales south of the coast was never the intention of its promoters, Edmund Sharpe M.A. instigated a 'Letter' to Lord Stanley of Alderley (President of the Board of Trade) in 1857 on 'Branch Railways' and used the Conway Valley as his yard-stick. He proposed a 3 ft gauge First Class Tramway from Conway down the west bank then to the east side at Llanrwst and terminating at Bettws-y-Coed. The section Llanrwst–Bettws-y-Coed would be a Second Class Tramway. Seven branches (to Eigiau, Cae Coch, The Abbey, Rhyd-y-Creau, Hafod-las, Penmachno and Dolwyddelan) would have been Mineral Tramways/Sidings and tapped lead mines, slate quarries, sulphur works etc. The intention was that locomotives would work south to Llanrwst, horses south to Bettws and (presumably) horses on the branches. Tourists were anticipated too. The 3 ft gauge was chosen to enable wagons to work right into the mines, quarries etc. and the main line would have been comparatively cheap to build in the wide near-level river valley.

This document set much enthusiasm ablaze. Not surprisingly some years before Hugh Beaver Roberts circularised all landowners likely to be involved in a Conway & Llanrwst Railway proposal of 28th February, 1853[1] (first mooted in 1845) and Sharpe's Letter brought about a meeting of interested persons at Llanrwst Town Hall, 6th July, 1858.[2]

A Conway & Llanrwst Branch Railway was planned on Sharpe's ideas for 15 miles of 3 ft 3 in. gauge and a prospectus issued in September 1858.[3] The amended gauge shows the influence of Charles Spooner's newest thinking to the nearest inch! Charles Holland of Liverpool (connected with the Festiniog Railway shortly afterward) and James Swinton Spooner – then a Llanrwst resident – were promoters; Sharpe was Engineer. The Secretary was none other than J.S. Hughes (later of the Festiniog too) a neighbour of Swinton Spooner. J. Fairbairn of Manchester also featured – it was quite a heady list.[4] A curious statement is that 'it is proposed to work it with small locos similar to those in use on the 3 ft mineral railways of North Lancashire,

Yorkshire and Scotland.' There was to be a central depot in Conway and conversion to standard gauge was envisaged. Charles E. Spooner was listed as owner of Hafod-Las Quarry in the Llugwy Valley and intending to use the railway. Some upset must have occurred because the scheme was re-cast, but only as between Conway and Llanrwst (12 miles) with Holland off the Board. Shortly afterwards,[5] and as if this was regretted, a further proposal was made, this time involving subscription by the L.N.W.R. (now working the Chester & Holyhead as from 1856), new junction arrangements with the main line and the Bettws portion was restored (1st December, 1860).

It must have been clear that the Valley was hardly likely to support a railway on each side of the river, but these last plans evolved despite an Act to build a Conway & Llanrwst Railway of 23rd July, 1860, a standard gauge line on the east side which reached Llanrwst 17th June, 1863 and Bettws-y-Coed five years later (6th April, 1868), having been formally embodied in the L.N.W.R. the year previously. Something of the doubts as to extension south of Llanrwst is perhaps reflected in the long delay for the 3¾ miles of an easy piece of construction.

Bettws now became the key; attention was focussed here as the N.W.N.G.Rlys No. 1 Undertaking would bring the narrow gauge from Portmadoc to Bettws via Beddgelert; No. 4 scheme would link No. 1 with the standard gauge terminus at Bettws before yet a further extension would take Railway No. 2 from Bettws to near Corwen. The spring of 1872 was the testing time and powerful landowning interests (though the N.W.N.G.R. had its own powerful figures) were among the factors preventing acceptance of Railways 2 and 4, in consequence of which No. 1 was dropped and the narrow gauge company concentrated on other routes.[6] It may be said that the L.N.W.R. had also opposed the N.W.N.G.R. but in view of its intention to scotch the G.W.R. who were likely to win much slate traffic from Blaenau Ffestiniog by their new railway from Bala, a truce had been arranged between them and Bettws would have been a mixed gauge station. The L.N.W.R.'s design was to extend south of Bettws by narrow gauge and make connection with the Festiniog and tap certain slate quarries which had long grown tired of the monopoly of the Festiniog. Festiniog interests were protected for the development of Euston's own slate traffic, and arrangements to provide the quarries with L.N.W.R.-built 2 ft gauge slate wagons would enable quarry lessees to have the choice of using either F.R. or L.N.W.R. wagons and outlets for their products. Meanwhile the L.N.W.R. produced two designs for standard gauge wagons 'to carry slate trucks' and to be built at Earlestown.

The first design (Jan. 1885) was for a six-wheeled flat wagon to carry six F.R. large slate wagons, three on each of two parallel bridge-railed tracks running the length of the wagon. Fall plates each end would allow whole trains to be loaded using an end-dock loading bay. The disadvantages were obvious; quarries did not load consistently into the

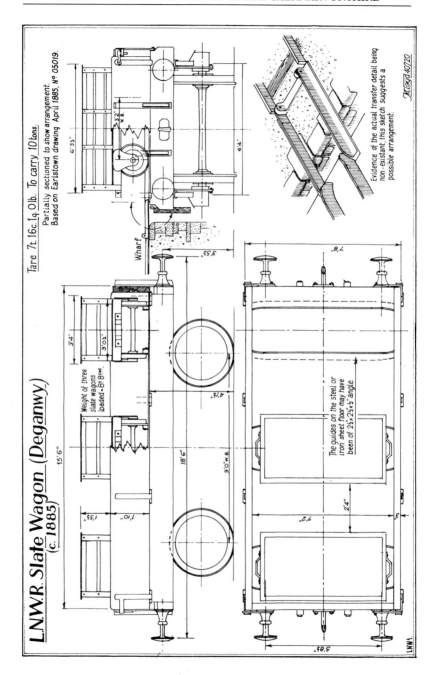

LNWR. Slate Wagon (Deganwy)
(c. 1885)

Tare 7t. 16c. 1q. 0lb. To carry 10 tons.
Partially sectioned to show arrangement.
Based on Earlstown drawing April 1885, No 05019.

Weight of three slate wagons loaded 81.8 cwt.

Wharf

Evidence of the actual transfer detail being non-existant, this sketch suggests a possible arrangement.

The guides on the steel or iron sheet floor may have been of 2½" x 2½" x ½" angle.

LNW1.

F.R.'s large wagons and there were limited locations for adopting the end-loading system. A new design of four-wheel wagon to be loaded from the side with three slate wagons to Earlestown's own design also, appeared in April following. By offering quarries a slate wagon of consistent size the 'athwart' position of those wagons on the transporter would create no fastening problems as their equal length could be held between the transporter's drop sides when they were raised. These special slate wagons (the 'Deganwy Flat') ran on and off the transporters by means of hinged rail sections on the wharf, and when on the transporter were held in place by angle iron at the wheel backs.

At Deganwy, the jetty of the St George's Harbour & Railway Co. (opened 1st October, 1858) was specially adapted to enable these wagons to run off the transporters, and either stock their loads on the jetty or offload from four landings.[7] To enable the L.N.W.R. to proceed an Act (35 and 36 Vic. Cap. 87 of 18th July, 1872) incorporated the Bettws & Festiniog Railway. Work started on the long tunnel at Blaenau under Moel Dyrnogydd to a narrow gauge loading gauge in February 1875 but the contractor (Gethin Jones, local contractor and quarry owner) failed and the L.N.W.R. took on the work themselves under William Smith, their Bangor District Engineer. Then came the failure of the L.N.W.R. scheme and a volte-face on the part of the L.N.W.R.[8] and with it passed the prospect of one of the most fascinating railway centres in Wales. (However, work on the transporter and slate wagons continued, and though the proposal of 3rd January, 1885 for a six wheeled wagon to carry six wagons on double-track lengthwise was not taken up, an alternative design dated 2nd April, 1885 was adopted, as above-mentioned.)

Neither Euston nor Paddington was destined to rob the Festiniog Railway of its slate traffic, for at the end of cut-throat competition the industry offered less tonnage and gave none of them the advantage. The standard gauge reached Blaenau two decades too late and Deganwy remained a monument to mistimed initiative.

The opportunities for building Light Railways under the Light Railway Act 1896 (59–60 Vic. Cap. 48) would next cast their shadow over the Valley, but a forecast of this era had come much earlier in late 1877 '. . . Tramways are extending in Caernarvonshire . . . a movement is in progress for the construction of one from the L.N.W.R. station at Llanrwst to Trefriw the village of the miners of that district and a favourite resort of summer visitors . . .'[9] As yet unproven, there may have been links with this and the erstwhile Gower Toll Bridge and Gower Road which linked Llanrwst station with the west bank and could have conveniently carried a light railway.

The Aluminium Corporation promoted The Abbey, Dolgarrog & Trefriw Light Railway (3¾ miles of 2 ft gauge) in May 1907, re-applying again in November with modifications. Clearly the line would form part of the Works of that Company in the district for its engineers were those of the Portmadoc, Beddgelert & South Snowdon line and the working by hydro-electric power with overhead supply line was intended;[10] the first intention had been for a standard gauge railway from the L.N.W.R. and for a short length to be used commonly by both concerns. Railway No. 1 would have a branch from a new station on the Conway Valley line (north of the Dolgarrog Halt opened 1st January, 1917) which entered the Works' complex after crossing the river at a disputed cost of £2,400 for a bridge (it would be but 6 fur. 7 ch. long). Railway No. 2 would have had a reversing junction with No. 1 and led southwards for 2 m. 7 fur. to Trefriw, sandwiched between river and roadway . . . and tightly so in places! Gradients were maximised at 1 in 30 and minimal curves at 4½ chain radius and the evidence is that thinking was keenly affected by the opening of the nearby Llandudno & Colwyn Bay Electric Railway – who had used the same Engineers – (opened 19th October, 1907). All this was taking place whilst the Corporation was heavily involved in dams and pipeline work in connection with lakes Eigiau and Cowlyd, and the means to drive turbines to generate sufficient electrical power for the manufacture of aluminium. It was said locally that the short link with the L.N.W.R. was vital to the Corporation but that the line to Trefriw was to ameliorate local support.[11]

The promotion then went to ground but resurfaced as The Dolgarrog Light Railway 1910 without any work being done (due to the liquidation of the Aluminium Corporation prior to reconstruction) for the first proposal.[12] Its aims were virtually identical so far as a railway was concerned. The scheme ran into difficulties, among them the acquisition of land, but an Order was granted on 3rd September, 1910 only to be blighted by a standard gauge scheme, The Conway Valley Light Railway[13] of November 1911. This would have linked Conway and Llanrwst along the west side of the valley and sought to amend both Railways of the Dolgarrog Light Railway. The C.V.L.R. had problems too and by various extensions of time its 1918 application for yet further time was too late to save it. The Light Railway era had by now almost ended, and narrow gauge railways of that order in the Valley were to remain a 'pipe dream'.

REFERENCES

1. C.R.O. Glynllifon Collection 2241.
2. C.R.O. Glynllifon Collection 2242.
3. NARROW GAUGE RAILWAYS IN SOUTH CAERNARVONSHIRE (*J.I.C. Boyd*) p.140 etc.
4. C.R.O. Glynllifon Collection 2243.
5. C.R.O. Glynllifon Collection 2244.
6. NARROW GAUGE RAILWAYS IN SOUTH CAERNARVONSHIRE (*J.I.C. Boyd*) p.146 etc.
7. S.G.H. & R.Co. incorp. Acts 1853, 1855, 1861: vested in L.N.W.R. 1873. Plans of 'Deganwy Pier' and 25 in. O.S. Map Caerns. IV 12 show considerable development 1885 – 1913. Movement of narrow gauge wagons was by capstan and cable.
8. NARROW GAUGE RAILWAYS IN SOUTH CAERNARVONSHIRE (*J.I.C. Boyd*) p.143–45.
9. THE MINING JOURNAL 5 January, 1878.
10. P.R.O. MT58/352.
11. THE WEEKLY NEWS 31 July, 1908; CARNARVON & DENBIGH HERALD 31 July, 1908.
12. P.R.O. MT58/352; MT6 1920/9, 2275/4, 2518/4.
13. P.R.O. MT6 2311/3.

PART 11
LLANBERIS LAKE RAILWAY (RHEILFFORDD LLYN PADARN)

Throughout the area covered by this book it has been necessary to describe the contents almost wholly in the past tense, but here is an exception although the site is an old one. So the very different Great Orme Tramway and the much more recent Llanberis Lake Railway, which runs alongside one of the largest natural lakes in North Wales, are the survivors. The Lake Railway was conceived at a time when word went about that the Padarn Railway serving the Dinorwic Quarry, might close; about the same period too, it became evident that British Rail would cut back its local railhead to Caernarvon – this has since become Bangor. Simultaneously with this forecast retrenchment the idea of creating a 'circle of railway' round Padarn Lake was born, perhaps using the P.R. site on the one shore and the standard gauge Llanberis branch course on the other? At the time the matter of gauge was unimportant. The line's headquarters might be at Pen-Llyn and perhaps the Dinorwic Quarry undertaking might be involved, using its Gilfach-Ddu Works for maintenance. Such speculation was shattered by the sudden disclosure of the bankruptcy of the Quarry concern in July 1969 and the sale of its effects which followed. Gilfach-Ddu was purchased by the County Council, the first stage in a broader concept of creating a Country Park; this was made no easier by the conflicting interests of various public bodies in the potential of the site.

The Llanberis Lake Railway is the fruition of an idea of A. Lowry Porter of Southend-on-Sea (who was the first Chairman of the Company). It operates as a tourist attraction along the former Padarn Railway site from Gilfach-Ddu – the headquarters – to the west end of Llyn Padarn; the Company holds two leases, one from Gwynedd County Council and the other from the Welsh Water Authority, being the bodies owning the relevant portions of the lake shore. There are other interesting areas of co-operation in the evolved Park and the inclusion of a steam railway along a historic right-of-way, adds life to the scheme. The railway opened on 28th May, 1971 as between Gilfach-Ddu and Cei Llydan (the old Padarn names are retained) after a preceding period notable for a rewarding search throughout the abandoned Quarry for suitable remaining track materials until November 1970. The pioneer phase ended on 3rd October, 1971 following the running of the last train of the season, and the track was extended during the ensuing winter to open to Pen-Llyn in the next season. Ten years had passed since Padarn trains had run along this length and eighteen months since the sale of assets; some features of the new railway could be recognised as having been obtained in that sale! The run was just a mile in length. A contretemps due to a slight derailment before the official party could board the inaugural train created an instant problem which was overcome by running it without any passengers! The complete reliability of the system has ever since been demonstrated, but it does seem that inaugural trains in this valley are fated!

The gauge is 1 ft 11½ in. so the four locomotives acquired from Dinorwic had to be re-gauged; the first mile was laid in 'Quarry main line' materials (double-headed rail in chairs) but the remainder used new flat-bottomed rail. In due course the Quarry materials were replaced by 45 and 60 lb./yd flat-bottomed rails from The North Devon Clay Co. Ltd., some of the lighter section having possible origins in the Lynton & Barnstaple Railway. Now all of this has been removed and new 50 lb./yd rails from British Steel Corporation are found throughout.

The line is single with an intermediate passing loop at Cei Llydan; headquarters and main station are in the area of the former 4 ft gauge loading dock at Gilfach-Ddu a portion of whose Works is used for maintenance. A considerable variety of steam and other motive power has been seen in the past; the same is true of the wagon stock, both classes of equipment having been inseparable to the casual on-looker at one period with that provided for Central Electricity Generating Board usage in connection with underground cable laying alongside the line started in winter 1975 and completed four years later. This stage of the electrical scheme caused some strange machinery and wagons to be seen in use; a single-slip point appeared in the layout to serve additional sidings (now gone) beside Gilfach-Ddu station. The former Padarn Railway's Workmen's Train Shed is now the Carriage Shed.

The steam stock currently on hand is (1984):

No.	Name	Type	Cylinders	Builder	Builders Works No.		Notes
No. 1	ELIDIR	0–4–0ST	Outside Cylinders	Hunslet	493/1889	ex Dinorwic Quarry	(A)
No. 2	WILD ASTER	0–4–0ST	Outside Cylinders	Hunslet	849/1904	ex Dinorwic Quarry	(B)
No. 3	DOLBADARN	0–4–0ST	Outside Cylinders	Hunslet	1430/1922	ex Dinorwic Quarry	(C)
No. 5	HELEN KATHRYN	0–4–0T	Outside Cylinders	Henschel 'REISA' Class	28035/1948	ex Bala Lake Rly	(D)

(A) ex-ENID later RED DAMSEL. Cab fitted from IRISH MAIL, not named ELIDIR until rebuilt by Lake Rly. Co. Out of use when purchased 1969

(B) ex-No. 7. Out of service when purchased 1969

(C) ex-No. 2. Purchased 1969

(D) German origin, built for clearing bomb-damaged buildings etc. in places where roads destroyed. From Bala 1975, where ran as No. 3

There are six rail tractors, these being:

No.	Name	Type		Builder	Builders Works No.	Notes
No. 7	—	4 wh. Diesel Mechanical	48DLZ	Ruston & Hornsby	441427/1961	(E)
No. 8	TWLL COED	4 wh. Diesel Mechanical	48DLZ	Ruston & Hornsby	268878/1956	(F)
No. 9	DOLGARROG	4 wh. Diesel Mechanical	40S	Motor Rail	22154/1962	(G)
No. 10	BRAICH	4 wh. Diesel Mechanical	44/48	Ruston & Hornsby	203031/1942	(H)
No. 11	—	4 wh. Diesel Mechanical	44/48	Ruston & Hornsby	198286/1939	(I)
No. 19	LLANELLI	4 wh. Diesel Mechanical	48DL	Ruston & Hornsby	451901/1961	(J)

(E) ex-National Coal Board, Bestwood, Notts. acquired 1977
(F) originally Lodge Hill & Upnor Rly., Kent, acquired 1976
(G) ex-Llyn Cowlyd maintenance tramway, Dolgarrog, acquired 1975
(H) ex-Munitions Tramway, Fauld, Staffs. acquired 1981
(I) ex-Munitions Tramway, Fauld, Staffs. acquired 1981
(J) ex-Thyssen Ltd., Llanelli, S. Wales, acquired 1974

The carriage stock (with doors on one side only and all on bogie chassis) comprises:

No.	Body type	Length/ Width (in feet)	Built	Compart- ments	Seats		Notes
21	Fully glazed	23 × 5	1972	5	30		C/SL B/T
22	Fully glazed	23 × 5	1972	5	30		C/SL B/T
23	Fully glazed	23 × 5	1973	5	30		C/SL B/T
24	Fully glazed	23 × 5	1973	4	30	Observation Saloon incl.	C/SL B/T
25	Fully glazed	23 × 5	1973	4	24	Guard's Van incl.	C/SL B/T
31	Part glazed	23 × 5	1972	5	30		C/RH B/TGD
32	Part glazed	23 × 5	1972	4	24	Guard's Van incl.	C/RH B/TGD
*(41)	Open above waist	16 × 4½	1971	3	18		C/RH B/GD
*(42)	Unglazed	16 × 4½	1971	4	24		C/RH B/D&GD
*(43)	Unglazed	16 × 4½	1971	4	24		C/RH B/D&GD
51	Fully glazed	15 × 5	1972	3	20	Observation Saloon incl.	C/GD B/GD
52	Fully glazed	15 × 5	1972	2½	15	Guard's Van incl.	C/GD B/GD
53	Fully glazed	15 × 5	1978	3½	21	(Seating is 6/6/6/3)	C/GD B/GD

54	Fully glazed	15 × 5	1979	3½	21	(Seating is 6/6/6/3)	C/GD B/GD
55	Fully glazed	15 × 5	1979	3½	21	(Seating is 6/6/6/3)	C/GD B/GD
56	Fully glazed	15 × 5	1980	3½	21	(Seating is 6/6/6/3)	C/GD B/GD

Carriage Nos. in brackets are removed from 1984 Stock List.

*now converted into other forms of stock e.g. "work vans"

C/SL	Chassis by Severn-Lamb Ltd., Stratford-on-Avon
C/RH	Chassis by Robert Hudson Ltd., Leeds
C/GD	Chassis by Gilfach-Ddu Workshops, L.L.R.
B/T	Body by Raymond Tisdale Ltd., Kenilworth
B/TGD	Body by Raymond Tisdale Ltd., Kenilworth in parts; assembled Gilfach-Ddu Workshops, L.R.R.
B/D&GD	Body by Davies & Son and Gilfach-Ddu Workshops, L.L.R.
B/GD	Body by Gilfach-Ddu Workshops, L.L.R.

Passenger stock runs on bogies designed and built in the Company's premises, and most stock incorporates considerable local construction.

Due to the initial phases to which the railway was put to use in the C.E.G.B. period, there are many modern-type wagons currently stored at Gilfach-Ddu; not all of these are required for the day-to-day upkeep of the railway. The origins of this considerable stock lie in:

30 4 wh. side-tippers from Penlee Quarry, Cornwall, purchased by C.E.G.B. (20 by Hudson and 10 by W.G. Allen Ltd. of Tipton);

16 4 wh. ammunition wagons by Hudson (with high wooden ends) from War Dept., Gretna (loaned to C.E.G.B. but bought by them (in lieu of returning same) then sold to L.L.R.);

5 bogie opens (timber sides and ends) by Hudson from War Dept., Barlow, Yorks. (loaned to C.E.G.B. but bought by them (in lieu of returning same) then sold to L.L.R.);

6 bogie opens (steel) by Hudson from Ministry of Defence, Fauld (purchased by L.L.R.);

Number of miscellaneous 4 wh. ammunition wagons by Hudson from Ministry of Defence, Fauld; Chilmark and Dinton (purchased by L.L.R.).

Presently there is a number of four-wheeled wagons of various types surviving from the above; the 'Gretna' chassis has become the Lake Railway 'standard' design. Eleven bogie wagons remain, all the C.E.G.B. Hudson tippers being sold at the end of the contract. The remaining ten are therefore all of Allen origin.

It is of passing interest that two units of the unconventional 87-vehicle articulated train (each unit having but a single axle) which was built to carry complete 350 metre lengths of heavy power cable for the C.E.G.B., have been preserved.

MAIN INDEX

A separate index is given for Drawings & Maps

(Place names will also be found under 'Routes')

INDEX TO DRAWINGS & MAPS